THE LITTLE FLOWERS OF
SAINT FRANCIS

THE LITTLE FLOWERS OF SAINT FRANCIS OF ASSISI

IN THE FIRST ENGLISH TRANS,
LATION REVISED & EMENDED
BY DOM ROGER HUDLESTON
WITH AN INTRODUCTION BY
ARTHUR LIVINGSTON

THE HERITAGE PRESS
NEW YORK

CONTENTS

VIII

IX

x

XI

INTRODUCTION

I

THE FIRST English translation of the *Fioretti di Santo Francesco d'Ascesi*, that of Lady Georgina Fullerton, appeared in the year 1864; and the first American translation, that by Abby Langdon Alger, was published in the year 1887. This is a good four centuries after the *princeps* edition of the *Fioretti* (Vicenza, 1476), and a half century after the "standard" Italian edition by Antonio Cesari (Verona, 1822). The tardiness of Anglo-Saxon recognition of this, one of the raciest, most spirited, and most beloved of the Italian classics is not to be grasped out of hand. Religious considerations, obvious as they might seem, could not account for the indifference of the fathers of English printing. Once published, moreover, the *Fioretti* made their way in their own right. The present century has witnessed numerous other translations in England and America and dozens of reprintings in America alone. I suspect, rather, that it was a strange case of editorial oversight, a nugget of gold that was there for anyone, yet was for centuries overlooked. The title may have had something to do with it. The phrase "Little Flowers" has, in English, a vague aroma of sentiment and propaganda, and by virtue of the diminutive it has acquired a similar flavor even in Italian. Suppose this collection of tales had been called the "Franciscan Anthology", a title at once more exact and more majestic in its associations? Or suppose, somewhat facetiously, but still within its spirit, it had been known as the "Selected Miracles of Saint Francis and his Brethren"? The story as regards the English-speaking world might, I believe, have been different.

I have called the *Fioretti* "tales"; and tales they are, fixed upon Saint Francis and his earliest disciples in the way in which legend accumulates about any celebrated character in history. But, in this case, and in contrast with the situation that usually prevails in folklore, the "stories" have a certain authority as history. One hundred years of Franciscan scholarship enable us even to evaluate the authenticity of the *Little Flowers*.

Saint Francis died in 1226. But his amanuensis, secretary, and confessor, his beloved brother Leo (who is quoted extensively in the *Little Flowers*), lived on till the year 1271. The Friar, Giovanni dalla Penna, one of the early missionaries of the Order in Germany, and another of the sources, did not die till 1274. In the year 1257 had come the great crisis in the Franciscan Order, whereby the Church, frowning darkly on an orgy of religious "revival" which enabled humble, ignorant and sometimes stuttering peasants to talk with God in His Three Persons *sicut amicus cum amico*, had given a more ecclesiastical temper to the Franciscan "Rule", and aimed at repressing mystical and miracle-working activity among the friars. This debate was conducted bitterly and with some show of force. John of Parma, leader of the "zealots" and Saint Bonaventura's predecessor as General of the Order, stood, at one moment (1257), condemned to imprisonment for life.

Already two conceptions of Saint Francis himself were current in the Order; and his biography was being recounted in different ways. Eventually Saint Bonaventura was to write the "official" biography, and to make it more "official" still by burning, so far as he could lay hands on them, all conflicting accounts of the Saint's life. Meantime, one thing is clear: the party "of good sense" was having many harsh things to say of those extremists who courted public ridicule for the benefit of their souls by preaching naked in the church pulpits, changing capon's drumsticks into nectarines, and doing other things disquieting to a theology which liked miracles in the principle but was inhospitable toward them in the fact. The harsh words hurt. They hurt directly men who had seen God walking in person among the hills of Umbria and believed He had rebegotten His Only Begotten in the guise of a lad of that humble country-side.

That was why, perhaps as early as the year 1250, and not much later than the year 1261, a monk of the March of Ancona, friend to the missionary, Giovanni dalla Penna, and known, or rather unknown, as Ugolino of Montegiorgio, began writing his *Floretum*, or "garden of flowers", the *flores* being simply "*notabilia*", or "more noteworthy things", things omitted from the formal biographies of the Saint, and the omission of which distorted and misrepresented, as old-timers knew, the spirit and the fact of those glorious days when the Saint was still on earth.

The *Floretum* of Ugolino of Montegiorgio, in the form in which that devoted monk composed it, has been lost to the world, though a copy of it seems to have been extant as late as 1623, when Wadding, the great Franciscan annalist, was writing his history of the Order in the Convent of Saint Isidore in Rome. Just what it contained is not known with certainty. Its text has to be reconstructed by inference from the numerous re-workings of it made at later times. The direct re-workings—they are substantial enlargements — are two in number: one, the *Actus beati Francisci et sociorum eius*, of which the earliest surviving trace is a mention in a catalogue of a convent in Assisi, dated 1381; and the other, the *Fioretti* themselves, of which the earliest known manuscripts date from 1390 (Berlin) and 1396 (Florence) respectively. Though the *Actus* and the *Fioretti*, as we know them at present, stand in such close relation that they could be word for word translations one of the other, the *Actus* contain twenty-two chapters not appearing in the *Fioretti*, and the *Fioretti* six chapters not appearing in the *Actus*. It seems necessary to suppose that they derive from some previous, and undiscovered, source, more comprehensive than either of them. Of this unknown anthology of Franciscan miracles something nevertheless may be said. While the *Floretum* of Ugolino did not extend beyond the year 1261, the source of the *Actus-Fioretti* dealt with episodes occurring late in 1322; and its compiler knew Ugolino personally and probably utilized other writings of Ugolino, which the latter had not exploited in the *Floretum*.

II

As is natural with a collection of wonder-stories, that same tendency to growth which is manifest in the *Actus-Fioretti* as compared with the reconstructed *Floretum*, is just as apparent in the history of the *Fioretti* themselves. Two themes in particular were provocative of such developments: on the one hand the life of Saint Francis, which moved copyists of the *Fioretti* to supplement their deficiencies as a biography with additions from other sources; the other, the parallelism between Saint Francis and Jesus, which was always challenging the ingenuity of the devout. These similitudes in the *Fioretti* are, with characteristic humility, three; Bartolommeo Pisano, by the end of the fourteenth century, increased them to forty; while Pedro Astorga, a Spanish monk of the seventeenth century, who wrote with all the characteristic vim of the Decadence, raised the number to four thousand. Meantime there was a tendency to make the *Fioretti* an archive of all Franciscan miracles — even at an early day those of Saint Anthony of Padua began creeping in. That naive briskness, that contagious chuckle, which is hidden in every paragraph of the fresh and vigorous Tuscan original of the *Fioretti* was not long in producing additions in the spirit of broad humor. We are encroaching on this sphere in the familiar stories of Brother Juniper. We are surely in an outright secular world in a *fioretto* which I picked up in Tuscany in my own youth — the story of the Franciscan novice, who, on climbing the blistering *scorciatoie* to his convent after the collect of alms on a summer's day, sets his bushel of chestnuts on the ground, wipes his brow, and then reflects, with a scepticism worthy of Brother Elias, and a Tuscan crudeness worthy of Brother Ruffino: "What a sell, if there should be no heaven!" (*Che fre...a se il cielo non c'è*).

As regards, therefore, the many texts of the *Fioretti*, some of very an‹ cient authority, which circulate in the various editions, it may be neces‹ sary to remember that, whatever the relation of the original of the *Actus-Fioretti* to the *Floretum*, the *Fioretti*, proper, must have contained fifty-three chapters, plus the five "considerations" on the Stigmata of Saint Francis. This content, in fact, aside from internal evidence, is vouched for by twenty-six manuscripts of the fifteenth century and some of the early printed editions. Without entering into the question of the varied adjuncts that were supplied at one time or another from one source or another, we may note, simply, the derivations of those additions which were accepted, with unsurpassed discernment and for their intrinsic me‹ rits of spirit or beauty, by Father Cesari in his classic edition of the *Fio‹ retti* (Verona, 1822). The "evidences" of the Stigmata presented in our chapters LIV-LVIII were derived early in the fifteenth century from the *Tractatus de miraculis* of Thomas of Celano, the earliest biographer and a contemporary of the Saint. The "life" of Brother Juniper comes from an early Latin manuscript (containing also a "life" of Brother Giles), in‹ dependent of the *Actus-Fioretti*, but which had been accreted to the *Fioretti* also in the fifteenth century. The "instructions and notable say‹ ings of Brother Giles" are by a known Florentine author, Feo Belcari, who died in 1484.

DESPITE the several hands that must have tinkered with the substance of the *Fioretti* before they reached their more extensive forms, one would not go far amiss in recognizing in a work of such surpassing literary charm the imprint of two unusual personalities.

The one must be that unknown monk of Tuscany who translated these stories (or compiled them, as the case may be) in such a sparkling and vivacious Tuscan idiom, an idiom as simple, direct, and limpid as may be imagined, but with an unfailing instinct for the enduring elements in a still future Italian language, and an idiom, withal, that retains the full vigor and picturesqueness of a peasant intelligence, wise in its worldly wisdom but unspoiled by any involutions of culture.

The second must be that same Ugolino of Montegiorgio, who somehow managed to condense into the pages of the old *Floretum* such a distillation of the pure spirit of early Franciscanism as to strike a tone and establish a mood which no later re-workings of his text could vitiate. In the sphere of fact, we may say that through Ugolino, who borrowed from Jacopo dalla Massa, an "eye-witness", and from legends going back to Brother Leo, these stories arrive at the very days of Saint Francis, without, for that matter, attaining any very great amount of historical plausibility. But it is a case where the truth of art transcends the truth of fact, and creates a verity more real than science or scholarship could by themselves attain. To possess the *Fioretti* is to re-live the early period of Franciscanism much as it was lived by the friends and disciples of the Saint.

But, in this connection, one must raise a warning against reading the *Little Flowers* with that long face of piety which is so easily put on in the presence of any literature that has a sacred look. Such sentimentalism, which blinds so many devout Christians to the art of the Bible for instance, is at variance with the shrewd simplicity of this folk masterpiece of Central Italy. What we have here, let us insist on the point, is humor; and one who cannot — I will not say laugh — one who cannot smile, will have read the *Little Flowers* in vain. I am not so sure that this smile did not, on occasion, play about the lips of Brother Ugolino himself. The world of humility, self-denial and "love" is one thing; and the world of self-assertion and competition is another thing; and they are things so antithetical to each other, in their perfection, that the wisdom of the one is the lunacy of the other, and vice versa.

One need not and perhaps should not further analyse the motivation of the smile, which is the smile the sophisticated must always have for the naive. The naive is always humor because it tends to simplify the majestic and the complex, making it mechanical, but at the same time more approachable and more lovable. The smile cannot be a laugh. A tear lingers just behind it.

The artless art of Ugolino (if it be his) was pure art in the sense that it presents concept as image, each image replete with conceptual suggestiveness. Saint Francis nibbling at his "second loaf", in order not to sin by presumption in equalling the Lord's fast of forty days; the Pope's curiosity to see Saint Clare make the Cross appear in the crust of her buns; the two dialogues of the friars with their translated brethren; the Saint's long wrestling with the Devil; Satan's revenge by causing a landslide with the swish of his tail; the astonishment of the "ladies and the cavaliers" at the holy spectacle of the first "Chapter"; Brother Bernard's founding of the Order at Bologna — the *Fioretti* are all scenes that could be painted (and were painted, as legend asserts, by Giotto). As the pictures multiply, the mood deepens in beauty and richness — and we must not forget to smile, meantime; for the perfection of humility and Christian love which the friars exemplify is attained by the most humble and direct of mechanical means. One can well understand the ancient quarrel in the Order. These untutored converts of Saint Francis were playing with a magic art, which evoked the Devil when it was black, and constrained the appearance of the Divinity when of brighter hue (XLIX).

There is little, if any, theology about these simple friars. Such questions belonged to those who were lettered and knew people off in the big towns, Rome, perhaps. They cared little about such things, having found in faith at all times, and now and again in "rapture", a direct access to the benign powers. One feels a sort of regional secretiveness in this technique of virtue, which also was practised in individual secretiveness, lest pride in success give Satan his chance. The sweetness of this child-like literalism resides in part, I believe, in an absence of a note of spiritual "arrivism", or spiritual "climbing", which one so minded can find even offensive in a Dante or a Savonarola. These straightforward souls of the

XVIII

brotherhood of Saint Francis wanted to keep out of Hell because it was hot, and to get out of Purgatory because it was uncomfortable. Yet they, too, like Jesus, visioned a love so great that willingly the least of them would have accepted damnation so only the world might have been saved. If one seek the moral theme in this early Franciscanism, one finds at last a morality that is made always for oneself and not for other people. Here again on earth were men who judged not, who loved the lost even more than the virtuous, and the bandit as much as the cavalier.

It was, after all, a snug and cosy world, the world in which these early Franciscans lived, a world personally supervised by its Creator, who walked the earth as a man among men, and who loved His creatures with a parent's love, assisted in His care of them by His Son and His Son's Mother. Thus warmly had Jesus thought of the world in His time — a projection, perhaps, as Renan suggests, of a verdant Galilee blossoming in the Syrian desert. This "naturalism" of the early Franciscans, so beautifully expressed in the lauds and in the "Canticle" of the Saint himself, finds surely in the *Little Flowers* its most complete and beautiful expression. It has been through them that the birds who stretched their throats and bowed their heads in approval of the Saint's exhortation to praise have ever since made their chirping voices heard above the noisy history of Europe. To savor this naturalism in its full freshness one need only turn to some expression of the naturalisms of a later day, that of the Rousseauians or of our own Emerson or Thoreau. These two were efforts to bring God back into the world (from which He had been exiled by Cartesian logic). But how vain the effort! How unsatisfactory a God that is only Nature, and how literary and metaphorical a Nature which we must think of as God! It is a more real and understandable thing, this Nature of the early Franciscans, the "useful", "humble", "comfortable" invention of a God who could be used, if one treated Him right, for the humble commonplace needs of common everyday people.

And we have said nothing about Frate Lupo! There are those who say he was a man, perhaps a bandit by that name. Anyone who can read the *Little Flowers* without understanding that Frate Lupo was a wolf, will, like those who cannot smile, have read them in vain!

ARTHUR LIVINGSTON

PART ONE

HERE BEGIN THE LITTLE FLOWERS
OF SAINT FRANCIS
OF ASSISI

CHAPTER I

IN THE NAME OF JESUS CHRIST OUR CRUCIFIED SAVIOUR, AND OF MARY HIS VIRGIN MOTHER. IN THIS BOOK ARE CONTAINED CERTAIN LITTLE FLOWERS — TO WIT, MIRA, CLES AND PIOUS EXAMPLES OF THE GLORIOUS SERVANT OF CHRIST ST FRANCIS, AND OF SOME OF HIS HOLY COMPAN, IONS; TO THE GLORY AND PRAISE OF JESUS CHRIST. AMEN

FIRST let us consider how the life of the glorious St Francis was conformed in every act with that of our Blessed Lord. For as Christ, before he began to preach, made choice of twelve Apostles, teaching them to despise all the things of this world, to follow him in poverty and in the practice of all other virtues, so St Francis, on the first founding of his Order, chose twelve companions, all lovers of poverty. And even as one of the twelve Apostles, being reproved by Christ, hanged himself by the neck, so among the twelve companions of St Francis was one, called Brother John della Capella, who apostatised, and finally hanged himself by the neck. This should be for the elect a great example and cause of humility and fear, when they consider how no one is certain of persevering in the grace of God to the end. As the holy Apostles, being filled with the Spirit of God, shone forth mightily before the world in holiness and humility, so too did the companions of St Francis; for from the time of the Apostles till this present day the world had never seen men so wonderful and so holy.

One of them, Brother Giles, like St Paul, was raised to the third heaven; another, Brother Philip the Tall, like the prophet Isaias, was touched upon the lips with a burning coal by an angel. Bro,

3

ther Silvester held converse with God, like one friend with another, as did Moses of old. Another, the most humble Brother Bernard, through the penetration of his intellect, reached the light of divine science, like the eagle — the emblem of St John

the Evangelist — and explained all the deepest mysteries of Holy Scripture. One there was who was sanctified and canonised in heaven, whilst still living on earth; this was Brother Ruffino, a nobleman of Assisi. And thus all bore singular marks of sanctity, as we shall see hereafter.

4

CHAPTER II

OF BROTHER BERNARD OF QUINTAVALLE, THE FIRST COMPANION OF ST FRANCIS

THE first companion of St Francis was Brother Bernard of Assisi, who was converted in the following way: St Francis had not yet taken the religious habit, though he had renounced the world, and had so given himself to penance and mortification that many looked upon him as on one out of his mind. He was scoffed at as a madman, was rejected and despised by his relations and by strangers, who threw stones and mud at him when he passed; yet he went on his way, accepting these insults as patiently as if he had been deaf and dumb. Then Bernard of Assisi, one of the richest and most learned nobles of the city, began to consider deeply the conduct of St Francis; how utterly he despised the world, how patiently he suffered injuries, and how his faith remained firm, though he had been for two years an object of contempt and rejected by all. He began to think and say within himself, "It is evident that this brother must have received great graces from God"; and so resolved to invite him to sup and to sleep in his house. St Francis having accepted the invitation, Bernard, who was resolved to contemplate the sanctity of his guest, ordered a bed to be prepared for him in his own room, where a lamp burned all night. Now St Francis, in order to conceal his sanctity, so soon as he entered the room, threw himself upon the bed, pretending to fall asleep. Bernard likewise soon after went to bed, and began to snore as if sleeping soundly. On this, St Francis, thinking that Bernard was really fast asleep, got up and began to pray. Raising his hands and eyes to heaven, he

5

exclaimed, with great devotion and fervour, "My God! my God!" at the same time weeping bitterly; and thus he remained on his knees all night, repeating with great love and fervour the words, "My God! my God!" and none others.

And this he did because, being enlightened by the Holy Spirit, he contemplated and admired the divine majesty of God, who deigned to take pity on the perishing world, and to save not only the soul of Francis, his poor little one, but those of many others also through his means. For, being enlightened by the Holy Ghost, he foresaw the great things which God would deign to accomplish through him and through his Order; and considering his insufficiency and unworthiness, he prayed and called upon the Lord, through his power and wisdom, to supply, help and accomplish that which of himself he could not do.

Then Bernard, seeing by the light of the lamp the devout actions of St Francis and the expression of his countenance, and devoutly considering the words he uttered, was touched by the Holy Spirit, and resolved to change his life. Next morning, therefore, he called St Francis, and thus addressed him: "Brother Francis, I am disposed in heart wholly to leave the world, and to obey thee in all things as thou shalt command me." At these words, St Francis rejoiced in spirit and said: "Bernard, a resolution such as thou speakest of is so difficult and so great an act, that we must take counsel of the Lord Jesus Christ, and pray to him that he may be pleased to show us what is his will, and may teach us to follow it. Let us then go together to the Bishop's palace, where we shall find a good priest who will say Mass for us. We will then remain in prayer till the third hour, imploring the Lord to point out to us the way he wishes us to select, and to this intent we will open the Missal three times." And when Bernard answered that he was well pleased with this proposal, they set out together, heard Mass, and after they had remained in prayer

6

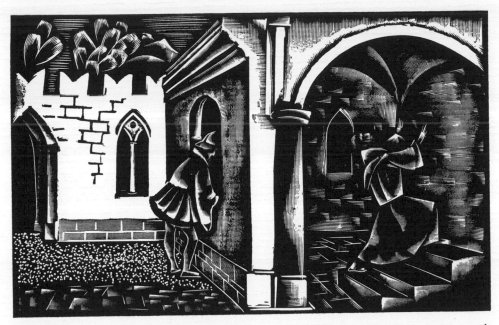

till the time fixed, the priest, at the request of St Francis, took
the Missal, then, having made the sign of the holy cross, he
opened it three times, in the name of our Lord Jesus Christ.

The first place which he lit upon was at the answer of Christ
to the young man who asked of him the way to perfection: *If
thou wilt be perfect, go, sell all that thou hast and give to the poor,
and come, follow me.* The second time he opened at the words
which the Saviour addressed to the Apostles when he sent them
forth to preach the Word of Truth: *Take nothing with you for
your journey: neither staff, nor scrip, nor bread, nor money;* wishing
to teach them thereby to commit the care of their lives to him,
and give all their thoughts to the preaching of the Holy Gospel.
When the Missal was opened a third time they came upon these
words: *If any one will come after me, let him deny himself, and
take up his cross, and follow me.*

Then St Francis, turning to Bernard, said: "This is the advice
that the Lord has given us; go and do as thou hast heard; and
blessed be the Lord Jesus Christ who has pointed out to thee the

way of his angelic life." Upon this, Bernard went and sold all that he had. Now he was very rich, and with great joy he distributed his wealth to widows, to orphans, to prisoners, to monasteries, to hospitals, and to pilgrims, in all which St Francis assisted him with prudence and fidelity.

Now it happened that a man of the name of Silvester, seeing how St Francis gave so much money to the poor, being urged on by avarice, went to him and said: "Thou didst not pay me enough for the stones I sold thee to repair the church; now that thou hast money, pay me what thou owest." St Francis, much surprised at such a demand, but, according to the precepts of the Scriptures, not wishing to dispute with him, put his hands into Bernard's lap, and filling them with money, gave it to Silvester, saying that, if he wanted more, he would give it to him. Silvester, being satisfied, returned home; but in the evening of the same day he reflected on his avarice, and on the holiness and the fervour of St Francis. That night also he saw St Francis in a vision, and it seemed to him as if a golden cross came out of his mouth, which reached up to heaven and extended to the extreme east and west. After this vision he gave all he possessed to the poor, for the love of God, and made himself a Brother Minor. He became so holy, and was favoured with such special graces, that he spake with the Lord as a friend speaks with a friend, of which St Francis was often a witness, as we shall see further on. Bernard likewise received from God many graces —he was ravished in contemplation, and St Francis said he was worthy of all reverence, and that he had founded the Order, because he was the first who had abandoned the world, giving all he possessed to the poor of Christ, keeping back nothing for himself; and practising evangelical poverty, placing himself naked in the arms of the Crucified, whom may we all bless eternally. Amen.

CHAPTER III

HOW ST FRANCIS, HAVING ALLOWED AN EVIL THOUGHT
TO ARISE IN HIS MIND AGAINST BROTHER BERNARD,
ORDERED HIM TO PLACE HIS FOOT THREE TIMES UPON
HIS NECK AND HIS MOUTH

ST FRANCIS, the devoted servant of the crucified Jesus, through constant weeping and penance, had become nearly blind, so that he could scarcely see. Wishing one day to speak with Brother Bernard on things divine, he left the place where he was and went to join him. Being told, upon arrival, that he was in the forest praying, St Francis proceeded thither, and, calling out, said; "Come, O Brother Bernard, and speak with this blind man." But Brother Bernard did not make answer; for, his soul being rapt in divine contemplation, he did not hear him call; one of the special graces of Brother Bernard being that of holding converse with God Almighty, of which St Francis had often been a witness. The saint, therefore, since he wished specially to speak with him at that hour, called him again a second time and a third. Brother Bernard, not having heard him, neither answered nor went to him; at which St Francis went away somewhat saddened, and wondering in himself how it was that, having called him three times, Brother Bernard had not come to him. With this thought on his mind, when he had proceeded a little way, he bade his companion wait for him, and retiring to a solitary spot, fell on his knees, praying that God would reveal to him why Brother Bernard had not answered his call. As he prayed, a voice came from God, which said, "O poor little man, why art thou troubled? Is it meet for man to leave God for the creature? When thou didst call Brother Bernard he was with me, and could nei-

9

ther hear thee, nor go to thee; be not then surprised if he answered thee not, for he was rapt out of himself, nor did he hear aught of all thou saidst." St Francis, having received this answer from God, went back with great haste to Brother Bernard, to accuse himself humbly of the thought he had allowed to enter his mind against him. Brother Bernard, seeing St Francis coming towards him, went to meet him, and threw himself at his feet. Then St Francis bade him rise, confessing most humbly what his thoughts had been and the answer which God had made him; and with these words he concluded: "I command thee, by virtue of holy obedience, to do whatsoever I shall order thee." Brother Bernard, fearing St Francis would oblige him to inflict upon him some great punishment, as was his custom, would most willingly have avoided obeying him. "I am ready," he answered, "to obey thee, father, if thou also wilt promise me to do whatsoever I shall command thee." To this St Francis consented; and Brother Bernard then asked him what he wished him to do. "I command thee," said St Francis, "under holy obedience, in order to punish my presumption and the evil thought of my heart, when I lie down on the ground to place one of thy feet on my neck, and the other on my mouth. And this shalt thou do three times, saying each time, 'Shame upon thee, shame upon thee! Be humbled, thou son of Peter Bernardoni, for thou art but a vile wretch; how camest thou to be so proud, thou miserable servant of sin!'" On hearing this Brother Bernard was much grieved, but out of holy obedience he did what St Francis had ordered him, striving withal to acquit himself thereof as lightly as possible. Then St Francis, having promised obedience to Brother Bernard, asked what he wished him to do, whereto the latter answered: "I command thee, in virtue of holy obedience, that whenever we are together thou reprove and correct with great severity all my defects." This order much surprised St Francis,

for Brother Bernard was so holy that he held him in great rev‹
erence, and did not believe it possible to find in him any fault.
From that time, therefore, the saint avoided being much with
Brother Bernard, fearing lest, out of holy obedience, he might
be obliged to reprove him; and when he was obliged to see or

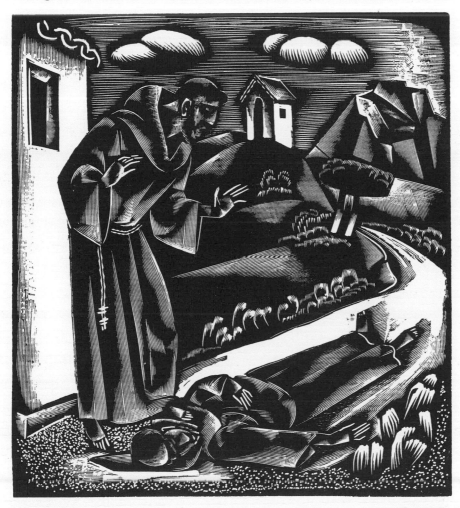

to speak with him, he parted from him as soon as possible. Most
edifying it was to hear with what charity, what admiration and
humility, St Francis, who was his superior, spoke of Brother Ber‹
nard, who was his first son in God — to the praise and glory of
Jesus Christ and his poor servant Francis. Amen.

CHAPTER IV

HOW THE ANGEL OF GOD PUT A QUESTION TO BROTHER ELIAS,
GUARDIAN OF VAL DI SPOLETO, AND HOW, WHEN BROTHER ELIAS
ANSWERED PROUDLY, THE ANGEL DEPARTED FROM HIM, AND TOOK
THE ROAD TO SAN GIACOMO, WHERE HE MET BROTHER BERNARD
AND TOLD HIM WHAT FOLLOWS

IN the first beginning of the Order, when there were as yet but few brothers and no convents established, St Francis went, out of devotion, to San Giacomo di Galicia, taking with him Brother Bernard and one or two other brothers. As they travelled on together, they met by the way a poor sick man. St Francis, moved with compassion at the sight of his sufferings, said to Brother Bernard: "My son, I will that thou stay here, and take care of this sick man." And Brother Bernard, meekly falling on his knees, received the order of his revered father and remained behind, whilst St Francis and the others proceeded to San Giacomo. On arriving there, they spent the night in prayer in the Church of St James, and God revealed to St Francis how he would found many convents all over the world, and how his Order would increase and multiply into a great multitude of brethren. After this revelation St Francis began to found convents in that country. Then returning by the way he had come, and finding Brother Bernard with the sick man, who had quite recovered, he allowed him to go the following year to San Giacomo, whilst he himself returned to Val di Spoleto, and took up his abode in a desert place with Brother Masseo, Brother Elias, and others. All these were very careful never to interrupt St Francis in his devotions; and this they did out of the great reverence they bore him, and because they knew that God revealed to him great things in prayer. Now it chanced one day, as St Francis was praying in the forest, that a handsome young man, dressed for travelling, presented himself at the convent-gate, knocking thereat so loudly, so quickly, and so long, that the brothers marvelled greatly at a way of knocking so strange and unusual. Brother Masseo, who went and opened the gate, thus addressed the young man: "Whence comest thou, my son? for the strange manner in which thou knockest makes me to think thou hast never been here before." At this the young man asked: "How then ought I to knock?" Brother Masseo answered: "Thou shouldst give three knocks, one after the other, and then wait time enough for a brother to say an 'Our Father', and come and open to thee; should he not arrive by that time, then thou mayest knock again." "I was in great haste," replied the stranger; "for I have made a long journey, and am come here to speak with St Francis, who at this hour is praying in the forest, wherefore I would not interrupt him. I pray thee, then, to call Brother Elias; for I wish to put a question to him, having heard that he is full of wisdom." Then Brother Masseo going, called Brother Elias; but he, being angry, refused to go, so that Brother Masseo was at a loss what answer to make the stranger. For if he told him Brother Elias could not wait on him, he would say an untruth; while if he told how he spoke in anger, he feared to give scandal. Whilst Brother Masseo was hesitating how he should act, whether or no he should return with the message, the stranger knocked again as he had knocked before. On this Brother Masseo hastened back to the convent-gate, and said reproachfully: "Thou hast not observed what I said to thee as to how thou shouldst knock." To this the young man made answer: "Since Brother Elias will not come to me, go, tell Brother Francis that I came here to speak with him; but, not wishing to interrupt his prayers, I beg him to order Brother Elias to come to me." Then

13

Brother Masseo went to St Francis, who was praying in the forest with his eyes lifted up to heaven, and gave him the message of the young man, with the answer of Brother Elias. Now the young man was the angel of God, under the form of a traveller. St Francis, without moving and still looking up to heaven, said to Brother Masseo: "Go, tell Brother Elias, in virtue of holy obedience, to go and speak with that young man." So Brother Elias, having received the order of St Francis, went to the convent-gate in an angry mood, and opening it with violence, asked of the young man what he wanted with him. The latter answered: "Beware of being angry, as thou appearest to be; for anger woundeth the soul, preventing it from discerning the truth." Brother Elias said again: "Tell me what thou wantest with me." "I wish to know," answered the stranger, "if it be permitted to such as follow the Holy Gospel to eat whatever is served before them, according to the words of Christ to his disciples; and I wish to ask thee, likewise, if it be lawful for any man to teach a doctrine contrary to the liberty preached in the Gospel." On this Brother Elias answered proudly: "I know what answer to make thee, but I am not inclined to give thee one. Be gone about thy business." The young man replied: "I know better than thou dost what answer to make to these questions." Then was Brother Elias much troubled; and, being very angry, he slammed to the door, and went his way. But afterwards, considering the questions which had been put to him, he doubted within himself whether he could answer them; for being Vicar of the Order, he had made a law which went beyond that of the Gospel, and passed the Rule of St Francis: to wit, that none of the brethren should eat flesh; so that the question was put expressly against himself. Not knowing in what way to clear his doubts, and being struck by the modest appearance of the young stranger, remembering also how he had said that he could answer the questions better

14

than himself, he hurried back to the convent-gate in hopes of finding him. But he had disappeared, for the pride of Brother Elias made him unworthy to converse with an angel. In the mean-time St Francis, to whom all had been revealed by God, return-ing from the forest, addressed himself reproachfully to Brother Elias, saying: "Thou doest wrong, proud Brother Elias; for thou hast sent away the holy angel of God, who came to instruct us. I tell thee that I greatly fear lest thy pride will make thee end thy days out of the Order." And so it happened even as St Francis said, for he died out of the Order. The same day and the same hour at which the angel had disappeared from the convent-gate, he appeared to Brother Bernard, who was making his way home-wards from San Giacomo, along the bank of a great river. The angel, clad in the same guise as a traveller, greeted him with the words, "God give thee peace, good brother." Now Brother Bernard, considering the beauty of the young man, who with so sweet a look pronounced the salutation of peace, according to the custom of his own country, asked of him whence he came. "I come," answered the angel, "from the convent where dwells St Francis. I went thither to speak with him, but to do so I was not able, for he was in the forest contemplating divine things, and I would not disturb him. In the same convent were Brother Giles, and Brother Elias, with Brother Masseo, who taught me how to knock at the convent-gate according to the custom of the brethren. Brother Elias would not answer the questions I put to him; but afterwards he repented, seeking to see and hear me; but it was too late." After these words, the angel asked Brother Bernard why he did not cross the river. "Because," answered Brother Bernard, "I fear to perish in the waters, which are very deep." The angel said to him, "Let us cross together; fear naught." And, taking him by the hand, in an instant they were both on the other side of the river. Then Brother Bernard knew him for the

angel of God, and with great joy and great reverence he ex‑
claimed: "Blessed angel of God, tell me thy name." The angel
answered: "Why dost thou ask my name, which is Wonderful?"
Having said these words, he disappeared, leaving Brother Ber‑
nard greatly comforted; so that he ended his journey with much

joy, noting the day and the hour when the angel had appeared.
On arriving at the convent, where St Francis was with his favou‑
rite companions, he related to them word for word his adven‑
ture; and they knew with a certainty that it was the very angel
who, on the same day and at the same hour, had appeared to
them also.

16

CHAPTER V

ST FRANCIS and his companions, being called by God to carry the cross of Christ in their hearts, to practise it in their lives, and to preach it by their words, were truly crucified men both in their actions and in their works. They sought after shame and contempt, out of love for Christ, rather than the honours of the world, the respect and praise of men. They rejoiced to be despised, and were grieved when honoured. Thus they went about the world as pilgrims and strangers, carrying nothing with them but Christ crucified; and because they were of the true Vine, which is Christ, they produced great and good fruits in many souls which they gained to God. It happened that, in the beginning of the Order, St Francis sent Brother Bernard to Bologna, there to accomplish many good works, according to the grace which God had given him. So Brother Bernard, making the holy sign of the cross, in the name of holy obedience, set out for Bologna; but when he arrived in that city, the little children in the streets, seeing him dressed so strangely and so poorly, laughed and scoffed at him, taking him for a madman. All these trials Brother Bernard accepted for the love of Christ, with great patience and with great joy, and seeking to be despised yet more, he went to the market-place, where, having seated himself, a great number of children and men gathered round him, and taking hold of his hood pushed him here and there, some throwing stones at him and others dust. To all this Brother Bernard submitted in silence, his countenance bearing an expression of holy joy, and for several days he returned to the same spot to receive the same insults. Now, patience being a work of perfection and a proof of virtue, a learned doctor of the law, seeing such virtue and constancy in Brother Bernard, who had endured for so many days such contempt and such injuries without losing his temper, said within himself: "Without doubt this man must be a great saint"; and going up to him, he asked him who he was, and whence he came. Brother Bernard put his hand into his bosom, and taking out the Rule of St Francis, gave it to him to read. The doctor, having read the Rule, was struck with wonder and admiration at the sublime perfection therein prescribed, and turning to his friends, he said: "Truly this is the most perfect state of Religion I have ever heard of, and this man and his companions are the holiest men I have met with in all the world; guilty indeed are those who insult him; we ought, on the contrary, to honour him as a true friend of God." And addressing Brother Bernard, he said to him: "If it is thy wish to found a convent in this town, in which thou mayest serve God according to thy heart's desires, I will help thee most willingly, for the salvation of my soul." Brother Bernard answered: "I believe that our Saviour Jesus Christ has inspired thee with this good intention, and most willingly do I accept thy offer, to the honour of Christ." Then the doctor, with much joy and great charity, conducted Brother Bernard to his house, and soon after gave to him a place as he had promised, which he arranged and furnished at his own expense, and from that moment he became a father to Brother Bernard, and the special defender of the Friars Minor. Brother Bernard, through his holy conduct, began to be much honoured by the people, so much so that those who could see and touch him accounted themselves as most blessed; but he, like a true disciple of Christ and a son of the humble Francis, fearing lest the honours of the world should disturb his peace and endanger

18

the salvation of his soul, set out one day and returned to St Francis, whom he thus addressed: "Father, the convent is founded at Bologna, send other brothers there to keep it up and reside there, as I can no longer be of any use; indeed, I fear that the too great honours I receive might make me lose more than I could gain." Now St Francis, having heard, one after another, all the things which the Lord had wrought through Brother Bernard, rendered thanks to God, who thus began to spread abroad the poor disciples of the Cross; then sent he others of the brethren to Bologna, and to Lombardy, and these founded many convents in divers countries.

CHAPTER VI

HOW ST FRANCIS, WHEN ABOUT TO DIE, BLESSED THE HOLY BROTHER BERNARD, NAMING HIM VICAR OF THE ORDER

THE holiness of Brother Bernard shone forth so brightly, that St Francis held him in great reverence, and often was heard to praise him. One day, as St Francis was in prayer, it was revealed to him by God that Brother Bernard, by divine permission, would sustain many painful combats with the devil. Now St Francis felt great compassion for Brother Bernard, whom he loved as a son; wherefore he wept and prayed for many days, imploring the Lord Jesus Christ to give him the victory over the evil one. As he was praying thus devoutly, the Lord answered his prayer, and said to him: "Fear not, Francis, for all the temptations which will assail Brother Bernard are permitted by God, to increase his virtue and win for him a crown of merit; for at length he will gain the victory over all his enemies, because he is one of the ministers of the kingdom of heaven." This answer to prayer

filled St Francis with joy; he thanked God; and from that mo‐
ment, Brother Bernard became even dearer to St Francis than
before, and many proofs of affection did he give him, not only
during his life but more especially at the hour of his death. For
when St Francis was about to leave this world, being surrounded
like the holy prophet Jacob by his devoted sons, all grieving at
the departure of so beloved a Father, he thus addressed them:
"Where is my first-born son? let him come to me, that my soul
may bless him before I die." Then Brother Bernard said in a
whisper to Brother Elias, who at that time was vicar of the Or‐
der: "Go to the right hand of the saint, that he may bless thee."
On this Brother Elias placed himself on the right side of St Fran‐
cis — who had lost his sight through much weeping — and the
saint, putting his right hand on the head of Brother Elias, said:
"This is not the head of my first-born, Brother Bernard." Then
Brother Bernard placed himself on the left side of St Francis,
who, crossing his arms in the form of a cross, put his right hand
on the head of Brother Bernard and his left on that of Brother
Elias. Then said he to Brother Bernard: "May God, the Father
of our Lord Jesus Christ, bless thee with every blessing, spiritual
and celestial; for thou art my first-born son in God, chosen in
this Order to set an example of every virtue, and to follow Christ
in evangelical poverty; for not only didst thou give all thy pos‐
sessions and distribute them freely and liberally to the poor, but
thou didst likewise offer thyself to God in this Order as a sacri‐
fice of love; blessed be thou, then, by our Saviour Jesus Christ
and by me, his poor servant, with eternal blessings, when thou
goest out and when thou comest in, when thou wakest and when
thou sleepest, both living and dying; he that blesseth thee shall
be blessed, he that curseth thee shall not remain unpunished.
Thou shalt be at the head of all thy brethren, and all thy com‐
mands the brethren shall obey. I give thee power to receive into

this Order whomsoever thou willest; no brother shall rule over thee. Thou art free to go where thou wilt, and to remain where it pleaseth thee best." So, after the death of St Francis, the brethren loved and revered Brother Bernard as their father, and when it was his turn to die, many brethren came from all parts of the world to take leave of him; amongst them the angelic Brother Giles, who when he saw Brother Bernard exclaimed, with great joy, *"Sursum corda!* Brother Bernard, *Sursum corda!"* and Brother Bernard ordered secretly one of the brothers to prepare for Brother Giles a place meet for contemplation, which was done even as he ordered. Now when the last hour of Brother Bernard arrived, he begged to be raised in his bed, and thus addressed the brethren who surrounded him: "Beloved brethren, I have not many words to say to you; but I wish you to consider that, as the religious order which has been my choice has been yours also, the hour which is now come for me will also come for you; and this I find in my soul to tell you, that for a thousand worlds I would not have served another Lord than our Saviour Jesus Christ. Now I accuse myself before my Saviour and before you all of every offence I have committed; and I pray you, my dear brethren, to love one another." And having said these words, and given other good advice, he lay down on his bed, his face radiant with joy and shining with celestial brightness, of which all the brethren were witnesses; and in that ecstasy of joy his holy soul, crowned with glory, passed from this present life to the blessed life of the angels.

CHAPTER VII

HOW ST FRANCIS PASSED THE TIME OF LENT IN AN
ISLAND, ON THE LAKE OF PERUGIA, WHERE HE FASTED
FORTY DAYS AND FORTY NIGHTS, EATING NO MORE
THAN HALF OF ONE LOAF

THE true servant of Christ, St Francis, was in certain things like unto a second Christ given to the world for the salva‹ tion of souls. Wherefore God the Father willed that in many points he should be conformed to his Son, Jesus Christ, as we have already explained in the calling of his twelve companions, as also in the mystery of the holy stigmata, and in a fast of forty days which he made in the manner following:

St Francis, one day of the Carnival, was near the Lake of Pe‹ rugia, in the house of one of his devout children, with whom he had spent the night, when he was inspired by God to go and pass the time of Lent in an island on the lake. Wherefore St Francis begged his friend, for the love of God, to convey him in his boat to an island uninhabited by man: the which he should do during the night of Ash-Wednesday, so that none might know where he was; and the friend, because of the great devotion he bore to St Francis, agreed to his request, and conveyed him to the said is‹ land, St Francis taking with him naught but two small loaves. When they had reached the island, his friend left him and re‹ turned home; the saint earnestly entreating him to reveal to no one where he was, and not to come and fetch him before Holy Thursday; to which he consented. St Francis being left alone, and there being no dwelling in the island in which he could take shelter, entered into a thick part of the wood all overgrown with brambles and other creeping plants, and forming as it were a

22

kind of hut, there he began to pray and enter into the contemplation of divine things. And there he passed the whole of Lent without drinking or eating aught save half of one of the small loaves he had taken with him, as we learned from his friend who, going to fetch him on Holy Thursday, found one of the loaves untouched and the other only half consumed. It is believed that St Francis ate this half out of reverence for our Blessed Lord, who fasted forty days and forty nights without taking any material food; for by eating this bit of bread he put aside the temptation to vainglory, and yet fasted forty days and forty nights in imitation of the Saviour. In later times God worked many miracles, through the merits of the saint, on the spot where St Francis had fasted so wonderfully, on which account people began to build houses and dwell there, and little by little a town rose up, with a convent called the Convent of the Isle; and to this day the inhabitants of that town hold in great respect and great devotion the spot in which St Francis passed the time of Lent.

CHAPTER VIII

ONE day in winter, as St Francis was going with Brother Leo from Perugia to St Mary of the Angels, and was suf⸗ fering greatly from the cold, he called to Brother Leo, who was walking on before him, and said to him: "Brother Leo, if it were to please God that the Friars Minor should give, in all lands, a great example of holiness and edification, write down, and note carefully, that this would not be perfect joy." A little farther on, St Francis called to him a second time: "O Brother Leo, if the Friars Minor were to make the lame to walk, if they should make straight the crooked, chase away demons, give sight to the blind, hearing to the deaf, speech to the dumb, and, what is even a far greater work, if they should raise the dead after four days, write that this would not be perfect joy." Shortly after, he cried out again: "O Brother Leo, if the Friars Minor knew all languages; if they were versed in all science; if they could explain all Scrip⸗ ture; if they had the gift of prophecy, and could reveal, not only all future things, but likewise the secrets of all consciences and all souls, write that this would not be perfect joy." After proceed⸗ ing a few steps farther, he cried out again with a loud voice: "O Brother Leo, thou little lamb of God! if the Friars Minor could speak with the tongues of angels; if they could explain the course of the stars; if they knew the virtues of all plants; if all the trea⸗ sures of the earth were revealed to them; if they were acquainted with the various qualities of all birds, of all fish, of all animals, of men, of trees, of stones, of roots, and of waters — write that

24

this would not be perfect joy." Shortly after, he cried out again:
"O Brother Leo, if the Friars Minor had the gift of preaching so
as to convert all infidels to the faith of Christ, write that this
would not be perfect joy." Now when this manner of discourse
had lasted for the space of two miles, Brother Leo wondered much
within himself; and, questioning the saint, he said: "Father, I
pray thee teach me wherein is perfect joy." St Francis answered:
"If, when we shall arrive at St Mary of the Angels, all drenched
with rain and trembling with cold, all covered with mud and ex-
hausted from hunger; if, when we knock at the convent-gate,
the porter should come angrily and ask us who we are; if, after
we have told him, 'We are two of the brethren', he should answer angrily, 'What ye say is not the truth; ye are but two impostors going about to deceive the world, and take away the alms
of the poor; begone I say'; if then he refuse to open to us, and
leave us outside, exposed to the snow and rain, suffering from
cold and hunger till nightfall — then, if we accept such injus-
tice, such cruelty and such contempt with patience, without being
ruffled and without murmuring, believing with humility and charity that the porter really knows us, and that it is God who maketh
him to speak thus against us, write down, O Brother Leo, that
this is perfect joy. And if we knock again, and the porter come
out in anger to drive us away with oaths and blows, as if we were
vile impostors, saying, 'Begone, miserable robbers! go to the hospital, for here you shall neither eat nor sleep!' — and if we accept all this with patience, with joy, and with charity, O Brother
Leo, write that this indeed is perfect joy. And if, urged by cold
and hunger, we knock again, calling to the porter and entreating
him with many tears to open to us and give us shelter, for the
love of God, and if he come out more angry than before, exclaiming, 'These are but importunate rascals, I will deal with them
as they deserve'; and taking a knotted stick, he seize us by the

25

hood, throwing us on the ground, rolling us in the snow, and shall beat and wound us with the knots in the stick — if we bear all these injuries with patience and joy, thinking of the sufferings of our Blessed Lord, which we would share out of love for him, write, O Brother Leo, that here, finally, is perfect joy. And now, brother, listen to the conclusion. Above all the graces and all the gifts of the Holy Spirit which Christ grants to his friends, is the grace of overcoming oneself, and accepting willingly, out of love for Christ, all suffering, injury, discomfort and contempt; for in all other gifts of God we cannot glory, seeing they proceed not from ourselves but from God, according to the words of the Apostle, 'What hast thou that thou hast not received from God? and if thou hast received it, why dost thou glory as if thou hadst not received it?' But in the cross of tribulation and affliction we may glory, because, as the Apostle says again, 'I will not glory save in the cross of our Lord Jesus Christ.' Amen."

CHAPTER IX

ONCE, at the beginning of the Order, St Francis was with Brother Leo in a convent, where they had no books wherewith to say divine office. So, when the hour of Matins arrived, St Francis said to Brother Leo: "My beloved brother, we have no Breviary wherewith to say Matins, but in order to employ the time in praising God, I will speak, and thou shalt answer me as I shall teach thee; and beware thou change not the words I shall bid thee say. Thus will I begin: 'O Brother Francis, thou hast done so much evil, and hast committed so many sins in the world, that thou art only worthy of hell'; and thou, Brother Leo, shalt answer: 'It is very true thou art worthy of the nethermost hell.'" And Brother Leo said, with the simplicity of a dove, "Right willingly, Father; begin, then, in the name of God." St Francis therefore began thus: "O Brother Francis, thou hast done so much evil, and hast committed so many sins in the world, that thou art worthy of hell." And Brother Leo made answer: "God will work so much good through thee, that thou wilt certainly go to heaven". "Do not speak thus, Brother Leo," said St Francis; "but when I say, 'Brother Francis, thou hast committed so many iniquities against God, that thou art worthy to be cursed by him,' thou shalt make answer: 'Yes, indeed, thou art worthy to be numbered among the cursed.'" And Brother Leo answered: "Most willingly, O my Father." Then St Francis, with many tears and sighs, striking his breast, cried with a loud voice: "O Lord of heaven and earth, I have committed against thee so many sins and so great iniquities, that I deserve to be cursed by thee." And Brother Leo answered: "O Brother Francis, among all the blessed the Lord will cause thee to be singularly blessed." And St Francis, much surprised that Brother Leo answered quite the contrary to what he had ordered him, reproved him for it, saying: "Why answerest thou not as I taught thee? I command thee, under holy obedience, so to do. When I say, 'O wicked Brother Francis, dost thou think God will have mercy on thee, when thou hast so sinned against the Father of mercies that thou art not worthy of finding mercy', then thou, Brother Leo, my little lamb, shalt answer: 'Thou art not worthy of finding mercy.'" But when St Francis began to repeat, "O wicked Brother Francis," and so on, Brother Leo answered: "God the Father, whose mercy is infinitely greater than thy sin, will show great mercy upon thee, and will grant thee likewise many graces." At this answer St Francis, being meekly angry, and patiently impatient, said to Brother Leo: "How canst thou presume to act against obedience? Why hast thou so often answered the contrary to what I ordered thee?" With great humility and respect Brother Leo answered: "God knows, my Father, that I had resolved in my heart each time to answer as thou didst command me, but the Lord made me to speak as it pleased him, and not as it pleased me." Then St Francis, being greatly astonished, said to Brother Leo: "I entreat thee, beloved, this time to answer as I command thee." And Brother Leo said: "Speak, in the name of God; for this time most certainly I will answer thee as thou desirest." And St Francis, weeping, said: "O wicked Brother Francis, dost thou think that God will have mercy on thee?" And Brother Leo answered: "Not only will he have mercy on thee, but thou shalt receive from him especial graces: he will exalt thee and glorify thee to all eternity, for he that humbleth himself shall be exalted; and I cannot speak otherwise, because it is God that speaketh by my lips." After this in humble contest, they watched till morning in many tears and much spiritual consolation.

CHAPTER X

HOW BROTHER MASSEO TOLD ST FRANCIS, AS IN JEST,
THAT THE WORLD WAS GONE AFTER HIM; AND HOW
ST FRANCIS ANSWERED THAT IT WAS INDEED SO, TO
THE CONFUSION OF THE WORLD AND THROUGH THE
GRACE OF GOD

ST FRANCIS once was living at the Convent of the Portiuncula, with Brother Masseo of Marignano, a man of great sanctity and great discernment, who held frequent converse with
God; for which reason St Francis loved him much. One day, as
St Francis was returning from the forest, where he had been in
prayer, the said Brother Masseo, wishing to test the humility of
the saint, went forth to meet him exclaiming: "Why after thee?
Why after thee?" To which St Francis made answer: "What is
this? What meanest thou?" Brother Masseo answered: "I mean,
why is it that all the world goeth after thee; why do all men wish
to see thee, to hear thee, and to obey thy word? For thou art neither comely nor learned, nor art thou of noble birth. How is it,
then, that all the world goeth after thee?" St Francis, hearing
these words, rejoiced greatly in spirit, and lifting up his eyes to
heaven, remained for a long space with his mind rapt in God;
then, coming to himself, he knelt down, returning thanks to God
with great fervour of spirit, and addressing Brother Masseo, said
to him: "Wouldst thou know why all men come after me? Know
that it is because the Lord, who is in heaven, who sees the evil
and the good in all places — because, I say, his holy eyes have
found among men no one more wicked, more imperfect, or a
greater sinner than I am; and to accomplish the wonderful work
which he intends to do, he has found no creature more vile than

29

I am on earth; for which reason he has chosen me, to confound all strength, beauty, greatness, noble birth, and all the science of the world, that men may learn that every virtue and every good gift cometh from him, and not from any creature, that

none may glory before him; but if any one glory, let him glory in the Lord, to whom belongeth all glory in eternity." Then Bro‑ ther Masseo, at such a humble answer, given with so much fer‑ vour, was greatly impressed, and learned of a certainty that St Francis was well grounded in humility.

CHAPTER XI

HOW ST FRANCIS MADE BROTHER MASSEO TURN ROUND AND ROUND LIKE A CHILD, AND THEN TO GO TO SIENA

ONE day, as St Francis was travelling with Brother Masseo, who was walking in front, they arrived at a spot where three roads met, one leading to Florence, one to Siena, and one to Arezzo, and Brother Masseo asked of St Francis which road they should take. "The one which God wills," answered St Francis. Said Brother Masseo: "And how are we to know the will of God?" "By the sign I shall show thee," answered St Francis; "I order thee, by the merit of holy obedience, on the spot where now thou art, to turn round and round, as children do in play, and not to stop or rest until I bid thee." On this Brother Masseo began to turn round and round, until his head became dizzy, as is wont to happen from such turning, and he fell down several times. But, as St Francis did not bid him to stop, he went on, out of obedience, till at last St Francis said: "Stand still, and move not; but tell me towards which of the three roads thou art turned?" "Towards that which leadeth to Siena," answered Brother Masseo. "That is the road," said St Francis, "which it pleaseth God we should take." As he went on his way, Brother Masseo wondered in himself why St Francis had made him to turn round like a child, in the presence of all those who passed that way, but out of reverence to the saint he did not dare ask him. As they reached Siena, the people of that city, having heard that the saint was approaching, went, out of devotion, to meet him, and taking him and Brother Masseo on their shoulders, carried them to the Bishop's palace, so that their feet touched not the ground.

In that same hour some of the inhabitants of Siena were fighting among themselves, and two of them had been killed. Then St Francis, hurrying to the spot, spoke to them so devoutly and in such holy words, that he constrained them all to make peace and give over quarrelling. The Bishop, having heard tell of the holy action of St Francis, invited him to his house, and received him with great honour, retaining him with him all that day and the following night. The next morning, St Francis, who in all his acts sought only the glory of God, rose very early with his companion, and went his way, without even taking leave of the Bishop; at which Brother Masseo murmured within himself, saying, as he went, "What is this that this good man has done? He has made me turn round and round like a child, and he leaves the Bishop, who has received him with such honour, without saying a word, or even thanking him"; for it seemed to Brother Masseo that St Francis had acted indiscreetly; but, inwardly checked by a divine inspiration, he thus reproached himself for indulging in such thoughts: "Thou art too proud who darest to judge the operation of divine grace; thine indiscreet pride makes thee worthy of hell; for Brother Francis yesterday performed such holy actions, that they could not be more wonderful had they been accomplished by an angel of God: so that even were he to order thee to throw stones, thou shouldst do so out of obedience; for that which he has done at Siena is the work of God, as the result proveth, for had he not pacified the men who were fighting together, not only would many have fallen victims, but the devil would have drawn many souls to hell. It is thy folly and thy pride which make thee to murmur at that which proceeds so manifestly from the will of God." Now all these things which Brother Masseo said in his heart were revealed to St Francis, who, coming up to him, said: "Hold fast the things which thou art thinking of at this moment, for they are good and useful, and inspired by God; but thy mur-

32

murings, which preceded them, were blind and vain and full of
pride, being sent into thy soul by the devil." Then Brother Masseo clearly saw that St Francis knew the secrets of his heart, and
understood of a certainty how the spirit of divine wisdom directed all the actions of his holy father.

CHAPTER XII

HOW ST FRANCIS GAVE TO BROTHER MASSEO THE OFFICE OF PORTER, OF ALMONER AND OF COOK; AND HOW, AT THE REQUEST OF THE OTHER BRETHREN, HE AFTERWARDS TOOK THESE DUTIES FROM HIM

ST FRANCIS, wishing to mortify Brother Masseo, that pride
should not enter his soul, because of the many graces and gifts
he had received from God, and also that, through the grace
of humility, he should advance from virtue to virtue, once when he
was residing in a solitary convent with his first companions, who
were all examples of holiness, of which number Brother Masseo
was one, he said unto the latter, before all the brethren: "O Brother Masseo, all these thy companions have the grace of contemplation and of prayer; but thou hast the grace of preaching the
word of God and of pleasing the people. I will therefore, in order
that they may give themselves to contemplation, that thou fill
the office of porter, of almoner and of cook, and that, when the
other monks shall be at their meals, thou alone shalt eat outside
the convent-gate, so as to be ready to say a few godly words to
such as come to the convent, before they knock at the gate, and
so that none other shall be obliged to go out but thee; this thou
shalt accomplish, through the virtue of holy obedience." Then
Brother Masseo put down his hood, bowed his head, and meekly
received and executed this order; filling for some days the offices

of porter, of almoner and of cook. At this his companions, who were all men enlightened by the Spirit of God, seeing him thus employed, began to feel in their hearts great remorse, considering how Brother Masseo had reached a greater state of perfection than any of them, and how all the work of the convent fell to his share, and none to theirs. Then went they all to St Francis, begging him to divide among them those charges, since they could not in conscience allow Brother Masseo to bear all the burden of the convent. At this St Francis, heeding their request, granted what they asked, and calling Brother Masseo, said unto him: "Brother Masseo, thy brethren wish to share the charges I have given thee, wherefore I will that the charges be divided among you all." Said Brother Masseo, with great humility and patience: "Father, whatever charge thou puttest upon me, be it small or be it great, I accept it as ordained by the Lord." Then St Francis, seeing the charity of the brethren and the humility of Brother Masseo, made them a most wonderful sermon on holy humility, teaching them that, the greater the gifts and graces we receive from God, so much greater must be our humility; for without humility no virtue can be acceptable to him. Then, having finished his sermon, he distributed the charges among them with great charity.

CHAPTER XIII

HOW ST FRANCIS AND BROTHER MASSEO PLACED THE BREAD
THEY HAD BEGGED UPON A STONE NEAR A FOUNTAIN; AND
HOW ST FRANCIS PRAISED THE VIRTUE OF HOLY POVERTY,
PRAYING ST PETER AND ST PAUL TO MAKE HIM LOVE HOLY
POVERTY GREATLY. AND HOW ST PETER AND
ST PAUL APPEARED TO HIM

THE wonderful servant and follower of Christ, St Francis, wishing to be in all things conformed to his Master — who, as the Gospel tells, sent his disciples two by two into all the cities and lands whither he intended to go to prepare the way for him — after he had assembled his twelve companions, sent them forth two by two into the world to preach. In order to set them an example of holy obedience; he first began to act himself like the Saviour Jesus Christ. Wherefore, having sent his companions to divers parts of the world, he took with him Brother Masseo, and set out towards the province of France. On arriving in a cer‹ tain town, being very hungry, they went, according to the Rule, begging their bread for the love of God. St Francis took one street, and Brother Masseo the other. St Francis, being a little man, with a mean exterior, did not attract much attention, and gathered only a few bits of dry bread, whereas Brother Masseo, being tall and good-looking, received many large pieces of bread, with several whole loaves. When they had ended their task of begging, they met on a spot outside the city where there was a beautiful fountain and a large stone, on which each placed what he had collected. St Francis, seeing that the pieces of bread which Brother Masseo had collected were much larger and better than those he had received, rejoiced greatly, and said: "O Brother

Masseo, we are not worthy of this great treasure"; and he repeated these words several times. At this Brother Masseo answered: "Father, how canst thou talk of a treasure where there is so much poverty, and indeed a lack of all things? for we have neither cloth, nor knife, nor dish, nor table, nor house to eat in, nor servant or maid to wait upon us." St Francis answered: "This is indeed the reason why I account it a great treasure, because man has had no hand in it, but all has been given to us by divine Providence, as we clearly see in this bread of charity, this beautiful table of stone, and this so clear fountain. Wherefore let us beg of God to make us love with all our hearts the treasure of holy poverty." Having spoken thus, they returned thanks; and when they had refreshed themselves with the bread and water, they rose and went on their way to France. And meeting with a church on the road, St Francis said to his companion, "Let us enter this church and pray." And entering in, St Francis cast himself down in prayer before the altar, and during his prayer the Lord visited him with a great increase of fervour, which so inflamed his soul with affection for holy poverty, that it seemed as if flames played around his head, and proceeded from his mouth; and going thus, all shining and burning with divine love, to his companion, he said to him, "Ah! ah! ah! Brother Masseo, give thyself to me"; and these words he repeated three times. At the third time he breathed on Brother Masseo, who, to his great surprise, was raised above the earth, and fell at some distance before the saint. He told his companion afterwards that, while thus raised in the air, he had felt such a sweet sensation in his soul, and had received such consolations from the Holy Spirit, as he had never before experienced. After this St Francis said to his companion: "Let us go to St Peter and St Paul, and let us pray them together that they may teach us and help us to possess the unbounded treasure of holy poverty, for it is a treasure

36

so great and so divine, that we are not worthy to possess it in these vile bodies of ours. It is this celestial virtue which teaches us to despise all earthly and transitory things, and through it every hindrance is removed from the soul, so that it can freely commune with God. Through this virtue it is that the soul, while still on earth, is able to converse with the angels in heaven. This virtue it is which remained with Christ upon the cross, was buried with Christ, rose again with Christ, and with Christ went up into heaven. This virtue it is which even in this world enables the souls who are inflamed with love of him to fly up to heaven; it is also the guardian of true charity and humility. Let us then pray the holy Apostles of Christ, who were perfect lovers of this evangelical pearl, to obtain for us from the Saviour Jesus the grace, through his great mercy, to become true lovers, strict observers, and humble disciples of this most precious, most beloved, and most evangelical grace of poverty." And thus conversing they arrived at Rome, and entered the church of St Peter, where St Francis knelt in prayer in one corner and Brother Masseo in another. After praying for some time with great devotion and many tears, the most holy Apostles Peter and Paul appeared to St Francis in much splendour, and thus addressed him: "As thy prayer and thy wish is to observe that which Christ and his holy Apostles observed, the Lord Jesus sends us to thee, to tell thee that thy prayer has been heard, and that it is granted to thee and to all thy followers to possess the treasure of holy poverty. We tell thee also from him, that whosoever, after thy example, shall embrace this holy virtue, shall most certainly enjoy perfect happiness in heaven; for thou and all thy followers shall be blessed by God." Having said these words they disappeared, leaving St Francis full of consolation. Then rising from prayer, and returning to Brother Masseo, he asked him if God had revealed anything to him in prayer. He answered, "No." Then St Francis told him how the holy Apostles had appeared to him, and what they had said. And both being filled with joy, they resolved to return to the Valley of Spoleto, giving up the journey into France.

CHAPTER XIV

HOW THE LORD APPEARED TO ST FRANCIS AND TO HIS BRETHREN AS HE WAS SPEAKING WITH THEM

IN the beginning of the Order, St Francis, having assembled his companions to speak to them of Christ, in a moment of great fervour of spirit commanded one of them, in the name of God, to open his mouth and speak as the Holy Spirit should inspire him. The brother, doing as he was ordered, spoke most wonderfully of God. Then St Francis bade him to be silent, and ordered another brother to speak in the same way, which having done with much penetration, St Francis ordered him likewise to be silent, and commanded a third brother to do the same. This one began to speak so deeply of the things of God, that St Francis was convinced that both he and his companions had spoken through the Holy Spirit. Of which also he received a manifest proof; for whilst they were thus speaking together, our Blessed Lord appeared in the midst of them, under the form of a beautiful young man, and blessed them all. And they, being ravished out of themselves, fell to the ground as if they had been dead, and were all unconscious of things external. And when they recovered from their trance, St Francis said to them: "My beloved brothers, let us thank God, who has deigned to reveal to the world, through his humble servants, the treasures of divine wisdom. For the Lord it is who openeth the mouth of the dumb, and maketh the tongues of the simple to speak wisdom."

CHAPTER XV

ST FRANCIS, when residing at Assisi, often visited St Clare, to give her holy counsel. And she, having a great desire to eat once with him, often begged him to grant her this request; but the saint would never allow her this consolation. His companions, therefore, being aware of the refusal of St Francis, and knowing how great was the wish of Sister Clare to eat with him, went to seek him, and thus addressed him: "Father, it seems to us that this severity on thy part in not granting so small a thing to Sister Clare, a virgin so holy and so dear to God, who merely asks for once to eat with thee, is not according to holy charity, especially if we consider how it was at thy preaching that she abandoned the riches and pomps of this world. Of a truth, if she were to ask of thee even a greater grace than this, thou shouldst grant it to thy spiritual daughter." St Francis answered: "It seems to you, then, that I ought to grant her this request?" His companions made answer: "Yea, father, it is meet that thou grant her this favour and this consolation." St Francis answered: "As you think so, let it be so, then; but, in order that she may be the more consoled, I will that the meal do take place in front of St Mary of the Angels, because, having been for so long time shut up in San Damiano, it will do her good to see the church of St Mary, wherein she took the veil, and was made a spouse of Christ. There, then, we will eat together in the name of God." When the appointed day arrived, St Clare left her convent with great joy, taking with her one of her sisters, and followed by the companions of St Francis. She arrived at St Mary of the Angels, and having devoutly saluted the Virgin Mary, before whose altar her hair had been cut off, and she had received the veil, they conducted her to the convent, and showed her all over it. In the meantime St Francis prepared the meal on the bare ground, as was his custom. The hour of dinner being arrived, St Francis and St Clare, with one of the brethren of St Francis and the sister who had accompanied the saint, sat down together, all the other companions of St Francis seated humbly round them. When the first dish was served, St Francis began to speak of God so sweetly, so sublimely, and in a manner so wonderful, that the grace of God visited them abundantly, and all were rapt in Christ. Whilst they were thus rapt, with eyes and hearts raised to heaven, the people of Assisi and of Bettona, and of all the country round about, saw St Mary of the Angels as it were on fire, with the convent and the woods adjoining. It seemed to them as if the church, the convent, and the woods were all enveloped in flames; and the inhabitants of Assisi hastened with great speed to put out the fire. On arriving at the convent, they found no fire; and entering within the gates they saw St Francis, St Clare, with all their companions, sitting round their humble meal, absorbed in contemplation; then knew they of a certainty, that what they had seen was a celestial fire, not a material one, which God miraculously had sent to bear witness to the divine flame of love which consumed the souls of those holy brethren and nuns; and they returned home with great consolation in their hearts, and much holy edification. After a long lapse of time, St Francis, St Clare, and their companions came back to themselves; and, being fully restored by the spiritual food, cared not to eat that which had been prepared for them; so that, the holy meal being finished, St Clare, well accompanied, returned to San Damiano, where the sisters received her with great joy, as they had feared that

40

St Francis might have sent her to rule some other convent, as he had already sent St Agnes, the sister of the saint, to be Abbess of the Convent of Monticelli, at Florence. For St Francis had often said to St Clare, "Be ready, in case I send thee to some other convent"; and she, like a daughter of holy obedience, had answered, "Father, I am always ready to go whithersoever thou shalt send me." For which reason the sisters greatly rejoiced when she returned to them, and St Clare was from that time much consoled.

CHAPTER XVI

HOW ST FRANCIS, HAVING BEEN TOLD BY ST CLARE AND THE HOLY BROTHER SILVESTER THAT HE SHOULD PREACH AND CONVERT MANY TO THE FAITH, FOUNDED THE THIRD ORDER, PREACHED TO THE BIRDS, AND REDUCED TO SILENCE THE SWALLOWS

THE humble servant of Christ, St Francis, a short time after his conversion, having already assembled and received many brothers into the Order, was much troubled and perplexed in mind as to what he ought to do; whether to give himself entirely to prayer, or now and then to preach the Word. Through his great humility, he had no opinion of himself or of the virtue of his prayers; and, wishing to know the will of God, he sought to learn it through the prayers of others. Wherefore he called to him Brother Masseo, and thus addressed him: "Go to Sister Clare, and bid her from me to set herself with some of the holiest of her sisters to pray the Lord that he may show me clearly whether he wills that I should preach or only keep to prayer. Then go to Brother Silvester, and ask of him the same favour." Now Brother Silvester had been in the world, and was the same who had seen in vision a golden cross come out of St Francis's mouth,

41

whose height reached up to heaven and its breadth to the farthest extremities of the world. Brother Silvester was so holy, that whatever he asked of God was granted to his prayer, and very often he held converse with the Lord; so that St Francis revered him greatly. Then Brother Masseo did as St Francis had commanded him; carrying the message first to St Clare, and then to Brother Silvester, who set about praying immediately; and, having received the answer from the Lord, returned to Brother Masseo, and said to him: "The Lord says, go and tell Brother Francis that he has not called him to this state to save merely his own soul but that he may produce fruits in those of others, and that through him many should be saved." Having received this answer, Brother Masseo returned to Sister Clare, to ask what she had learnt from God; and she told him that she and all her companions had received from God the same answer as the Lord had given to Brother Silvester. Then Brother Masseo hastened to St Francis to bring him these answers; and St Francis received him with great charity, washing his feet, and serving him at dinner. When the repast was over, he called Brother Masseo into the forest, and, kneeling down before him, put back his hood; and crossing his arms on his breast, he said to him: "What answer dost thou bring me? what does my Lord Jesus Christ order me to do?" Brother Masseo answered: "The Lord Jesus Christ has revealed both to Brother Silvester and to Sister Clare, that it is his will thou shouldst go about the world to preach; for thou hast not been called for thyself alone, but for the salvation of others." Then St Francis, having received the answer, and knowing it to be the will of the Lord Jesus Christ, arose with fervour, saying, "Let us go in the name of God"; and taking with him Brother Masseo and Brother Agnolo, both holy men, he let himself be guided by the Spirit of God, without considering the road he took. They soon arrived at a town called Savurniano, where

St Francis began to preach, first ordering the swallows, who were
calling, to keep silence until he had finished; and the swallows
obeyed his voice. He preached with such fervour, that the inhabitants of the town wished to follow him out of devotion; but
St Francis would not allow them, saying: "Be not in such haste,
and leave not your homes. I will tell you what you must do to
save your souls." Thereupon he founded the Third Order for
the salvation of all; and leaving them much consoled and well
disposed to do penance, he departed thence, and reached a spot
between Cannaio and Bevagno. And as he went on his way, with
great fervour, St Francis lifted up his eyes, and saw on some trees

by the wayside a great multitude of birds; and being much surprised, he said to his companions, "Wait for me here by the way,
whilst I go and preach to my little sisters the birds"; and entering into the field, he began to preach to the birds which were on
the ground, and suddenly all those also on the trees came round
him, and all listened while St Francis preached to them, and did
not fly away until he had given them his blessing. And Brother
Masseo related afterwards to Brother James of Massa how St
Francis went among them and even touched them with his garments, and how none of them moved. Now the substance of the
sermon was this: "My little sisters the birds, ye owe much to God,
your Creator, and ye ought to sing his praise at all times and in
all places, because he has given you liberty to fly about into all

43

places; and though ye neither spin nor sew, he has given you a twofold and a threefold clothing for yourselves and for your offspring. Two of all your species he sent into the Ark with Noe that you might not be lost to the world; besides which, he feeds you, though ye neither sow nor reap. He has given you fountains and rivers to quench your thirst, mountains and valleys in which to take refuge, and trees in which to build your nests; so that your Creator loves you much, having thus favoured you with such bounties. Beware, my little sisters, of the sin of ingratitude, and study always to give praise to God." As he said these words, all the birds began to open their beaks, to stretch their necks, to spread their wings, and reverently to bow their heads to the ground, endeavouring by their motions and by their songs to manifest their joy to St Francis. And the saint rejoiced with them. He wondered to see such a multitude of birds, and was charmed with their beautiful variety, with their attention and familiarity, for all which he devoutly gave thanks to the Creator. Having finished his sermon, St Francis made the sign of the cross, and gave them leave to fly away. Then all those birds rose up into the air, singing most sweetly; and, following the sign of the cross, which St Francis had made, they divided themselves into four companies. One company flew towards the east, another towards the west, one towards the south, and one towards the north; each company as it went singing most wonderfully; signifying thereby, that as St Francis, the bearer of the Cross of Christ, had preached to them and made upon them the sign of the cross, after which they had divided among themselves the four parts of the world, so the preaching of the Cross of Christ, renewed by St Francis, would be carried by him and by his brethren over all the world, and that the humble friars, like little birds, should possess nothing in this world, but should cast all the care of their lives on the providence of God.

CHAPTER XVII

HOW A LITTLE CHILD WHO HAD ENTERED THE ORDER SAW
ST FRANCIS IN PRAYER ONE NIGHT, AND SAW ALSO THE
SAVIOUR, THE VIRGIN MARY, AND MANY OTHER
SAINTS TALK WITH HIM

A CERTAIN pure and innocent child was received into the
Order during the lifetime of St Francis, and the convent
in which he lived was so small that the monks were obliged
to sleep on mats. It chanced that St Francis came one day to that
convent, and in the evening, after Compline, he went to rest, so
as to rise up early to pray, as was his custom, when all the other
friars were still asleep. The said little child had made up his mind
carefully to watch St Francis, to learn something of his sanctity,
and find out more especially what he did in the night when he
got up; and in order that he might not be overtaken by sleep,
he laid him down by St Francis, tying the end of the cord he wore
round his waist to the one which the saint wore, so that he was
sure of being awakened when the latter got up in the night; and
this he did so gently, that St Francis was not aware of his contri-
vance. When all the other friars were fast asleep, St Francis rose
from sleep, and finding the child's cord tied to his own, he carefully untied it so as not to awake him and went alone into the
wood which was near the convent. Entering into a little cell
which was there, he began to pray. Shortly after, the child
awoke, and finding St Francis gone, and the cord untied, he rose
up quickly and went to seek him. Perceiving the door open which
led to the wood, he thought St Francis had gone that way; and
entering into the wood, and hurrying on to the little cell, he heard
the sound of many voices. Approaching near to hear and see

whence they came, he saw a great and wonderful light all round
the saint, and in the light was Jesus Christ, with the Virgin Mary,
St John the Baptist, St John the Evangelist, and a great multitude
of angels, all talking with St Francis. On seeing this the child fell
to the ground as if he had been dead. The miracle of this holy
vision being ended, St Francis rose to return to the convent, and
stumbling in the way against the child, who appeared to be dead,

with great compassion he took him up in his arms and carried
him in his bosom, as the good shepherd is wont to carry his lambs.
Having learned from him how he had seen the vision, he forbade
him to tell any man thereof so long as he, St Francis, lived. The
little child grew up in the grace of God, and had a great devotion to St Francis. He became one of the most distinguished men
of the Order. After the death of St Francis, he related the vision
to the brethren.

CHAPTER XVIII

THE faithful servant of Christ, St Francis, once held a general chapter at St Mary of the Angels, at which chapter more than five thousand friars were present. Amongst them also was St Dominic, the head and founder of the Order of Friars Preachers, who chanced to be on his way from Bologna to Rome: for having heard of the chapter which St Francis had called together in the plain of St Mary of the Angels, he went there with seven friars of his Order. A certain Cardinal also, much devoted to St Francis, to whom the saint had foretold that he would one day be Pope, came expressly from Perugia to Assisi, and every day he went to visit St Francis and his brethren. Sometimes he sang Mass and preached to them; and each time the said Cardinal visited the holy company he experienced much pleasure and devotion. Seeing the friars all seated in the plain round St Mary of the Angels, in groups — here forty, there a hundred, and elsewhere eighty, all occupied in conversing about God, or in prayer, or in works of charity — seeing them all so silent and so grave, and wondering how such a multitude could be so orderly, he was moved to tears, and exclaimed, with great devotion, "Truly this is the field of God; this is the army, and these are the knights of the Lord." No vain or useless word was to be heard in all that multitude; each group of friars was engaged either in prayer, or saying their office, in weeping over their sins and those of their benefactors, or in reasoning on the salvation of souls. Many tents made of mats had been pitched in that field, divided

47

in groups, according to the different provinces from whence the friars came; so that this Chapter was called the "Chapter of mats".

The friars had no other beds but the bare ground, with here and there a little straw; for pillows they had stones or pieces of wood. For which reasons they were held in much devotion; and so great was the fame of their sanctity, that many came to see and hear them from the court of the Pope which was at Perugia, and from other parts of the Valley of Spoleto. Many counts and barons, many knights and other gentlemen, many Cardinals, Bishops and Abbots, many priests and much people, came to see this great and holy and humble congregation; for the world had never yet witnessed so many holy men assembled together; and most especially they went thither to see the saintly founder and father of the Order, who had taken from the world so many gifted men, and had formed so beautiful and devout a flock to follow the steps of the true Pastor, Jesus Christ. The chapter being assembled, St Francis, the father of all those holy men, expounded with great fervour of spirit the Word of God, speaking to them in a loud voice that which the Holy Spirit dictated. Now the subject he took for his sermon was this: "My children, we have promised great things to God, and God has promised even greater things to us. If we observe what we have promised him, we shall certainly receive what he has promised to us. The pleasures of this world pass quickly away, but the punishment which follows them is eternal. The sufferings of this world are trifling, but the glory of the life to come is without bounds." And, preaching on these words most devoutly, he comforted the brethren, encouraging them to holy obedience, to reverence for holy Mother Church, to charity among themselves, to pray God for all people, to bear with patience the adversities of life, to be temperate in prosperity, to keep angelic purity and chastity, to

be at peace with God, with men and with their own conscience, to love, to observe, and to practise holy poverty. He then added: "I command you all here present, through holy obedience, to take no thought what you shall eat or what you shall drink, or of aught else that is necessary to the body, but only to meditate, to pray, and to praise God, casting on him the thought of all the rest, for he has you all in his especial care; and let each of you receive this command with a happy heart and a joyful countenance." St Francis having finished his sermon, all the friars began to pray. Yet St Dominic, who was present, wondered much at this order of St Francis, considering it as indiscreet, for he could not understand how such a great multitude could exist without taking thought for the body. But the heavenly Pastor, our Blessed Saviour, wishing to show the care he takes of his lambs, and with what singular love he loves his poor servants, put into the hearts of all the people of Perugia, of Spoleto, of Foligno, of Spello, of Assisi, and of all the neighbouring country, to take meat and drink to that holy congregation; and presently men came from all these places with horses, and asses, and carts, laden with bread

49

and wine, with beans and cheese, and other good things of which the poor of Christ had need. Besides all this, they brought napkins and knives, jugs and glasses, and all that was needed for such a multitude; and those who could carry most and serve the best rejoiced greatly, and the knights, barons and other noblemen, who were present, waited on the brethren with great devotion and humility. St Dominic, seeing this, and knowing of a certainty that it was the divine providence of God which had provided for them thus, acknowledged most humbly that he had unjustly accused St Francis of giving indiscreet orders; and going to him, he knelt humbly before him and confessed his fault, adding: "The Lord truly hath especial care of all these holy servants of poverty. I knew it not till now, and henceforth I promise to observe holy evangelical poverty; and, in the name of God, I condemn all friars of my Order who shall seek to have possessions of their own." And St Dominic was greatly edified by the faith of the most holy Francis, by the obedience and poverty of so large and well-ordered a chapter, and he blessed the providence of God, who had given them every grace in such abundance. In that same chapter also it was revealed to St Francis that many brethren wore on their flesh small hearts and bands of iron, for which reason many were ill and hindered in their prayers; and St Francis, like a discreet father, gave order, under holy obedience, that all who wore such things should take them off and place them before him; and more than five hundred little hearts and bands of iron were placed before him — some destined to be worn round the arms, and others round the waist — and all together formed a large heap, which St Francis ordered to be left in that field. The chapter being ended, he encouraged them all in well-doing, warning them how to avoid sin in this wicked world, and sent them back to their divers provinces, with his blessing and that of God, filled with spiritual joy and consolation.

CHAPTER XIX

HOW THE VINE OF THE PRIEST OF RIETI, WHOSE HOUSE ST FRANCIS
ENTERED TO PRAY, WAS TRAMPLED UNDER FOOT BY THE GREAT
NUMBERS WHO CAME TO SEE HIM, AND HOW IT YET PRODUCED
A GREATER QUANTITY OF WINE THAN USUAL, AS ST FRANCIS HAD
PROMISED; AND HOW THE LORD REVEALED TO THE SAINT THAT
HEAVEN WOULD BE HIS PORTION WHEN HE LEFT THIS WORLD

ST FRANCIS at one time being grievously tormented with a disease in his eyes, the Cardinal Ugolino, protector of his Order, who loved him dearly, wrote to him to come to Rieti, where there were excellent oculists. St Francis, having received the Cardinal's letter, set off first to San Damiano, where was Sister Clare, the devout spouse of Christ, to give her some spiritual consolation, intending afterwards to go on to the Cardinal. On arriving at San Damiano, the following night his eyes grew so much worse that he could not see the light, and was obliged to give up going any farther. Then Sister Clare made him a little cell of reeds, in order that he might repose the better; but St Francis, owing partly to the pain he suffered, and partly to the multitude of rats, which much annoyed him, could rest neither day or night. After suffering for several days this pain and tribulation, he began to think that it was sent to him by God as a punishment for his sins, and he thanked the Lord in his heart and with his lips, crying out with a loud voice: "My God, I am worthy of this, and even of worse. My Lord Jesus Christ, thou Good Shepherd, who hast shown thy mercy to us poor sinners in the various bodily pains and sufferings it pleaseth thee to send us; grant to me, thy little lamb, that no pain, however great, no infirmity nor anguish, shall ever separate me from thee." Having made this prayer, a voice came from heaven, which said: "Fran-

51

cis, if all the earth were of gold, if all the seas and all the foun‹
tains and all the rivers were of balm, if all mountains, all hills,
and all rocks were made of precious stones, and if thou couldst
find a treasure as much more precious again as gold is more pre‹
cious than earth, and balm than water, and gems than mountains
and rocks, if that precious treasure were offered to thee in the
place of thy infirmity, wouldst thou not rejoice and be content?"
St Francis answered: "Lord, I am unworthy of such a treasure."
And the voice of God said again: "Rejoice with all thy heart,
Francis, for such a treasure is life eternal, which I have in keep‹
ing for thee, and even now promise to thee; and this thine infir‹
mity and affliction is a pledge of that blessed treasure." Then was
St Francis filled with joy at so glorious a promise; and calling his
companion, he said to him: "Let us go to the Cardinal." He
humbly took leave of Sister Clare, after having comforted her
with holy words, and took the road to Rieti. When he approach‹
ed the town, such a multitude came out to meet him, that he
would not go into the city, but went to a church which was about
two miles off. But the people, hearing where he was gone, went
thither to see him; so that the vine which surrounded the church
was greatly injured, and all the grapes were gathered; at which
the priest, to whom it belonged, was very grieved in his heart,
and repented of having received St Francis in his church. The
thought of the priest being revealed to the saint, he called him
to him and said: "Dearest father, tell me, how many measures
of wine does this vine produce when the year is a fertile one?"
He answered: "Twelve measures." Then said St Francis: "I pray
thee, father, have patience and endure my presence here a few
days longer, as I find great rest in this church; and, for the love of
God and of me his poor servant, let the people gather the grapes
off thy vine; for I promise thee, in the name of my Saviour Jesus
Christ, that it shall produce every year twenty measures of wine."

And St Francis remained there for the benefit of the souls of all who went to see him, for many went away filled with divine love, and gave up the world. The priest, having faith in the promise of St Francis, left the vineyard open to all those who came to see him. And, wonder of wonders! although the vine was entirely ruined, so that there scarcely remained, here and there, a few small bunches of grapes, when the time of vintage arrived, the priest gathered the few bunches which were left, and put them

into the winepress; and according to the promise of St Francis, these few little bunches did not fail to produce twenty measures of excellent wine. This miracle teaches us that as, in consequence of the merits of St Francis, the vine, though despoiled of its grapes, produced an abundance of wine, so in the same way many Christians, whose sins had made them barren of virtue, through the saint's preaching and merits, have often come to abound in the good fruit of repentance.

CHAPTER XX

A YOUNG man, of noble birth and of delicate habits, who had entered the Order of St Francis, was seized after a few days, through the devil's suggestions, with a violent dislike of the habit that he wore: he hated the shape of the sleeves; he felt a horror for the hood, for the length of the dress, and the coarseness of the material; so that it seemed to him as if he carried about him an insupportable weight; and, disliking the Order more and more, he determined to leave it and return to the world. It was the custom of this young man, at whatever hour he passed before the altar in the convent at which the Blessed Sacrament was reserved, to kneel down with great respect and, covering his head with his hood and crossing his arms on his breast, to prostrate himself, as he had been taught to do by the master of novices. It so happened, that the night when he had made up his mind to leave the convent, he passed before the altar, and, kneeling down as he was wont to do, he prostrated himself to the ground, and, being ravished in spirit, the Lord sent him a most wonderful vision. He saw before him a great multitude of saints ranged in procession, two by two, clothed in vestments made of precious material: their faces and their hands shone like the sun; they sang, as they walked, to the sound of celestial music. Two of them were more nobly and more richly dressed than the rest, and surrounded by such a blaze of light that none could look on them without being dazzled. At the end of the procession was one so gloriously adorned, that he seemed, like a new knight, to be more favoured than the others. Now the young man, seeing such a beautiful procession, was struck with wonder; but although he could not guess the meaning of the vision, he dared not ask, and seemed struck dumb with amazement. When the procession had almost passed away, he took courage, and addressing himself to those who were in the rear, he said: "O beloved, I pray you tell me who are these wonderful beings who form this venerable procession." They answered: "Know, my son, that we are all Friars Minor, who are come from the glories of Paradise; and those two who shine forth brighter than the rest, are St Francis and St Anthony; and the last one you saw so especially honoured is a holy friar, lately dead, who having fought with courage against temptation and having persevered to the end, we lead in triumph to the glories of Paradise; and these splendid vestments which adorn us have been given to us by God, in exchange for the coarse tunic we wore with so much patience in religion; and the glorious light which shines upon us has been given in reward for the humility, the holy poverty, the obedience, and chastity that we observed to the end of our lives. Now, my son, do not find the robe of religion too rough to wear; for if, clothed in the sackcloth of St Francis, and out of love to Christ, thou dost despise the world, mortifying thy flesh, and fighting valiantly against the devil, thou too shalt receive these splendid vestments, and shine with this glorious light." On hearing these words the young man came to his senses, and feeling himself much strengthened, he put far from him all temptation to leave the Order, confessed his sin to the guardian and to the brethren, and from that moment dearly loved the coarse vestment of St Francis and the severity of penance, and at length ended his life in the Order in a state of great sanctity.

CHAPTER XXI

OF THE MOST HOLY MIRACLE OF ST FRANCIS IN TAMING THE FIERCE WOLF OF GUBBIO

AT the time when St Francis was living in the city of Gub, bio, a large wolf appeared in the neighbourhood, so terrible and so fierce, that he not only devoured other animals, but made a prey of men also; and since he often approached the town, all the people were in great alarm, and used to go about armed, as if going to battle. Notwithstanding these precautions, if any of the inhabitants ever met him alone, he was sure to be devoured, as all defence was useless: and, through fear of the wolf, they dared not go beyond the city walls. St Francis, feeling great compassion for the people of Gubbio, resolved to go and meet the wolf, though all advised him not to do so. Making the sign of the holy cross, and putting all his confidence in God, he went forth from the city, taking his brethren with him; but these fearing to go any farther, St Francis bent his steps alone toward the spot where the wolf was known to be, while many people fol, lowed at a distance, and witnessed the miracle. The wolf, seeing all this multitude, ran towards St Francis with his jaws wide open. As he approached, the saint, making the sign of the cross, cried out: "Come hither, brother wolf; I command thee, in the name of Christ, neither to harm me nor anybody else." Marvellous to tell, no sooner had St Francis made the sign of the cross, than the terrible wolf, closing his jaws, stopped running, and coming up to St Francis, lay down at his feet as meekly as a lamb. And the saint thus addressed him: "Brother wolf, thou hast done much evil in this land, destroying and killing the creatures of God without his permission; yea, not animals only hast thou de, stroyed, but thou hast even dared to devour men, made after the image of God; for which thing thou art worthy of being hanged like a robber and a murderer. All men cry out against thee, the dogs pursue thee, and all the inhabitants of this city are thy enemies; but I will make peace between them and thee, O brother wolf, if so be thou no more offend them, and they shall forgive thee all thy past offences, and neither men nor dogs shall pursue thee any more." Having listened to these words, the wolf bowed his head, and, by the movements of his body, his tail, and his eyes, made signs that he agreed to what St Francis said. On this St Francis added: "As thou art willing to make this peace, I promise thee that thou shalt be fed every day by the inhabitants of this land so long as thou shalt live among them; thou shalt no longer suffer hunger, as it is hunger which has made thee do so much evil; but if I obtain all this for thee, thou must promise, on thy side, never again to attack any animal or any human being: dost thou make this promise?" Then the wolf, bowing his head, made a sign that he consented. Said St Francis again: "Brother wolf, wilt thou pledge thy faith that I may trust to this thy promise?" and putting out his hand he received the pledge of the wolf; for the latter lifted up his paw and placed it familiarly in the hand of St Francis, giving him thereby the only pledge which was in his power. Then said St Francis, addressing him again: "Brother wolf, I command thee, in the name of Christ, to follow me immediately, without hesitation or doubting, that we may go together to ratify this peace which we have concluded in the name of God"; and the wolf, obeying him, walked by his side as meekly as a lamb, to the great astonishment of all the people. Now, the news of this most wonderful miracle spreading quickly through the town, all the inhabitants, both men and women, small and great, young and old, flocked to the market-place to see St Francis and the wolf. All the people being assembled, the saint got up to preach, saying, amongst other things, how for our sins God permits such calamities, and how much greater and more dangerous are the flames of hell, which last for ever, than the rage of a wolf, which can kill the body only; and how much we ought to dread the jaws of hell, if the jaws of so small an animal as a wolf can make a whole city tremble through fear. The

sermon being ended, St Francis added these words: "Listen, my brethren: the wolf who is here before you has promised and pledged his faith that he consents to make peace with you all, and no more to offend you in aught, and you must promise to give him each day his necessary food; to which, if you consent, I promise in his name that he will most faithfully observe the compact." Then all the people promised with one voice to feed the wolf to the end of his days; and St Francis, addressing the latter, said again: "And thou, brother wolf, dost thou promise to keep the compact, and never again to offend either man or beast, or any other creature?" And the wolf knelt down, bowing his head, and, by the motions of his tail and of his ears, endeavoured to show that he was willing, as far as was in his power, to hold to the compact. Then St Francis continued: "Brother wolf, as thou gavest me a pledge of this thy promise when we were outside the town, so now I will that thou renew it in the sight of all this people, and assure me that I have done well to promise in thy name"; and the wolf lifting up his paw placed it in the hand of St Francis. Now this event caused great joy in all the people, and a great devotion towards St Francis, both because of the novelty of the miracle, and because of the peace which had been concluded with the wolf; and they lifted up their voices to heaven, praising and blessing God, who had sent them St Francis, through whose merits they had been delivered from such a savage beast. The wolf lived two years at Gubbio; he went familiarly from door to door without harming anyone, and all the people received him courteously, feeding him with great pleasure, and no dog barked at him as he went about. At last, after two years, he died of old age, and the people of Gubbio mourned his loss greatly; for when they saw him going about so gently amongst them all, he reminded them of the virtue and sanctity of St Francis.

CHAPTER XXII

HOW ST FRANCIS TAMED THE WILD DOVES

A CERTAIN young man having caught one day a great number of doves, as he was going to sell them he met St Francis, who always felt a great compassion for such gentle animals; and, looking at the doves with eyes of pity, he said to the young man: "O good young man, I entreat thee to give me those harmless birds, emblems in Scripture of humble, pure, and faithful souls, so that they may not fall into cruel hands, which would put them to death." And the young man, inspired by God, immediately gave them to St Francis, who, placing them in his bosom, addressed them thus sweetly: "O my little sisters the doves, so simple, so innocent, and so chaste, why did you allow yourselves to be caught? I will save you from death, and make you nests, that you may increase and multiply, according to the command of God." Then St Francis made nests for them all, and they began to lay their eggs and hatch them in presence of the brethren, and were as familiar and as tame with St Francis and the friars as if they had been hens brought up amongst them, nor did they ever go away until St Francis had given them his blessing. Then said St Francis to the young man who had given them to him: "My son, thou shalt become a friar in this Order; and shalt serve most fervently the Lord Jesus Christ"; and so it came to pass, for the young man became a friar, and lived in the Order in great holiness.

CHAPTER XXIII

HOW ST FRANCIS DELIVERED THE BROTHER WHO, BEING
IN SIN, HAD FALLEN INTO THE POWER OF THE DEVIL

ST FRANCIS, being one day in prayer in the Convent of
the Portiuncula, saw, by the revelation of God, that all the
convent was surrounded and besieged by devils, as by a great
army; but none could penetrate into the convent, because the
brothers were so holy that the demons could not enter into any
one of them. They remained, however, on the watch, until one
day a certain brother being offended by another, thought in his
heart how he could accuse and do him harm. Having yielded to
this evil thought, the devil, seeing a way open to him, entered the
convent and took possession of the brother. On this St Francis,
like a vigilant pastor, ever watching over his flock, seeing that
the wolf had entered in to devour one of his lambs, called the
brother, and commanded him to confess immediately the hatred
he had nourished in his heart towards his neighbour, which had
caused him to fall into the power of the enemy. The brother,
much alarmed, and seeing that his saintly father had penetrated
into his deepest thoughts, confessed the evil feeling which had
entered into his heart, and humbly asked pardon and penance.
When he had done this, and being absolved of his sin had accepted his penance, St Francis beheld the devil to flee away; and
the brother, being freed from such a cruel monster through the
charity of his good shepherd, thanked God, and returned to the
little flock of the saintly pastor corrected and strengthened, and
lived afterwards in great sanctity.

CHAPTER XXIV

HOW ST FRANCIS CONVERTED TO THE FAITH THE SULTAN OF BABYLON

ST FRANCIS, urged by zeal for the faith of Christ and by a wish to suffer martyrdom, took with him one day twelve of his most holy brethren, and went beyond the sea with the intention of going straight to the Sultan of Babylon. They arrived in a province belonging to the Saracens, where all the passes were guarded by men so cruel, that no Christian who passed that way could escape being put to death. Now it pleased God that St Francis and his companions should not meet with the same fate; but they were taken prisoners, and after being bound and ill-treated, were led before the Sultan. Then St Francis standing before him, inspired by the Holy Spirit, preached most divinely the faith of Christ; and to prove the truth of what he said, professed himself ready to enter into the fire. Now the Sultan began to feel a great devotion towards him, both because of the constancy of his faith, and because he despised the things of this world (for he had refused to accept any of the presents which he had offered to him), and also because of his ardent wish to suffer martyrdom. From that moment he listened to him willingly, and begged him to come back often, giving both him and his companions leave to preach wheresoever they pleased; he likewise gave them a token of his protection, which would preserve them from all molestation.

At length St Francis, seeing he could do no more good in those parts, was warned by God to return with his brethren to the land of the faithful. Having assembled his companions, they went together to the Sultan to take leave of him. The Sultan said to him:

"Brother Francis, most willingly would I be converted to the faith of Christ; but I fear to do so now, for if the people knew it, they would kill both me and thee and all thy companions. As thou mayest still do much good, and I have certain affairs of great importance to conclude, I will not at present be the cause of thy death and of mine. But teach me how I can be saved, and I am ready to do as thou shalt order." On this St Francis made answer: "My lord, I will take leave of thee for the present; but after I have returned to my own country, when I shall be dead and gone to heaven, by the grace of God, I will send thee two of my friars, who will administer to thee the holy baptism of Christ, and thou shalt be saved, as the Lord Jesus has revealed to me; and thou in the meantime shalt free thyself from every hindrance, so that, when the grace of God arrives, thou mayest be found well disposed to faith and devotion." The Sultan promised so to do; and did as he had promised. Then St Francis returned with his company of venerable and saintly brethren, and after a few years ending his mortal life, he gave up his soul to God. The Sultan, having fallen ill, awaited the fulfilment of the promise of St Francis, and placed guards in all the passes, ordering them if they met two brothers in the habit of St Francis to conduct them immediately to him. At the same time St Francis appeared to two of his friars, and ordered them without delay to go to the Sultan and save his soul, according to the promise he had made him. The two set out, and having crossed the sea, were conducted to the Sultan by the guards he had sent out to meet them. The Sultan, when he saw them arrive, rejoiced greatly, and exclaimed: "Now I know of a truth that God has sent his servants to save my soul, according to the promise which St Francis made me through divine revelation." Having received the faith of Christ and holy baptism from the said friars, he was regenerated in the Lord Jesus Christ; and having died of his disease, his soul was saved, through the merits and prayers of St Francis.

CHAPTER XXV

THE true disciple of Christ, St Francis, as long as he lived in this miserable life, endeavoured with all his might to follow the example of Christ the perfect Master; whence it happened often, through the operation of grace, that he healed the soul at the same time as the body, as we read of Jesus Christ himself; and not only did he willingly serve the lepers himself, but he willed that all the brethren of his Order, both when they were travelling about the world and when they were halting on their way, should serve the lepers for the love of Christ, who for our sake was willing to be treated as a leper. It happened once, that in a convent near the one in which St Francis then resided there was a hospital for leprosy and other infirmities, served by the brethren; and one of the patients was a leper so impatient, so insupportable, and so insolent, that many believed of a certainty that he was possessed of the devil (as indeed he was) for he ill-treated with blows and words all those who served him; and, what was worse, he blasphemed so dreadfully our Blessed Lord and his most holy Mother the Blessed Virgin Mary, that none was found who could or would serve him. The brethren, indeed, to gain merit, endeavoured to accept with patience the injuries and violences committed against themselves, but their consciences would not allow them to submit to those addressed to Christ and to his Mother, wherefore they determined to abandon this leper, but this they would not do until they had signified their intention to St Francis, according to the Rule. On learning this, St Francis, who was

64

not far distant, himself visited this perverse leper, and said to him: "May God give thee peace, my beloved brother!" To this the leper answered: "What peace can I look for from God, who has taken from me peace and every other blessing, and made me a putrid and disgusting object?" St Francis answered: "My son, be patient; for the infirmities of the body are given by God in this world for the salvation of the soul in the next; there is great merit in them when they are patiently endured." The sick man answered: "How can I bear patiently the pain which afflicts me night and day? For not only am I greatly afflicted by my infirmity, but the friars thou hast sent to serve me make it even worse, for they do not serve me as they ought." Then St Francis, knowing through divine revelation that the leper was possessed by the malignant spirit, began to pray, interceding most earnestly for him. Having finished his prayer, he returned to the leper and said to him: "My son, I myself will serve thee, seeing thou art not satisfied with the others." "Willingly," answered the leper; "but what canst thou do more than they have done?" "Whatsoever thou wishest I will do for thee," answered St Francis. "I will then," said he, "that thou wash me all over; for I am so disgusting that I cannot bear myself." Then St Francis heated some water, putting therein many odoriferous herbs; he then undressed him, and began to wash him with his own hands, whilst another brother threw the water upon him, and, by a divine miracle, wherever St Francis touched him with his holy hands the leprosy disappeared, and his flesh was perfectly healed; and as his body began to be healed, so likewise was his soul healed also. On this the leper, seeing his leprosy beginning to vanish, felt great sorrow and repentance for his sins, and began to weep bitterly. While his body was being purified externally of the leprosy through the cleansing of the water, so his soul internally was purified from sin by the washing of tears and repentance; and feeling himself completely healed both in his body and his soul, he humbly confessed his sins, crying out in a loud voice, with many tears: "Unhappy me! I am worthy of hell for the wickedness of my conduct to the brethren, and the impatience and blasphemy I have uttered against the Lord"; and for fifteen days he ceased not to weep bitterly for his sins, imploring the Lord to have mercy on him, and then made a general confession to a priest. St Francis, perceiving this evident miracle which the Lord had enabled him to work, returned thanks to God, and set out for a distant country; for out of humility he wished to avoid all glory, and in all his actions he sought only the glory of God, and not his own. It pleased God that the leper, who had been healed both in his body and in his soul, after having done penance for fifteen days, should fall ill of another infirmity; and having received the sacraments of the Church, he died a most holy death. His soul on its way to heaven appeared in the air to St Francis, who was praying in a forest, and said to him: "Dost thou know me?" "Who art thou?" asked the saint. Said he: "I am that leper whom our Blessed Lord healed through thy merits, and to-day I am going to life eternal, for which I return thanks to God and to thee. Blessed be thy soul and thy body, blessed be thy holy words and works, for through thee many souls are saved in the world; and know that there is not a single day in which the angels and other saints do not return thanks to God for the holy fruits of thy preaching and that of thy Order in various parts of the world. Be comforted, then, and thank the Lord, and may his blessing rest on thee." Having said these words, he went up to heaven, leaving St Francis much consoled.

CHAPTER XXVI

HOW ST FRANCIS CONVERTED CERTAIN ROBBERS AND ASSAS-
SINS, WHO BECAME FRIARS; AND OF A WONDERFUL VISION
WHICH APPEARED TO ONE OF THEM WHO WAS
A MOST HOLY BROTHER

AS St Francis went one day through the desert of Borgo di San Sepolcro, and was passing by a castle called Monte Casale, he saw a young man of noble mien, and elegant in appearance, coming towards him, who thus addressed him: "Father, I would willingly be one of thy monks." St Francis answered: "My son, thou art young, noble, and delicate; perhaps thou wouldst not be able to endure poverty and hardships." The young man said again: "Father, are you not men, like me? If you, then, can support these things, through the grace of God I shall be able to do so likewise." This answer greatly pleased St Francis, and giving the young man his blessing, he received him immediately into the Order, and gave him the name of Brother Angelo. And this young man was so remarkable and so distinguished, that shortly after he was named Guardian of the Convent of Monte Casale. At that time there were three famous robbers in that part of the country, who did much evil in all the neighbourhood. Coming one day to the said convent, they asked Brother Angelo, the guardian, to give them something to eat. The guardian, reproving them harshly, answered them thus: "Cruel robbers and murderers, you are not ashamed to deprive others of the fruits of their labours, and you have the audacity to come here and devour that which is given in charity to the servants of God — you who are not worthy of the earth which bears you, for you neither respect man nor the Lord who made you. Go

67

about your business, and do not appear here again." Then the robbers went away in anger, much troubled by these words. Shortly after, St Francis arrived at the convent with a sack of bread and a little vessel of wine, which he and his companion had begged; and the guardian related to him how he had sent away the robbers. On this St Francis reproved him sharply, saying that he had behaved most cruelly, for sinners are brought back to God more easily by kindness than by harsh words. "Wherefore," said he, "our Master Jesus Christ, whose Word we have promised to observe, says that the whole need not a physician, but they that are sick, and that he came not to call the just, but sinners, to repentance; for which reason he often sat down to meat with them. As, then, thou hast acted against charity, and against the Gospel of Christ, I command thee, in the name of holy obedience, to take with thee this sack of bread, which I have begged, and this little vessel of wine, and go after the robbers, over the hills and across the valleys, until thou meet with them. And when thou hast found them, give them from me this bread and wine; and then, kneeling down before them, thou shalt humbly confess thy fault, begging them, in my name, not to do evil any more, but to fear God and never again offend him. If they consent to this, I promise to provide for all their wants, and to give them continually both meat and drink; and when thou hast told them this, thou shalt humbly come back here." Whilst the guardian went on the errand of St Francis, the latter began to pray, asking God to touch the hearts of the robbers and bring them to repentance. The obedient guardian, having found out their retreat, presented to them the bread and wine, and said and did what St Francis had commanded; and it pleased God that as the robbers ate the bread of charity which St Francis had sent them, they reasoned thus among themselves: "Alas for us, miserable men that we are! What pains await us in hell; for not only have we robbed, beaten and wounded our neighbours, but we have likewise taken away their lives, and yet for all these cruel deeds we feel no remorse of conscience, and no fear of God! and behold this holy friar who is come to us, for a few unkind words, which we merited most justly, has humbly confessed that he was wrong, and has brought us likewise bread and wine, with a most gracious promise from the holy St Francis. These men indeed are holy religious of God who merit his Paradise, and we are sons of perdition, worthy of the pains of hell; and each day we add to our perdition, and we know not whether yet, because of the sins we have committed hitherto, we can find mercy in the sight of God." One of them having spoken thus, the other two answered, saying: "Most certainly thou speakest truly; but what are we to do?" "Let us go," said one of the others, "to St Francis; and if he gives us a hope that our sins may find mercy in the sight of God, we will do what he shall command us to save our souls from the punishment of hell." This counsel pleasing the others, they agreed to go immediately to St Francis; and having found him, they thus addressed him: "Father, because of the multitude of our sins we dare not look for mercy from God; but if thou hast a hope that he may have pity on us, we are ready to do what thou shalt order, and do penance for our sins with thee." Then St Francis bade them stay, and with much kindness and charity comforted them, giving them many proofs of the mercy of God, and promising them to ask the Lord to have pity on their sins. He told them that his mercy knows no bounds, and that were their sins without number the mercy of God is even greater, according to the word of the Gospel and of the Apostle St Paul, who says our Blessed Lord *came into the world to save sinners*. The three robbers on hearing these words resolved to renounce the devil and his works; and St Francis received them into the Order, in which they did great penance. Two of them died shortly after their conversion, and went to heaven; but the third survived, and, reflecting on his sins, he did penance during fifteen years. Besides the ordinary fasts which he observed with the brethren, he fasted at other times three days in the week on bread and water, went barefooted, wore no other vestment but his tunic, and never slept after Matins. During this time St Francis passed from this miserable life. The converted robber having continued to do penance for many years, it so happened that one night, after Matins, he was visited by such a strong temptation to sleep, that he could neither pray nor watch according to his custom. At last, finding it impossible to resist any longer, he threw himself on his bed to sleep. No sooner had he laid down his head than he was rapt in spirit and led up into a very high mountain, on the side of which was a deep precipice bordered with sharp stones and large rocks all broken to pieces, so that the precipice was frightful to look at; and the angel who conducted the brother pushed him with such violence, that he fell into the abyss, and, rolling down from stone to stone and from rock to rock, he reached the bottom shattered all to pieces, as it seemed to him. As he lay on the ground in this pitiable condition, the angel said to him: "Arise, for thou hast a much longer journey to take." And the brother answered: "Thou art both cruel and unreasonable. Thou seest that I am about to die from my fall, which has shattered me all to pieces, and thou tellest me to arise." On this the angel, coming near him, touched him, healing all his wounds. He then showed him an immense plain, full of sharp and pointed stones, covered with thorns and brambles, and told him that he was to run all over the plain, and cross it barefooted till he reached the other end, where was a burning furnace, which he was to enter. And the brother having crossed the plain with great pain and suffering, the angel ordered him to enter the furnace, as it was meet for him to do. The brother exclaimed: "Alas, what a cruel

70

guide thou art! Thou seest that I am nearly dead, having crossed this horrible plain; and to rest me thou commandest me to enter this burning furnace"; and looking up, he saw all around many demons with iron pitchforks in their hands; and as he hesitated

to obey the angel, they pushed him into the furnace. When he was in the furnace, he looked around and saw one who had for‹ merly been his companion burning all over from head to foot; and he said to him: "O my unhappy companion, how camest thou here?" And he answered: "Go a little farther, and thou

71

shalt find my wife; she will tell thee why we are damned." Then
the brother, going a little farther, saw the said woman surrounded
with flames; and he said to her: "O unfortunate and miserable
woman, why art thou condemned to suffer such a cruel torment?"
"Because," she answered, "at the time of the great famine which
St Francis had foretold, my husband and I cheated the people,
and sold them wheat and oats in a false measure. It is for this that
I am condemned to burn in this dreadful place." Having heard
these words, the angel who conducted the brother drew him out
of the furnace, and said to him: "Prepare thyself now for a very
horrible journey." Then the brother answered him sorrowfully:
"O cruel guide, thou hast no compassion on me. Thou seest how
I am almost burnt to death in this furnace, and thou preparest
for me another horrible and dangerous journey." Then the angel touching him, he became whole and strong; after which he
led him to a bridge, which it was impossible to pass without
great danger, for it was slightly built, very narrow, and very
slippery, without any parapets, while underneath there flowed
a terrible river full of serpents, scorpions and dragons, which
produced a great stench. Then said the angel to him: "Go over
the bridge, as by all means thou must cross it." And the brother
answered: "How can I cross it without falling into that dangerous river?" The angel said to him: "Follow me, and place thy
foot where thou shalt see me place mine, and thou shalt cross it
safely." Then the brother walked behind the angel as he had ordered him, and reached the middle of the bridge, when suddenly
the angel flew away, and leaving the brother, went on to a very
high mountain at a great distance from the bridge. When the
brother saw whither the angel had flown, being without his guide
and looking down, he saw all those terrible animals with their
heads out of the water, and their mouths open ready to devour
him, if he were to fall into the river; and he trembled much with

fear, not knowing what to do or what to say, as he could neither go back nor go forward. Seeing himself in such tribulation, and having no refuge but in God, he bent down, and clinging to the bridge, with all his heart and with many tears he recommended himself to the Lord, praying him to have mercy on him. Having finished his prayer, it seemed to him as if wings were growing out of his back, and he waited with great joy till they should be large enough to enable him to fly away from the bridge, and go to the spot whither the angel had flown. After waiting a little time, his impatience to leave the bridge became so great that he tried to fly; but his wings not having reached their growth, he fell on the bridge, and the feathers came off; upon which he clung again to the bridge as he had done before, and recommended himself to God. Having finished his prayer, it seemed to him as if the wings were growing again; but losing patience a second time, he tried to fly before the wings were fully grown, and falling down on the bridge as before, the feathers came off. And seeing that it was his impatience to fly away which made him fall down thus, he said within himself: "If my wings begin to grow a third time, I will most certainly wait until they are large enough to enable me to fly away without falling." And having come to this decision, he saw the wings begin to grow for the third time, and waited so long that they might attain their growth, that it seemed to him as if more than a hundred and fifty years had elapsed between the first growth of his wings and the third. At last he arose for the third time, and exerting all his strength, he flew up to the spot whither the angel had flown before him; and knocking at the gate of the place into which he had entered, the porter asked of him who he was and whence he came. To this he answered: "I am one of the Friars Minor." The porter said to him: "Wait a little whilst I go and fetch St Francis, to see if he knows thee." While the porter was gone to fetch St Francis, the

73

brother began to examine the wonderful walls of the palace, which appeared so luminous and so transparent, that he could see through them the choirs of saints, and what they were doing. As he was struck with wonder at this sight, St Francis came towards him, with Brother Bernard and Brother Giles, followed by a great multitude of saints, both men and women, who had followed him in life, and they appeared to be innumerable. Then St Francis said to the porter: "Let him come in, for he is one of my friars." As soon as he had entered, he felt such consolation and such sweetness, that he forgot all the tribulations he had gone through, as if they had never been. And St Francis, taking him inside, showed him many wonderful things, and said to him: "My son, it is meet that thou return to the world: thou shalt remain there seven days, during which thou shalt prepare thyself with great devotion and great care; for after the seven days I will come and fetch thee, and then thou shalt be with me in this abode of the blessed." St Francis wore a most wonderful cloak, adorned with beautiful stars, and his five stigmata were like five stars, so bright that all the palace was illumined by their rays. And Brother Bernard likewise had on his head a crown of stars, and Brother Giles was adorned with a blazing light, and he saw there many other holy brothers whom he had not known in the world. Having taken leave of St Francis, he returned, much against his will, to the world. When he awoke and came back to himself, the brothers were singing prime; so that the vision had lasted only from matins to prime, though it seemed to him as if many years had elapsed. He related to the guardian all the vision from beginning to end. After seven days he fell ill of a fever, and on the eighth day St Francis came to him, as he had promised, with a great multitude of glorious saints, and conducted his soul to life eternal in the kingdom of the blessed.

CHAPTER XXVII

ST FRANCIS coming one day to the city of Bologna, all the inhabitants went out to meet him, and the crowd was so great that it was with much difficulty he made his way to the market-place, which was filled with men, women, and scholars. And St Francis, on arriving there, stood upon an elevated spot, and began to preach that which the Holy Spirit put into his mind to say; and he preached so wonderfully that he appeared to be an angel, not a man; and his words were like sharp arrows, which pierced through the hearts of those who listened to them. And many men and women were brought to repentance through that sermon; of this number were two noble students of the March of Ancona — one named Pellegrino and the other Rinieri. These two being touched in their hearts by divine inspiration, through the said sermon, went to St Francis, saying that they wished to leave the world and become friars in his Order. And it having been revealed to St Francis that they had been sent by God to be examples of virtue in the Order, he received them joyfully, on account of the great fervour they showed, saying to them: "Thou, Pellegrino, shalt follow in the Order the ways of humility; and thou, Rinieri, shalt serve the brethren" — and so it fell out; for Brother Pellegrino would never be treated as a cleric but as a lay-man, though he was a learned man and deeply versed in the Sacred Canons; and through his humility he reached a high degree of perfection in virtue; so that Brother Bernard, the first son of St Francis, said of him that he was one of the most perfect friars in the world; and finally Brother Pellegrino passed from this world full of virtue, having wrought many miracles both before his death and after. And Brother Rinieri served the brothers most devoutly and most faithfully, living in great sanctity and great humility, and becoming very intimate with St Francis. And having been named Minister of the province of the March of Ancona, he governed it for a long time with much discretion and most peaceably; and St Francis revealed to him many secrets. Now after some time the Lord allowed a great temptation to take possession of his soul, which greatly grieved and troubled him; he observed severe penance, subjected himself to much rigorous discipline, and endeavoured day and night, with prayers and tears, to drive away the temptation, but not succeeding he believed that God had abandoned him. Being in a state of great despair he determined as a last remedy to go to St Francis, thinking thus within himself: "If the saint receives me kindly and is familiar with me, as he is wont, I may hope that God will have pity on me; but if not, this will be the sign that I am abandoned by the Lord." And setting out, he went to St Francis, who at that time was lying grievously ill, in the palace of the Bishop of Assisi; and God revealed to him the whole temptation which had assailed Brother Rinieri, and his intention of coming to him. Then St Francis, calling immediately Brother Leo and Brother Masseo, said to them: "Go forth to meet my beloved Brother Rinieri, and having embraced him salute him from me, and tell him that of all the brothers scattered abroad in the world I love him most particularly." And they set out, and meeting Brother Rinieri in the way, they embraced him, telling him what St Francis had ordered them to say. The message brought such sweetness and such consolation to him, that he was quite beside himself with joy; and thanking God with all his heart, he reached the place where St Francis was lying ill. Now though St Francis was grievously ill, yet when he heard that Brother Rinieri was approaching, he arose and went to meet him; and embracing him with much affection he said to him: "My very dear Brother Rinieri, of all the brothers in the world I love thee most especially"; and making the sign of the holy cross on his forehead, he kissed him, adding: "My beloved son, the Lord hath permitted this temptation that thou mayest gain a great increase of merit; but if thou dost not wish this gain, the temptation shall be removed"; and, O miracle! no sooner had St Francis pronounced these words than immediately the temptation left him, and it seemed to him as if in all his life he had never been tempted, and he was greatly comforted.

CHAPTER XXVIII

OF AN ECSTASY WHICH CAME TO BROTHER BERNARD,
AND HOW HE REMAINED FROM MATINS UNTIL NONE
IN A STATE OF RAPTURE

BROTHER BERNARD of Quintavalle was an example of the manifestation of the grace of God in the poor followers of the Gospel, who gave up the world to follow Christ. For since he had taken the habit of St Francis, he was often rapt in God through the contemplation of celestial things. It happened one day, as he was in a church hearing Mass, his mind was so raised to God that he was transfixed and enraptured, so as not to be aware of the moment of the elevation of the Body of Christ; for he neither knelt down nor removed his hood, as did the others, but remained motionless, with his eyes intently gazing upwards, and remained so even from Matins till the hour of None. On coming back to himself, he went about the convent crying out with a loud voice: "O brothers! O brothers! O brothers! there is not a man in all this land, however great and however noble he may be, who, if a palace full of gold were offered him, would not willingly carry on his back a sack of copper to acquire so rich a treasure." Now this celestial treasure, promised to the lovers of Christ, had been revealed to Brother Bernard; and his mind was so fixed upon it, that for fifteen years his heart and countenance were raised alway to heaven. In all that time he never satisfied his hunger, though he ate a little of whatever was set before him; wherefore he used to say that if a man does not taste what he eats his abstinence has no merit, for true abstinence is to moderate oneself in those things which are agreeable to the palate. His intelligence also became so enlightened that many great divines had recourse to him to solve difficult questions and explain obscure passages of Scripture, which he did with great facility. So completely was his mind detached and withdrawn from all things earthly, that he soared like the swallows above the earth, and remained sometimes twenty, sometimes thirty days at the top of a high mountain contemplating things divine. For which reason Brother Giles said that he had received a gift from God which had been given to no other human being — namely, that in his divine flight he was fed like the swallows. And, because of this wonderful grace of contemplation which he had received from God, St Francis willingly and frequently held converse with him day and night; and often they were found to be in a state of ecstasy all night long, in the wood where they used to meet together to talk on things divine.

CHAPTER XXIX

HOW THE DEVIL OFTEN APPEARED TO BROTHER RUFFINO IN THE FORM
OF A CRUCIFIX, TELLING HIM THAT ALL THE GOOD HE DID WAS OF NO
AVAIL, SEEING HE WAS NOT OF THE NUMBER OF THE ELECT OF GOD;
WHICH BEING REVEALED TO ST FRANCIS, HE MADE KNOWN TO BROTHER
RUFFINO THE ERROR INTO WHICH HE HAD FALLEN

BROTHER RUFFINO, one of the most noble men of the city of Assisi, a companion of St Francis and a man of great sanctity, was one day violently tempted in mind on the subject of predestination, so that he grew quite melancholy and sorrowful; for the devil put it into his heart that he was damned, and not of the number of those predestined to life eternal, making him believe that all he did in the Order was of no avail. And this temptation increasing more and more, he had not the courage to reveal it to St Francis, though he never ceased to pray and to fast: for the enemy of his soul added sorrow to sorrow, not only fighting inwardly but likewise outwardly, taking various forms in order better to deceive him. One day he appeared to him under that of a crucifix, and said to him: "O Brother Ruffino, why dost thou inflict on thyself penance and prayer, as thou art not of the number of the predestinate to life eternal? Believe me — for I know whom I have chosen and predestined — and believe not the son of Peter Bernardoni if he tell thee the contrary; and do not take his advice in this matter, since neither he nor any man knows the truth but I, who am the Son of God. Know of a certainty that thou art of the number of the damned; and the son of Peter Bernardoni, thy father, and his father likewise, are damned, and whosoever followeth them is damned also." On hearing these words, Brother Ruffino was so blinded by the spirit of dark-

79

ness, that he lost all the faith and love he had felt for St Francis hitherto, and would not even communicate to him what was passing within him. But that which Brother Ruffino did not reveal to his saintly father was revealed to him by the Holy Spirit. When, therefore, the saint learned to what dangers his son was exposed, he sent to him Brother Masseo; but Brother Ruffino refused to listen to him, saying: "What have I to do with Brother Francis?" And Brother Masseo, enlightened by the Spirit of God and knowing the deceits of the devil, answered: "O Brother Ruffino, thou knowest that St Francis may be compared to an angel of God, who has made known the truth to many souls in the world, and through whom we have received the grace of God; wherefore I will at all events that thou come with us to him, for I clearly see that thou art deceived by the devil." On hearing these words, Brother Ruffino arose and went to St Francis; and the saint, perceiving him at a distance, cried out: "O Brother Ruffino, thou foolish one, whom hast thou believed?" Then coming up to him, he related to him one by one all the temptations, both internal and external, to which he had been exposed, showing him clearly that he who had appeared to him was the devil and not Christ, and that he was by no means to listen to his suggestions; but if he appeared to him again and said unto him "Thou art damned", he was to say to him these words: "Open thy mouth!" and by this sign he would clearly know that he was the devil and not Christ; for no sooner should the words be uttered than he would immediately disappear. "Thou shouldst have known," added the saint, "with whom thou wast dealing, when he hardened thy heart against all that was good, for such is his especial office; but Christ, the blessed one, never hardens the heart of the faithful; for on the contrary his office is to soften the heart of man, according to the words of the prophet: *I will take away from thee the heart of stone, and will give thee a heart of flesh.*" Then Brother Ruffino, seeing that St Francis was acquainted with all his temptations in the order they had come to him, was deeply touched by his exhortations, and beginning to weep bitterly, he humbly confessed his guilt in concealing from him his trouble. He was greatly consoled and comforted by the admonitions of his saintly father, which St Francis ended by saying: "My son, go to confession, and give not up the practice of thine accustomed prayers; know of a certainty that this temptation will be to thee a source of great consolation and humility, as thou shalt shortly see." Then Brother Ruffino returned to his cell in the wood; and as he was praying and weeping bitterly the enemy approached, bearing in his exterior the semblance of Christ himself. He thus addressed him: "O Brother Ruffino, did I not tell thee not to listen to the son of Peter Bernardoni, nor to weary thyself with prayer and fasting, inasmuch as thou art damned? What is the use of inflicting on thyself privations in this world, seeing thou hast no hope of salvation after death?" And immediately Brother Ruffino said, "Open thy mouth!" upon which the devil left him in so great rage and fury, that all Monte Subasio, which was close by, was shaken to the very foundation, and large stones rolled down the sides, knocking against each other as they fell, and producing a great fire in all the valley; and the noise they made was so terrible that St Francis and all his companions went out to see what had taken place: and even to this day those large stones are to be seen lying in great confusion. Then Brother Ruffino saw plainly that it was the devil who had deceived him, and returning to St Francis he threw himself at his feet, acknowledging his fault. St Francis comforted him with kind words, and sent him back to his cell full of consolation. As he was praying there most devoutly, Christ, the blessed one, appeared to him, and filling his soul with the fire of divine love, he thus addressed him: "Thou didst well, my son, to be-

81

lieve in St Francis; for he who made thee so unhappy was the
devil. But I am Christ, thy Master; and in order to prove to thee
that I am he, I promise thee that thou shalt never again be troubled in this way." Having said these words, he departed, leaving
the brother so happy, and enjoying such peace and sweetness of
spirit, with his mind so raised above the things of this world,
that for a whole day and night he was rapt in God, and from that
moment he had no doubts as to his salvation, and became quite
a new man. Most willingly would he have remained day and
night in prayer and in the contemplation of divine things, had
he been permitted to do so. Wherefore St Francis said of him
that he had been canonised during his lifetime by Christ, and
that, save in his presence, he would not hesitate to call him St
Ruffino, even though he were still on earth.

CHAPTER XXX

OF THE BEAUTIFUL SERMON WHICH ST FRANCIS
AND BROTHER RUFFINO PREACHED AT ASSISI

THE said Brother Ruffino, through constant contemplation, was so absorbed in God that he became almost insensible to things external, and very seldom spoke; added to which he never had possessed the gift of speech, neither was he eloquent nor self-possessed. Notwithstanding this, St Francis ordered him one day to go to Assisi and preach to the people that which God should dictate to him. On this Brother Ruffino expostulated, saying: "Reverend Father, I pray thee excuse me, and send some other brother in my stead; for thou knowest that I have not the grace of preaching: I am simple and ignorant." At this St Francis answered: "Inasmuch as thou hast not obeyed immediately, I command thee to take off thy cloak and thy hood and go to Assisi, where thou shalt enter a church and preach to the people; and this shalt thou do out of holy obedience." Having received this order, Brother Ruffino, taking off his mantle and his hood, proceeded to Assisi, and entering the church, after having bowed before the altar, he mounted into the pulpit and began to preach to the people, who, seeing him in so strange a dress, laughed at him, saying: "These men do such penance that they are quite out of their mind." In the meantime St Francis, reflecting how promptly Brother Ruffino, who was one of the most noble men of Assisi, had obeyed the harsh command he had given, reproached himself, saying: "How couldst thou, who art but the humble son of Peter Bernardoni, send one of the most distinguished men of Assisi to preach to the people as if he were a madman? May God forgive thee! But thou shalt do the same thing which thou hast ordered him to do." And immediately taking off his cloak and his hood with great fervour of spirit, he went to Assisi, taking with him Brother Leo, who carried his mantle and that of Brother Ruffino. The inhabitants of Assisi, seeing him thus accoutred, reviled him, believing that both he and Brother Ruffino were out of their minds through much penance. St Francis entered the church as Brother Ruffino was saying these words: "O beloved, flee from the world, and leave sin; render to all men that which is their due, if thou wilt avoid hell; keep the commandments of God and love the Lord and thy neighbour, if thou wilt possess the kingdom of heaven." Then St Francis ascended the pulpit, and began to preach in so wonderful a way on holy penance, on the world, on voluntary poverty, on the hope of life eternal, on the nakedness of Christ and on the shame of the Passion of our Blessed Saviour, that all they who heard him, both men and women, began to weep bitterly, being moved to devotion and compunction; and in all Assisi the Passion of Christ was commemorated as it never had been before; so that the people were greatly edified by this action of St Francis and of Brother Ruffino. Then St Francis put on the cloak of Brother Ruffino and his own, and returned to the convent of the Portiuncula, praising and glorifying God, who had given them grace to conquer and despise themselves, to the edification of the flock of Christ, and enabled them, by their example, to show how the world ought to be despised. And from that day the people greatly revered them, so that those who could touch but the hem of their garments esteemed themselves blessed.

CHAPTER XXXI

HOW ST FRANCIS WAS ACQUAINTED WITH THE SECRETS OF THE CONSCIENCES OF ALL HIS BRETHREN

AS our Lord Jesus Christ says in his Gospel, *I know my sheep, and mine know me,* so the holy St Francis, like a good shepherd, knew, through divine revelation, all the merits and virtues of his companions, and also their defects and faults, and was enabled to deal with them according to their needs — humbling the proud and exalting the humble, rebuking vice and praising virtue — as we read in the wonderful revelations which were made to him by God with regard to his first children. Amongst others, we are told that once St Francis was with his companions in a convent talking of God, when Brother Ruffino was absent, being in contemplation in the forest; and, as the saint was conversing with them, Brother Ruffino passed by at some distance, whereon St Francis asked them whom they believed to be the holiest soul in the world. They answered immediately, that they believed it to be St Francis. The saint reproved them, saying: "Beloved brothers, I am the most unworthy and the vilest of all men in the world; but see there Brother Ruffino, who is now coming out of the forest; the Lord has revealed to me that his soul is one of the three most holy on earth; and I tell you candidly, I should not hesitate to call him St Ruffino even during his lifetime, his soul being full of grace, and sanctified and canonised in heaven by our Lord Jesus Christ." This opinion St Francis never expressed in the presence of Brother Ruffino. That he was equally acquainted with the defects of his brethren, we learn in the case of Brother Elias, whom he often reproved for his pride;

and of Brother John della Cappella, to whom he foretold that he would hang himself; and of that brother who was seized by the devil as a punishment for his disobedience; and of many others whose defects and virtues were clearly revealed to him by Christ.

CHAPTER XXXII

HOW BROTHER MASSEO OBTAINED FROM CHRIST
THE VIRTUE OF HUMILITY

THE first companions of St Francis set themselves with all their might to follow holy poverty with regard to earthly things, and to acquire every other virtue, as the sure means of obtaining celestial and eternal riches. It happened, therefore, that one day, as they were assembled together to speak of things divine, one of them related the following example: "There was a man, a great friend of God, to whom had been given the grace of a life contemplative as well as active. He was at the same time so humble, that he looked upon himself as a very great sinner; and his humility was to him a means of sanctification, and confirmed him in the grace of God; for it caused him to increase in virtue, and saved him from falling into sin." And Brother Masseo, hearing such wonderful things of humility, and knowing it to be one of the greatest treasures of life eternal, was so inflamed with a love and desire of this virtue of humility, that he lifted his eyes to heaven with much fervour, and made a vow and firm resolution never again to rejoice until he should feel the said virtue to be firmly established in his soul. From that moment he was constantly shut up in his cell, macerating his body with fasts and vigils and prayers, weeping before the Lord, and earnestly imploring him to grant him this virtue, without which he felt that he was only worthy of hell, and with which the friend of God of whom he had heard was so richly endowed. Brother Masseo having passed several days in this state of mind, as he was entering the forest and asking the Lord, who willingly listens to the prayers of the humble, with cries and tears to grant him this divine virtue, he heard a voice from heaven, which called him twice: "Brother Masseo! Brother Masseo!" And he, knowing in his spirit that it was the voice of Christ, answered: "My Lord." Then Christ answered: "What wilt thou give in exchange for this virtue which thou askest for?" And Brother Masseo answered: "Lord, I will willingly give the eyes out of my head." Christ answered: "I grant thee the virtue, and command at the same time that thou keep thine eyes." And having said these words, the voice was silent; and Brother Masseo was so filled with the grace of humility, that from thenceforward he was constantly rejoicing. And often when he was in prayer he was heard to utter a joyful sound, like the song of a bird, resembling "U-u-u", and his face bore a most holy and happy expression. With this he grew so humble that he esteemed himself less than all other men in the world. And Brother James of Fallerone having asked him why in his joy he used always the same sound, he replied gaily, that when in one way he found all good he saw no reason to change it.

CHAPTER XXXIII

HOW ST CLARE, BY ORDER OF THE POPE, BLESSED THE
BREAD WHICH WAS ON THE TABLE, AND HOW ON EACH
LOAF APPEARED THE SIGN OF THE HOLY CROSS

ST CLARE, a most devout servant of the Cross of Christ, and one of the sweetest flowers of St Francis, was so holy, that not only the Bishops and Cardinals but the Pope himself wished to see and hear her, and went often to visit her in person. One day, amongst others, the holy Father went to her convent to hear her speak of things celestial; and having long reasoned together, St Clare ordered the table to be laid and bread to be placed upon it, in order that the holy Father might bless it. Their spiritual conclave being at an end, St Clare, kneeling down with great reverence, begged him to bless the bread which had been placed on the table. To whom the holy Father answered: "Most faithful sister, I will that thou bless this bread by the sign of the cross to which thou hast devoted thyself." St Clare said: "Most holy Father, excuse me. I should indeed be worthy of reproof if I, a miserable woman, should presume to give such a blessing in the presence of the Vicar of Christ." Then the Pope answered: "In order that such an act be not looked upon as presumptuous, but that it may bear on it the marks of obedience, I command thee, in the name of holy obedience, to make on this bread the sign of the cross, and to bless it in the name of God." At this St Clare, like a true daughter of obedience, blessed the loaves most devoutly, making over them the sign of the holy cross; and, wonderful to relate, on all those loaves appeared a cross, most clearly marked; and some of them were eaten, but the rest were put aside, in order to testify of the miracle. And the holy Father, having seen the miracle, thanked God; and taking some of the bread, went away, leaving his blessing with Sister Clare. At that time Sister Ortolana, mother of St Clare, and Sister Agnes, her sister, were living together in the convent with St Clare, both most virtuous women, full of the Holy Spirit, likewise many other nuns; to whom St Francis sent a great number of sick persons, who were all healed by their prayers and by the sign of the most holy cross.

CHAPTER XXXIV

HOW ST LOUIS, KING OF FRANCE, WENT IN PERSON IN A PILGRIM'S GARB TO VISIT THE HOLY BROTHER GILES

ST LOUIS, King of France, went on a pilgrimage to visit the sanctuaries in the world. And having heard of the fame of the sanctity of Brother Giles, who was one of the first companions of St Francis, he determined in his heart to go and visit him in person; for which object he set out for Perugia, where the said brother then lived. He arrived at the convent-gate as if he had been a poor unknown pilgrim, and asked with great importunity for Brother Giles, without telling the porter who it was who wished to see him; and the porter went to Brother Giles, and told him there was a pilgrim at the gate who asked for him. But the Lord having revealed to Brother Giles that the pilgrim was the King of France, he left his cell in haste, and ran to the gate without asking any questions. They both knelt down and embraced each other with great reverence and many outward signs of love and charity, as if a long friendship had existed between them, though they had never met before in their lives. Neither of them spoke a word; and after remaining clasped in each

other's arms for some time, they separated in silence, St Louis to
continue his journey, and Brother Giles to return to his cell. As
the king departed, a certain friar inquired of one of those who
accompanied him who it was that had embraced Brother Giles,
and he answered that it was Louis, King of France; and when
the other brothers heard this, they were all sorrowful because
Brother Giles had not spoken to him; and giving vent to their
grief, they said: "O Brother Giles, why hast thou been so uncivil
as not to say a word to so holy a king, who has come from France
to see thee, and hear from thee some good words?" Brother Giles
answered: "Beloved brothers, be not surprised at this, that nei‹
ther could I say a word to him nor he to me; for no sooner had
we embraced each other than the light of divine wisdom re‹
vealed his heart to me, and mine to him; and by a divine opera‹
tion we saw into each other's hearts, and knew far better what
we had to say than if we had explained in words that which we
felt in our hearts. For so imperfectly the tongue of man reveals
the secret mysteries of God, that words would have been to us
rather a hindrance than a consolation. Know, then, that the king
went away from me well satisfied, and greatly comforted in
mind."

90

CHAPTER XXXV

HOW ST CLARE, BEING ILL, WAS MIRACULOUSLY CARRIED,
ON CHRISTMAS NIGHT, TO THE CHURCH OF ST FRANCIS,
WHERE SHE ASSISTED AT THE OFFICE

ST CLARE was at one time so dangerously ill that she could not go to church with the other nuns to say the Office on the night of the Nativity of Christ. All the other sisters went to Matins; but she remained in bed, very sorrowful because she could not go with her sisters to receive spiritual consolation. But Jesus Christ, her Spouse, unwilling to leave her comfortless, carried her miraculously to the church of St Francis, so that she was present at Matins, assisted at the Midnight Mass, and received the Holy Communion, after which she was carried back to her bed. When the nuns returned to their convent, the ceremonies being ended at St Damiano, they went to St Clare and said to her: "O Sister Clare, our Mother, what great consolations we have experienced at this feast of the Holy Nativity! Oh, if it had but pleased God that you should have been with us!" To this St Clare answered: "Praise and glory be to our Lord Jesus Christ, the blessed one, my beloved sisters and daughters; for I have not only assisted at all the solemnities of this most holy night, but I have experienced in my soul even greater consolations than those which have been your share; for by the intercession of my father, St Francis, and through the grace of our Saviour Jesus Christ I have been personally present in the church of my venerable father, St Francis, and with the ears of my body and those of my spirit have heard all the Office, and the sounds of the organ, and the singing, and have likewise received there the most Holy Communion. Rejoice, then, because of these graces which I have received, and return thanks to our Lord Jesus Christ."

CHAPTER XXXVI

HOW ST FRANCIS EXPLAINED TO BROTHER LEO
A BEAUTIFUL VISION THAT HE HAD SEEN

ST FRANCIS being once grievously ill, Brother Leo, as he was in prayer by his bedside, was rapt in ecstasy, and carried in spirit to a great, wide and rapid river; and watching those who crossed it, he saw some brothers enter the river heavily laden, who were carried away by the current and were drowned; some contrived to reach one third of the way; others arrived as far as the middle of the stream; yet none could resist the rapidity of the waters, but fell down and were drowned. Presently he saw other brothers arrive; these carried nothing on their backs, but all bore upon them the marks of holy poverty. They entered the river, and passed over to the other side without any danger to themselves. Having seen this, Brother Leo came to himself; and St Francis knowing in spirit that he had had a vision, called him to him, and asked what he had seen. When Brother Leo had related to him the vision, St Francis said: "What thou hast seen is indeed true. The great river is the world; the brothers who were drowned are those who do not follow their evangelical profession, or practise the great virtue of poverty; but they who passed the river are those who neither seek nor possess in this world any earthly riches, who having food and raiment are therewith content, and follow Christ naked on the cross, bearing joyfully and willingly his sweet and easy yoke and loving holy obedience: these pass easily from this earthly life to life eternal."

CHAPTER XXXVII

HOW JESUS CHRIST, THE BLESSED ONE, AT THE PRAYER OF
ST FRANCIS, CONVERTED A RICH NOBLEMAN WHO HAD MADE
GREAT OFFERS TO ST FRANCIS, AND INSPIRED HIM WITH A
WISH TO BECOME A RELIGIOUS

ST FRANCIS, the servant of Christ, arriving late one evening with one of his brothers at the house of a rich and powerful nobleman, the two were received by him as if they had been angels of God, with so much courtesy and respect that the saint felt himself drawn to love him greatly; for he considered how on entering his house he had embraced him with much affection; how he had washed his feet, and humbly wiped and kissed them; how he had lighted a great fire, and prepared a supper composed of the choicest meats, serving him himself with a joyful countenance. When the supper was ended, the nobleman thus addressed St Francis: "Behold, my father, I offer thee myself and all I possess. If ever thou art in want of a tunic, or a mantle, or any other thing, purchase them, and I will pay thee. And see, I am ready to provide for all thy wants, as, through the grace of God, it is in my power to do so; for I abound in all temporal riches, and out of love to God, who gave them to me, most willingly do I bestow my goods on his poor." St Francis, seeing so much courtesy and generosity, felt great affection towards him; and having taken leave of him, he said to his companion: "Truly this nobleman would be a great gain to our Order, seeing he is so grateful to God, and so kind and courteous to his neighbour and to the poor. For know, dear brother, that courtesy is one of the attributes of God, who sendeth his rain on the just and on the unjust; for courtesy is the sister of charity, it ex-

93

tinguisheth hatred and kindleth love. I have discovered in this good man such divine virtues, that I would most willingly have him as a companion. On some future day we will pay him another visit, for possibly the Lord may touch his heart, and induce him to follow us in his service; in the meantime we will pray God to put this desire into his heart, and give him grace to execute it." Now a few days after St Francis had made this prayer, the Lord touched the heart of the nobleman; and the saint said to his companion: "Let us go, my brother, to the dwelling of that courteous nobleman, as I hope in God that, amongst his temporal gifts, he will offer himself and join our Order"; and they set out accordingly. As they arrived near the house, St Francis said to his companion: "Wait for me a little, that I may first ask the Lord to prosper our journey, and pray that it may please our Saviour Jesus Christ, through his holy Passion, to take from the world this virtuous nobleman, and confide him to us, his poor weak servants." Having said this, he knelt down in a spot where he could be seen by the nobleman, who was walking to and fro in his rooms; and it pleased God that he should perceive St Francis as he prayed in the presence of Christ, who appeared in great glory and stood before him; he saw, too, that for a long space of time the saint was raised above the earth. On seeing this he felt in his heart so great a desire to leave the world, that he hastened out of his palace, and with great fervour of spirit ran to St Francis, and kneeling at his feet implored him earnestly and devoutly to receive him into his Order, and allow him to do penance with him. Then the saint, seeing that his prayer was granted, and that the nobleman asked of him the accomplishment of his wish, arose and embraced him joyfully, devoutly returning thanks to God, who had made such a present to his Order. And the nobleman said to St Francis: "What wilt thou have me to do, my father? I am ready to obey thee, and give all I possess to the poor, in order to follow Christ with thee, without any hindrance from things temporal." And following the advice of the saint, he distributed all he possessed to the poor, and entered the Order, living a life of holiness and penance, and speaking always of divine things.

CHAPTER XXXVIII

HOW IT WAS REVEALED TO ST FRANCIS THAT BROTHER ELIAS
WAS DAMNED AND WAS TO DIE OUT OF THE ORDER; AND HOW
AT THE DESIRE OF THE SAID BROTHER, HE PRAYED TO CHRIST
FOR HIM, AND HOW HIS PRAYER WAS GRANTED

AS St Francis and Brother Elias were living together in a convent, it was revealed by God to St Francis that Brother Elias was damned, seeing he was about to apostatise, and that he would die out of the Order. In consequence of this revelation, the saint took such a dislike to him that he neither spoke to him nor conversed with him; and when Brother Elias went towards him, he turned away and took another direction, in order not to meet him. Now Brother Elias perceiving, and seeing that St Francis disliked him, was anxious to know the reason. He therefore accosted him one day in order to speak with him, the saint endeavouring, as usual, to avoid him; but Brother Elias retained him courteously, and begged him to say why he avoided his company, and refused to speak to him. St Francis answered: "This is the reason: it has been revealed to me by God that thou wilt apostatise, and die out of the Order; also that, because of thy sins, thou art damned." On hearing this Brother Elias said: "My reverend father, I implore thee, by the love of Christ Jesus, not to despise me for this reason, nor send me from thee; but like a good shepherd, following the example of thy Master, to seek and

95

save the lamb which will perish without thy help. Pray to God for me, that, if possible, he may revoke the sentence of my dam, nation; for it is written, that the Lord will forgive the sinner if he repent of his sin; and I have such faith in thy prayers that were I even in hell and thou wert to pray for me, I should find refreshment. I implore thee, then, that thou recommend me, a sinner, to God, who came into the world to save sinners, that he may have mercy on me." This request Brother Elias made with so much fervour and so many tears, that St Francis had compas, sion on him, and promised to pray for him, which he did; and as he prayed most devoutly, the Lord revealed to him that his prayer was granted; that the sentence of damnation pronounced on Brother Elias had been revoked; that his soul would be finally saved; but that he would leave the Order and die out of it; and so it happened. For Frederick, King of Sicily, having rebelled against the Church, was excommunicated by the Pope, with all those who gave him aid or counsel. Brother Elias being looked upon as one of the most learned men in the world, King Frede, rick sent for him, wishing to see him. He obeyed the summons, and thus rebelled against the Church; for which reason he was excommunicated by the Pope, and deprived of the habit of St Francis. Soon after the excommunication he fell dangerously ill; and a lay brother who belonged to the Order, a man of holy life, having heard of his illness, went to visit him, and amongst other things said to him: "My dear Brother, I grieve to see thee thus excommunicated and out of the Order, and that probably thou wilt die in this state. If there is any way by which I can deliver thee from this danger, most willingly would I undergo any trou, ble and fatigue to help thee." Brother Elias answered: "My Bro, ther, I see no other way but that thou go to the Pope and entreat him, for the love of God and of St Francis his servant, upon whose teaching I gave up the world, to absolve me from this excommu,

nication, and restore to me my religious habit." And the lay bro⸱
ther said he would most willingly undertake the journey for his
salvation; and taking leave of him, he went to the Pope, and
humbly kneeling before him implored him to take pity on Bro⸱
ther Elias, for the love of Christ and of St Francis his servant.
And it pleased God that the holy Father granted his request, tell⸱
ing him to return to him, and if he found him alive to tell him
in his name that he was absolved from the excommunication,
and that the habit of his Order was restored to him. He hastened
back to Brother Elias with this joyful news, and, finding him on
the point of death, gave him the message of the Pope, telling him
that he was absolved from the excommunication, and that his
habit was restored to him. On this Brother Elias departed from
this world, his soul being saved by the merits and prayers of St
Francis, in which he had placed such great faith.

CHAPTER XXXIX

OF THE WONDERFUL DISCOURSE WHICH ST ANTHONY
OF PADUA, A FRIAR MINOR, MADE IN THE CONSISTORY

THAT wonderful vessel of the Holy Spirit, St Anthony of Padua, one of the chosen disciples and companions of St Francis, whom the latter called his Vicar, was preaching one day before the Pope and the Cardinals in Consistory; there being present men of divers nations — Greeks, Latins, French, Germans, Slavs, English, and others; and he was so inflamed by the Holy Spirit, and explained the word of God so devoutly, so sweetly, so clearly, and in a manner so efficacious and so learned, that all those who were in the Consistory, though they spoke different languages, understood what he said as perfectly as if he had spoken the language of each. And they were all full of wonder, for it seemed to them as if the miracle of the Apostles at the time of Pentecost had been renewed, when the Holy Spirit taught them to speak all languages; and they said among themselves: "Does not he that preacheth come from Spain? How is it, then, that in his words we each hear our own tongue spoken?" And the Pope, as much surprised as the others, considering the deep meaning of his words, exclaimed: "In truth this man is the ark of the Testament, and the treasure of the Holy Scriptures."

98

CHAPTER XL

OF THE MIRACLE WHICH GOD PERFORMED WHEN ST ANTHONY,
BEING AT RIMINI, PREACHED TO THE FISHES OF THE SEA

CHRIST, the blessed one, was pleased to show forth the great
sanctity of his most faithful servant St Anthony, and how
men ought devoutly to listen to his preaching, by means of
creatures without reason. On one occasion, amongst others, he
made use of fish to reprove the folly of faithless heretics: even as
we read in the Old Testament that in ancient times he reprov﹣
ed the ignorance of Balaam by the mouth of an ass. St Anthony
being at one time at Rimini, where there was a great number of
heretics, and wishing to lead them by the light of faith into the
way of truth, preached to them for several days, and reasoned
with them on the faith of Christ and on the Holy Scriptures.
They not only resisted his words, but were hardened and obsti﹣
nate, refusing to listen to him. At last St Anthony, inspired by
God, went down to the sea-shore, where the river runs into the
sea, and having placed himself on a bank between the river and
the sea, he began to speak to the fishes as if the Lord had sent
him to preach to them, and said: "Listen to the word of God,
O ye fishes of the sea and of the river, seeing that the faithless
heretics refuse to do so." No sooner had he spoken these words
than suddenly so great a multitude of fishes, both small and great,
approached the bank on which he stood, that never before had
so many been seen in the sea or in the river. All kept their heads
out of the water, and seemed to be looking attentively on St An﹣
thony's face; all were ranged in perfect order and most peace﹣
fully, the smaller ones in front near the bank, after them came

those a little bigger, and last of all, where the water was deeper, the largest. When they had placed themselves in this order, St Anthony began to preach to them most solemnly, saying: "My brothers the fishes, you are bound, as much as is in your power, to return thanks to your Creator, who has given you so noble an element for your dwelling; for you have at your choice both sweet water and salt; you have many places of refuge from the tempest; you have likewise a pure and transparent element for your nourishment. God, your bountiful and kind Creator, when he made you, ordered you to increase and multiply, and gave you his blessing. In the universal deluge, all other creatures perished; you alone did God preserve from all harm. He has given you fins to enable you to go where you will. To you was it granted, according to the commandment of God, to keep the prophet Jonas, and after three days to throw him safe and sound on dry land. You it was who gave the tribute-money to our Saviour Jesus Christ, when, through his poverty, he had not wherewith to pay. By a singular mystery you were the nourishment of the eternal King, Jesus Christ, before and after his resurrection. Because of all these things you are bound to praise and bless the Lord, who has given you blessings so many and so much greater than to other creatures." At these words the fish began to open their mouths, and bow their heads, endeavouring as much as was in their power to express their reverence and show forth their praise. St Anthony, seeing the reverence of the fish towards their Creator, rejoiced greatly in spirit, and said with a loud voice: "Blessed be the eternal God; for the fishes of the sea honour him more than men without faith, and animals without reason listen to his word with greater attention than sinful heretics." And whilst St Anthony was preaching, the number of fishes increased, and none of them left the place that he had chosen. And the people of the city hearing of the miracle, made haste to go and witness it. With them also came the heretics of whom we have spoken above, who, seeing so wonderful and manifest a miracle, were touched in their hearts; and threw themselves at the feet of St Anthony to hear his words. The saint then began to expound to them the Catholic faith. He preached so eloquently, that all those heretics were converted, and returned to the true faith of Christ; the faithful also were filled with joy, and greatly comforted, being strengthened in the faith. After this St Anthony sent away the fishes, with the blessing of God; and they all departed, rejoicing as they went, and the people returned to the city. But St Anthony remained at Rimini for several days, preaching and reaping much spiritual fruit in the souls of his hearers.

CHAPTER XLI

HOW THE VENERABLE BROTHER SIMON DELIVERED A BROTHER
FROM A GREAT TEMPTATION, ON ACCOUNT OF WHICH HE WAS
ON THE POINT OF LEAVING THE ORDER

ABOUT the beginning of the Order, and during the lifetime of St Francis, a young man from Assisi took the habit, whose name was Simon; and the Lord adorned him with such graces and such elevation of mind, that all his life long he was a mirror of sanctity, as I have heard from those who lived with him for a long time. He very seldom left his cell, and whenever he was in company with the brothers he spoke always of God. He had never learned grammar, yet he talked of divine things and of the love of Christ in so elevated a way and with such profound wisdom, that his words seemed to be supernatural. One evening he went into the wood with Brother James of Massa to speak of God, and they spent the whole night conversing sweetly on divine love. When morning dawned they seemed to have been together but a few minutes, as the said Brother James told me himself. Brother Simon was so completely absorbed by the joy of these divine communications with God, and his spirit was so overflowing with love, that he was often obliged to lie down, as the tranquil sweetness which came over him with the Holy Spirit required not only the repose of the soul, but likewise that of the body; and during these divine visitations he was often rapt in God, and quite insensible to all bodily things. On one occasion, as he was thus rapt in God, and insensible to the world, his heart was so burning with divine love that his bodily senses were dead to all things external. A brother wishing to convince himself if this really was the case, as it appeared to be, took a piece of burning coal out of the fire, and put it on his foot; and Brother Simon neither felt it, nor did it leave any mark, though it was left there some time, until it went out of itself. The said Brother Simon, when he sat down to his meals, before nourishing his body took and gave to those around him the nourishment of the soul, by speaking of God. A young man of San Severino, who had been excessively vain and worldly, and who was of noble blood and of delicate habits, was converted by means of the holy conversation of Brother Simon, and entered the Order. When he received him into the convent he took from him his secular dress, and the young man remained with Brother Simon, to be instructed in the Rule. The devil, who is ever on the watch to do evil, tempted him so strongly in the flesh, that he felt it impossible to resist; and going to Brother Simon, he said to him: "Give me back my clothes which I wore in the world, as I cannot resist this temptation of the flesh." Brother Simon, feeling for him great compassion, said to him: "Sit down here awhile with me, my son"; and he spoke to him of God so earnestly, that the temptation left him. Shortly after, however, it returned, and he went again and asked for his clothes, and Brother Simon delivered him from it by speaking to him of God; and he did the same thing several times. At last, one night the temptation assailed him again with such force, that he felt it was quite impossible to resist; and he went to Brother Simon, and implored him to give him back his scholar's dress, as he could no longer remain in the convent. Then Brother Simon, as usual, made him sit down by his side, and talked to him of God; the young man listened, and bowing his head sorrowfully, laid it on Brother Simon's breast. The latter, filled with compassion, raised his eyes to heaven, and prayed that the Lord would have pity on him. As he prayed he was rapt in ecstasy, and his prayer was granted. When he came back to himself, he found the young man quite freed from the temptation, and as calm as if he had never been assaulted; the evil spirit which had raged in his heart was, as it were, converted into the Spirit of God, for he had approached the burning coal of divine love — that is to say, Brother Simon — and his heart henceforth was inflamed with the love of God and of his neigh‹ bours. Finding himself on one occasion with a malefactor who had been condemned to have both his eyes torn out, this young man felt such compassion for him that he went bodily to the gov‹ ernor, and in full council implored him with tears and prayers to allow him to give one of his eyes, so that the malefactor might not lose both. The governor and all those who composed his council were so touched by the charity of the monk, that they pardoned the culprit. Brother Simon being one day in prayer in the forest, and being greatly annoyed by a flock of crows who dis‹ turbed him in his meditations by their cries, he ordered them in the name of Christ, to go away, and never to return again; and the birds flew away at his command, and were never again seen or heard in all the country round about. And all the custo‹ dy of Fermo, where the convent was situated, bore testimony to this miracle.

CHAPTER XLII

OF SEVERAL WONDERFUL MIRACLES WHICH THE LORD PERFORMED
THROUGH THE MEANS OF BROTHER PETER OF MONTICELLO, AND
BROTHER CONRAD OF OFFIDA. HOW BROTHER BENTIVOGLIO CARRIED
A LEPER FIFTEEN MILES IN A VERY SHORT TIME; HOW ST MICHAEL
SPOKE TO ANOTHER BROTHER, AND HOW THE VIRGIN MARY AP,
PEARED TO BROTHER CONRAD AND PLACED HER
DIVINE SON IN HIS ARMS

AS the sky is adorned with stars, so the province of the March of Ancona was in former times adorned with holy and exemplary friars, who, like the bright luminaries in heaven, ornamented the Order of St Francis, and enlightened the world by their doctrine and example. Foremost amongst these was Bro, ther Lucido Antico, in whom indeed shone forth the fire of di, vine charity and the light of holiness; for, taught by the Spirit of God, his preaching produced innumerable fruits. Another brother, Bentivoglio of Severino, was seen by Brother Masseo raised above the earth as he was praying in the forest, at the sight of which miracle Brother Masseo became a Friar Minor, and grew so holy that he worked many miracles, both during his life, time and after his death: he is buried at Murro. The said Bro, ther Bentivoglio being once all alone at Trave Bonanti, nursing and serving a leper, received an order from his superior to go to another convent fifteen miles off. Not wishing to abandon the poor leper, he placed him carefully on his back, and charitably took him with him. Between the dawn of day and the rising of the sun he accomplished the fifteen miles, and arrived with his burden at the convent to which he had been sent, which was call, ed Monte Sancino. Had he been an eagle he could not have flown as quickly, and such a miracle caused great wonder and

surprise in all that country. Another Brother, Peter of Monticello, who was the guardian of the old Convent of Ancona, was
raised several feet above the earth, to the foot of the crucifix before which he was in prayer. This same Brother Peter having
once observed the Lent of St Michael with great devotion, as he
was praying on the last day of the feast in the church, was heard
to speak with St Michael by a young man who had hidden himself behind the high altar, in hopes of seeing something wonderful; and the words which he heard were these. The saint said to
Brother Peter: "Thou hast suffered faithfully for my sake, and
during many days hast mortified thy body; wherefore I am come
to comfort thee, and whatever grace thou askest of God, I will
obtain for thee." Brother Peter answered: "Most holy prince of
the celestial host of saints, faithful servant of divine love, and
pious protector of souls, this is the grace I ask of thee, namely,
that thou obtain from God the pardon of my sins." And St
Michael answered: "Ask some other grace, as this I will most
easily obtain." And as Brother Peter asked for nothing else,
the Archangel added: "Through the faith and devotion which
thou hast to me, I will obtain for thee not this grace only, but
many others likewise." And when the conversation, which had
lasted some time, was ended, the Archangel Michael departed,
leaving Brother Peter greatly comforted. At the same time lived
Brother Conrad of Offida in the Convent of Forana in the custody of Ancona, where resided Brother Peter. Having gone one
day into the forest to meditate on God, Brother Peter followed
him to see what would befall him; and Brother Conrad began to
implore the Virgin Mary, with great fervour and devotion, to
obtain from her Blessed Son that he might experience somewhat
of the sweetness which St Simeon experienced the day of the Pu-
rification, when in his arms he held Jesus the Blessed Saviour.
Having finished his prayer, the Virgin Mary obtained his re-

quest; and, behold! the Queen of Heaven appeared in great splendour, with her Blessed Son in her arms, and approaching Brother Conrad placed the Holy Child in his arms. He received him most reverently, and embracing him clasped him to his breast, his heart overflowing and burning with divine love and inexpressible consolation. Brother Peter, who witnessed this scene at a distance, felt likewise in his soul great sweetness and joy. When the Virgin Mary had departed from Brother Conrad, Brother Peter hastened back to the convent that he might not be seen; but when Brother Conrad arrived, full of joy and happiness, Brother Peter said to him: "O brother, thou hast received great consolation to-day!" And Brother Conrad answered: "What sayest thou, Brother Peter? How dost thou know? Hast thou seen me?" "I know," answered Brother Peter, "that the Virgin Mary, with her Blessed Son, has visited thee." And Brother Conrad, who, through great humility, wished to keep secret the grace with which God had favoured him, entreated Brother Peter to tell no one what he had witnessed; and from henceforth so great was the love which existed between these two brethren, that they seemed to have but one soul and one heart in all things. The said Brother Conrad, being once in the Convent of Siruolo, delivered a woman who was possessed by a devil, by praying for her a whole night; and her mother coming to know it, he left the place in the morning, that he might not be discovered and honoured by the people.

CHAPTER XLIII

HOW BROTHER CONRAD OF OFFIDA CONVERTED A YOUNG
BROTHER, WHO WAS A STUMBLING-BLOCK TO THE OTHER
BROTHERS; AND HOW AFTER DEATH HIS SOUL APPEARED TO
BROTHER CONRAD, BEGGING HIM TO PRAY FOR HIM; AND
HOW THROUGH HIS PRAYERS HE WAS DELIVERED FROM THE
GREAT PAINS OF PURGATORY

THE life of the said Brother Conrad of Offida, the great advocate of evangelical poverty and of the Rule of St Francis, was so exemplary and so meritorious in the sight of God, that Christ, the blessed one, honoured him with many miracles, not only after death, but likewise during his life. Amongst others, being once on a visit to the Convent of Offida, the brothers begged him, for the love of God and of holy charity, to reprove a young brother in the said convent, whose conduct was so puerile and disordered, and his manners so dissolute, that he distracted all the brethren, both young and old, at divine office, and cared little or nothing for any of the observances of religious life. At the request of the brothers, and out of compassion for the said young man, Brother Conrad called him to him one day, and reproved him with so much charity, that a complete change took place in his heart, and the said young man, putting off his former childish way of life, became so obedient, so meek, so devout, so anxious to do what was right, so ready to serve others, and so zealous in the practice of every virtue, that the brethren, to whom he had hitherto been a stumbling-block, found in him much comfort and satisfaction, so that they loved him dearly. Shortly after this conversion it pleased God to take him out of the world; and his death caused great sorrow to the brethren. A few days after his soul had left the body, it appeared to Brother

107

Conrad as he was in prayer before the altar of the convent, devoutly saluting him as his father. On Brother Conrad asking who he was, he answered: "I am the soul of the young brother who died a few days ago." Said Brother Conrad to him: "My beloved son, how is it with thee?" And the soul answered: "By the grace of God, and through thy teaching, I have cause to be thankful, for I am not damned; but because of certain sins of which I had not time to repent while I was in the world, I am suffering the extremest pain of purgatory; and I pray thee, Father, as thou hadst compassion on me when living, to help me now by thy prayers, and say for me some *Paters,* for thy prayers are most acceptable to God." Then Brother Conrad, continuing his devotions, said for him a *Pater* with a *Requiem aeternam.* At this the soul said: "Holy Father, I am greatly refreshed already, and I pray thee to repeat thy prayer for me." Brother Conrad did as he was begged, and the soul said again: "As thou prayest for me, my sufferings are relieved; wherefore I implore thee, cease not to pray for me." Then Brother Conrad, seeing that the soul of the young man was relieved by his prayers, said for his intention a hundred *Paters;* and when they were finished the soul said to him: "I thank thee, dearest Father, in the name of God, for thy great charity towards me; through thy prayers I have been delivered from the pains of purgatory, and am going to heaven," and with this the soul departed. Brother Conrad, in order to comfort and console the brethren, related to them the vision. And on this wise the soul of the young brother went to heaven, through the merits of Brother Conrad.

CHAPTER XLIV

HOW THE MOTHER OF CHRIST AND ST JOHN THE EVAN,
GELIST APPEARED TO BROTHER CONRAD, AND TOLD HIM
WHO HAD SUFFERED THE GREATEST SORROW
AT THE PASSION OF CHRIST

WHEN Brother Conrad and the aforenamed Brother Peter, the two shining lights of the custody of Ancona, were living together in the Convent of Forano, such love and charity existed between them that they seemed to have but one heart and one soul; and they made between them a pact that they would make known to each other and share every mercy which the Lord should send them. Having made this agreement, it happened one day, as Brother Peter was praying, devoutly meditating on the Passion of Christ, and how his Blessed Mother, with St John the Evangelist and St Francis, were represented at the foot of the cross, as having been crucified with Christ in mental sufferings, he felt a great wish to know which of the three had suffered the greatest sorrow on account of the Passion of Christ — the Mother who had given him birth, the disciple who had laid his head on his bosom, or St Francis, who was, as it were, crucified with him. As he was meditating on this, the Virgin Mary appeared to him, with St John the Evangelist and St Francis, all clothed in the heavenly garb of glorified souls; and St Francis seemed to be dressed more richly than St John. At this vision Brother Peter was greatly terrified, but St John comforted him by saying: "Fear not, dear brother; for we are come to enlighten thee in thy doubt: know, then, that the Mother of Christ, and I, his disciple, have suffered above every other creature at his Passion, and after us St Francis has suffered more than all others, and this is why thou seest him in such glory." And Brother Peter said: "Why then, most holy Apostle of Christ, are the vestments of St Francis more beautiful than thine?" "Because," answered St John, "when he was in the world, he wore a humbler dress than I." And having said these words, he gave to Brother Peter a glorious vestment that he had in his hand, saying: "Take this dress which I have brought for thee." Then St John being about to put it on him, Brother Peter fell down in terror, and began to cry out: "Brother Conrad, Brother Conrad, haste thou to help me! come and see most wonderful things!" And as he said these words, the vision disappeared. Then Brother Peter related to Brother Conrad all he had seen, and they together returned thanks to God.

CHAPTER XLV

OF THE CONVERSION, LIFE, MIRACLES, AND DEATH OF THE HOLY BROTHER JOHN DELLA PENNA

WHEN Brother John della Penna was still in the world as a boy in the province of Ancona, a beautiful child appeared to him one night, and calling him, said: "John, go to Santo Stefano, where one of my Friars Minor is preaching; take heed to his words, and believe the doctrine he teaches, for I have sent him to thee. After that thou shalt make a great journey, and then come to me." Then the boy John arose, being greatly troubled in mind, and reaching Santo Stefano, he found a great multitude of men and women waiting to hear a sermon. Now he who was about to preach was a friar named Philip, who was one of the first brethren to visit Ancona, for as yet there were but few convents established in the province. And the said Brother Philip stood up to preach; and he did so most devoutly, not with words of worldly widsom, but, inspired by the Spirit of Christ, he announced the kingdom of eternal life. The sermon being ended, the boy went to Brother Philip, and said to him: "Father, if thou wilt receive me into the Order, most willingly will I do penance, and serve our Lord Jesus Christ." And Brother Philip seeing the great innocence of the child, and his earnest desire to serve God, said to him: "Come to me on such a day at Ricanati, and I will receive thee." Now a provincial chapter was to be held at Ricanati, and the boy in his simplicity fancied that this was the journey he was to make according to the vision, and that after having accomplished it he would go to heaven, which he thought likewise would be as soon as he had been received into the Order. He went, therefore, to Ricanati, where he was received into the Order by Brother Philip. Seeing that it did not happen to him as he had expected, and the Minister having said in chapter that if anyone wished to go to the province of Provence, for merit of holy obedience, he would most willingly give him permission, and Brother John feeling a great desire to go there — thinking in his heart that that would be the journey he was to make before he went to heaven, but lacking courage to say so — he confided his wish to Brother Philip, and entreated him to obtain for him permission to go to the province of Provence. Then Brother Philip, seeing his purity and the holiness of his intentions, obtained for him the permission he wished for; and the little Brother John set out on his way most joyfully, as he believed that, his journey being ended, he would go to heaven. But it pleased God that he should remain in the said province five-and-twenty years, always looking forward to the day of his departure, living in great sanctity, setting a most holy example, and increasing in virtue and in favour with God and man; so that he was much beloved by seculars as well as by the brethren. Now Brother

John being one day in prayer, weeping and lamenting that his wish was never accomplished, and his pilgrimage here below so lengthened, Christ, the blessed one, appeared to him, and he felt his soul melt within him. Then said the Lord to him: "My son, Brother John, ask of me what thou wilt." And he answered: "My Lord, I have naught else to ask thee but thyself, as I desire naught else; but I ask thee to forgive my sins, and to grant me the grace that I may see thee once more, when I shall have the greatest need of thy presence." And Christ the blessed answered: "Thy request is granted"; and having said these words he departed, leaving Brother John much comforted. At last the brothers of the province of Ancona, having heard of the fame of his sanctity, persuaded the General of the Order to command him, out of holy obedience, to return to Ancona. No sooner had the order reached him than he set out most joyfully, hoping that on arriving he would go to heaven, according to the promise of Christ. On arriving in the province he lived there thirty years, not being recognised by any of his relations; and every day he expected that, through the mercy of God, the promise would be accomplished. During this time he often filled the office of guardian with much discretion, and the Lord performed many miracles through him. Amongst other gifts that he received from God was the spirit of prophecy. Being once absent from the convent, one of his novices was so strongly tempted by the devil that he determined to leave the Order as soon as Brother John should return. On this Brother John, being informed, by the spirit of prophecy, of the temptation and of the decision of the novice, hastened back to the convent, and calling the novice, ordered him to go to confession; but before he did so he related to him all his temptations, as the Lord had revealed them to him, and ended by saying: "My son, as thou hast waited for me, and wouldst not go away without my blessing, the Lord has had pity on thee, for not only wilt thou not leave the Order, but thou shalt die in it, in the grace of God." And the said novice remain‹ ed in the Order, and became a holy brother. These things were related to me by Brother Ugolino. The said Brother John, albeit his mind was so happy and so calm, spoke but seldom; he was a man of prayer, and rarely returned to his cell after Matins, but remained in the church till morning. One night after Matins an angel of God appeared to him, saying: "Brother John, thy life is ended, for the moment thou hast desired so ardently is come; and I make known to thee from God that thou mayest ask of him what grace soever thou wilt; likewise I announce to thee that thou mayest choose between one day in purgatory, or seven days of suffering in this world." And Brother John, having chosen the seven days of suffering in this world, immediately fell ill, and was afflicted with divers diseases; for he had a great fever, and the gout in his hands and feet, besides a pain in his side, and many other sufferings; but, worse than all this, a devil stood before him, holding a large paper on which were written all the sins he had ever committed in thought, word, or deed. Then said the devil to him: "Because of these sins which thou hast committed, in thought, word and deed, thou art condemned to the depths of hell." And it seemed to him as if he had never done any good actions; he even forgot that he was in the Order, or ever had been in it, believing that he was damned, as the devil said; so that when the brothers asked him how he was, he answered: "I am most unhappy, because I am damned." The brothers seeing this, sent for an aged friar named Brother Matthew of Monte Robbiano, who was a holy man and a great friend of Brother John. When the said Brother Matthew arrived, the seventh day of his sufferings was approaching, and going near him he asked him how he was. "I am in evil case," was the answer, "because I am damned." Then said Brother Matthew to him: "Dost thou not remember that thou hast often confessed to me, and I have absolved thee of all thy sins? Dost thou not remember likewise that thou hast served God for many years in this holy Order? Dost thou not know that the mercy of God is greater than all the sins in the world, and that Jesus Christ, the blessed one, our Saviour, gave himself for our salvation? Have good hope; for I know of a certainty that thou wilt be saved." And as he spoke the end of the trial arrived, and the temptation disappeared; then was Brother John greatly comforted, and he said to Brother Matthew: "My dear brother, thou art tired, and it is late; I pray thee go and take a little rest"; but Brother Matthew would not leave him. Yielding, however, at last to his prayers, he went to take a little rest, and Brother John remained alone with the friar who served him. And lo! Christ, the blessed one, appeared in great glory, as he had promised to appear to him once more when he should be in most need of him, and he healed him of all his infirmities. Then Brother John joined his hands, thanking God for having permitted him to end the long journey of this present miserable life in the arms of Jesus, to whom he confided his soul, passing from this mortal life to life eternal with Christ, the blessed one, whom he had so long awaited and desired to see. The said Brother John was buried in the Convent della Penna di San Giovanni.

CHAPTER XLVI

HOW BROTHER PACIFICO, BEING IN PRAYER, SAW THE SOUL OF
BROTHER UMILE, HIS BROTHER IN THE FLESH, GO UP TO HEAVEN

THERE were two brothers of the province of Ancona who
entered the Order after the death of St Francis — one was
named Brother Umile, and the other Brother Pacifico —
both of whom attained a great degree of perfection and sanctity.
Brother Umile lived in the Convent of Soffiano, and there died;
Brother Pacifico lived in another convent, at some distance. It
pleased God that Brother Pacifico, being one day in prayer in a
solitary place, was rapt in ecstasy, and saw the soul of his brother, which had just left his body, go straight to heaven without
any hindrance. Many years after this, Brother Pacifico was sent
to the Convent of Soffiano, where his brother had died, at the
time when the friars, at the demand of the Lords of Bruforte,
changed their convent for another, and were removing the remains of the holy brothers who had died there. When the grave
of Brother Umile was opened, his brother took his bones, and
having washed them in wine, wrapped them carefully in a white
napkin, and weeping over them, kissed them with great devotion. The other brothers were much surprised that he should set
them such bad example, for they could not understand how a
man so holy could show such carnal affection towards his brother,
honouring his remains so far above those of the other friars, who,
not being less holy than Brother Umile, were worthy of like
honour. Then Brother Pacifico, knowing how he was misjudged
by the brethren, humbly explained to them his conduct, saying:
"My most dear brothers, be not surprised if I honour the bones of
my brother above those of the other friars; for, thanks be to God,

it is not through carnal affection that I do this, but because when my brother left this life I was praying in a solitary place, very far from the convent where he lay dead, and I saw his soul go straight to heaven; wherefore I am sure that his bones are holy, and will

be honoured in heaven. If the Lord had revealed to me the same things of the other friars, I would treat their bones also with equal reverence." Then the brethren being convinced that his intentions were holy and just, were greatly edified by what he had told them, and praised God who did such wonderful things for his holy friars.

CHAPTER XLVII

IN the above-mentioned Convent of Soffiano there lived formerly a Friar Minor so holy that he appeared to be almost supernatural, and he was often rapt in God. He possessed the grace of contemplation in a notable degree; and often when he was ravished and raised above the earth in ecstasy, all kinds of birds used to come and perch on his head, his arms, and his hands, singing most wonderfully. He was very fond of solitude, and rarely spoke; but when anyone asked him a question he answered so wisely and so graciously that he seemed to be an angel rather than a mortal. He was a man wholly devoted to prayer and contemplation, and the brothers held him in great reverence. Having finished the course of his virtuous life, it was the will of God that he should fall dangerously ill, so that he could take no nourishment, and he refused all human remedies, placing all his hope in the celestial Physician, Jesus Christ, the blessed one, and his divine Mother, by whom, through the mercy of God, he was visited and healed. For as he was lying on his bed, preparing for death with all his heart and with great devotion, the glorious Virgin Mary, Mother of Christ, appeared to him with a great multitude of angels and holy virgins, and surrounded by much splendour. She approached his bed, and on seeing her, he experienced the greatest comfort and joy both in soul and body, and began to pray to her humbly, to ask of her divine Son to deliver his soul from its miserable prison of flesh. As he persevered in prayer, with many tears, the Virgin Mary called him by his name, saying to him: "My son, have no doubts; for thy prayer is granted, and I am come to comfort thee a little before thou leavest this world." By the side of the Virgin Mary there stood three holy virgins, holding in their hands three vases filled with a sweet ointment; and the Virgin Mary taking one of the vases opened it, when all the house was filled with the odour thereof; then taking a spoonful of the contents she gave it to the sick brother. No sooner had he tasted it than he experienced so sweet a sensation, that it seemed as if his soul could no longer remain in his body, and he cried out: "No more, O blessed Virgin Mary; no more, O blessed Physician, whose pleasure it is to save the human race from perishing; I cannot endure such sweetness." But the compassionate Mother of God continued to give him the ointment, until the vase was emptied. The first vase being emptied, the Blessed Virgin took the second, and was about to give him the contents; but he said: "O blessed Mother of God, if my soul is, as it were, melted by the sweetness and virtue of the ointment thou hast already given me, how shall I ever be able to support the effect of a second vase? I pray thee, O Virgin, blessed above all the saints and all the angels, not to give me any more." The glorious Virgin Mary answered: "Taste, my son, a little of the second vase"; and having given him a little, she said: "Thou hast sufficient, my son, for to-day; soon I will come again to conduct thee to the kingdom of my Son, whom thou hast ever sought and desired"; and having said these words, she took leave of him and departed. And the brother was so strengthened and comforted by the medicine she had given him, that he lived for several days in perfect health, without taking any nourishment. Shortly after, as he was talking gaily with the brethren, he passed from this miserable life most joyfully.

CHAPTER XLVIII

BROTHER James della Massa, to whom the Lord revealed many secrets, and to whom he gave a perfect knowledge of the Holy Scriptures and of the future, was so holy, that Brother Giles of Assisi, Brother Mark of Montino, Brother Juniper, and Brother Lucido said of him, that they knew no one in the world who was greater in the sight of God than this Brother James. I had a great wish to see him; for having asked Brother John, the companion of Brother Giles, to explain to me certain spiritual things, he said to me: "If thou wilt be well directed in things spiritual, try to speak with Brother James della Massa; for his words being the words of the Holy Spirit, one can neither add to nor take away from them anything, and there is not a man on earth whom I have a greater wish to see." When Brother John of Parma was minister of the convent, this Brother James was once, in prayer, ravished in God, remaining for three days in ecstasy, quite insensible to all bodily feeling, so that the brethren thought him to be dead; and during this ecstasy many things with regard to the Order were revealed to him. Having learnt this, my wish to speak to him and to hear him greatly increased. When the Lord permitted me to see him, I thus addressed him: "If that which I have heard of thee be true, I pray thee not to conceal it from me. I have heard that when thou wast three days as if thou hadst been dead, the Lord revealed to thee, amongst other things, what was to take place in our Order; and this was told me by Brother Matthew, to whom thou didst reveal it out of obedience." Brother James confessed most humbly that what Brother Matthew had said was true: now this is what Brother Matthew told me: "I know a brother to whom the Lord has made known that which will take place in our Order; for Brother James della Massa has told me that, after the Lord had revealed to him many things concerning the Church militant, he saw in a vision a large and beautiful tree, the root of which was of gold, and all the branches were men, and these men were all Friars Minor; and there were as many large branches as there were provinces in the Order, and each branch was composed of as many brethren as there were friars in each province; and he was informed of the number of friars in the Order, and in each province — with their names, their ages, their rank, and the different offices they filled — also their various merits and defects. And he saw Brother John of Parma at the summit of the highest branch of the tree, and round him were the ministers of each province; and he saw Christ, the blessed one, sitting on a throne, who, calling St Francis to him, gave him a chalice full of the spirit of life, saying, 'Go to thy brothers, and give them to drink of this spirit of life, as Satan will rise up against them, and many will fall and not rise again.' And Christ, the blessed one, gave to St Francis two angels to accompany him; and St Francis took the chalice to his brothers, and offered it first to Brother John of Parma, who taking it drank all its contents in haste, but with great reverence, and having done so he became luminous, like the sun. After him St Francis offered it to all the others; and very few there were who took it, and drank with devotion: those who did so, were filled with light, like the sun; but those who took the chalice, and threw away its contents most irreverently, became black and deformed, and horrible to look at; those who drank a part of the contents and threw away the rest, were partly bright and partly dark, in proportion to the quantity they drank or threw away. The brightest of all was the said Brother John, who, having drained to the dregs the cup of life, had seen by the aid of a celestial light the tempests and troubles which were about to rise against the tree, shaking and tearing its branches; for which reason the said Brother John left the top of the tree where he was, and placing himself under its branches hid himself close to the roots. A brother who had drunk some and thrown away some of the contents of the chalice, took possession of the place on the branch he had left; no sooner was he there, than the nails of his fingers became like points of iron; on seeing this, he hastened to leave the place he had taken, and in his fury he sought to vent his rage on Brother John; and Brother John perceiving his intention, cried out to Christ, the blessed one, who was seated on his throne, to help him; and Christ, hearing his cry, called St Francis, and giving him a sharp stone, said: 'Take this stone, and going cut the nails of the brother who seeks to tear Brother John, so that he may not be able to do him any harm.' And St Francis did as he was ordered. In the meantime a great tempest arose, and the wind shook the tree in such a way that all the brethren fell to the ground. First fell those who had thrown away the contents of the chalice of the spirit of life: these were carried by devils to dark regions, full of pain and anguish; but Brother John, and others who had drunk of the chalice, were carried by angels to the regions of life eternal, full of light and splendour. And Brother James, who witnessed the vision, saw clearly the names, the condition and the fate of each brother. And the tempest did not cease till the tree was blown down, and carried away by the wind; and immediately another tree arose out of the golden roots of the old one, and it was entirely composed of gold, with its leaves and fruits; but for the present we will not describe the beauty, the virtues, and the delicious fragrance of this wonderful tree."

CHAPTER XLIX

AMONG the learned and holy brethren and sons of St Francis, who, as Solomon says, form the glory of their father, was the venerable and holy Brother John of Fermo, of the province of Ancona, who lived in our times. Having spent the greater part of his life in the holy house of Alvernia, he died there, and was known by the name of Brother John of Alvernia; he was a man of great holiness and great sanctity. This Brother John, when he was a child, greatly loved the ways of penance, which preserve the purity both of the body and of the soul; and at a very tender age he began to wear a belt of iron, and to observe great fasting and abstinence; more especially he used these mortifications when he was residing with the Canons of San Pietro di Fermo, who lived in great luxury; he avoided all pleasures, and macerated his body with great severity. His companions, being against such penitential ways, tried by every means to turn him from them, taking from him his instruments of penance, and preventing him from fasting; wherefore the holy child, inspired by God, resolved to leave the world and its worshippers, and to put himself in the arms of his crucified Lord, taking the habit of the crucified St Francis; which he did. Being received into the Order so young, and confided to the care of the master of the novices, he grew so spiritual and so devout, that whenever he heard the said master speak of God, he felt his heart to burn within him, as if it had been on fire, so that it was impossible for him to remain quiet, and he ran to and fro in the garden, in the forest, and even in the church; for so sweet was the sensation he

122

experienced, that it seemed to him as if his heart was melted like wax before the fire. As time went on, this holy youth advanced from virtue to virtue, and his soul was adorned and enriched with spiritual gifts; he was often rapt in ecstasy, so that his mind was raised at times to the splendours of the cherubim, at times to the ardour of the seraphim and the joys of the beatified. At one time this ecstasy of divine love, which seemed, as it were, to set his heart on fire, lasted for three years, and this took place on the holy mountain of Alvernia. But as God takes especial care of his children, sending them at divers times consolation or tribula,tion, adversity or prosperity, according to their need, in order to preserve in them the grace of humility, or to awaken in their hearts a greater thirst after spiritual things, so it pleased his di,vine bounty, when the three years were ended, to withdraw from Brother John this flame of celestial love, and take from him every spiritual consolation. Then was Brother John most disconsolate and sorrowful, and this great trial made him so miserable, that he wandered about the forest, crying out with sighs and tears for the beloved Spouse of his soul, for without his presence his soul could enjoy neither peace nor rest. Yet nowhere could he find his Beloved, or recover those sweet spiritual sensations to which the love of Christ had accustomed him. Now this trial lasted sev,eral days, during which time he persevered in prayer, weeping and sighing, and imploring the Lord to take pity on his soul, and restore to him his Beloved. At last, his patience having been suf,ficiently tried, as he was wandering one day sorrowfully in the forest he sat down, overcome with fatigue; and as he was gazing up to heaven, with his eyes full of tears, Jesus Christ, the blessed one, appeared to him, standing in silence on the path by which he himself had come. Brother John knew him to be the Christ, and throwing himself at his feet he burst into a flood of tears, and thus addressed him: "Help me, O my Lord! for without thee, my sweet Saviour, I am all in sorrow and in darkness; without thee, gentle Lamb, I am in anguish and fear; without thee, Son of the most high God, I am in confusion and in shame; without thee, I am despoiled of every good, for thou art Jesus Christ, the true light of my soul; without thee, I am lost and damned, for thou art the life of souls, the life of life; without thee, I am sterile and unfruitful, for thou art the fountain of every grace; without thee, I can have no consolation, for thou, O Jesus, art our Redeemer, our love, our desire, the bread of comfort, the wine which rejoices the hearts of angels and of saints; enlighten me, O pitying Shepherd, for I am thy lamb, albeit most unworthy." When the Lord delays to grant the desires of holy men, their love towards him greatly increaseth; for the which reason Christ, the blessed one, left Brother John, going from him without granting his request, and without speaking to him. Then Brother John arose, and running after him threw himself again at his feet, imploring him not to leave him, and crying out: "O Jesus Christ, most sweet Saviour, have mercy on me in my trouble; by the truth of thy salvation and the multitude of thy mercies, restore to me the joy of thy countenance, and cast upon me a look of pity; for the earth is full of thy mercy"; but the Lord Jesus went from him without saying a word, or leaving him any consolation. Then Brother John followed him with great fervour, and when he came up to him, Christ, the blessed one, turned round, and looking at him most sweetly, he opened his holy and merciful arms and embraced him; and when he opened his arms Brother John saw rays of light come from his holy bosom, which lighted up all the forest, as well as his own soul and body. Then Brother John knelt down at the feet of Christ, the blessed one, who, as he had given his foot to Mary Magdalene to kiss, so now gave he it to Brother John. Then Brother John, taking it with great reverence, bathed it with his tears like another Magdalene, saying most devoutly: "I pray thee, my Lord, look not at my sins, but, by thy holy Passion and by the precious Blood which thou hast shed, awaken my soul to the grace of thy love; for thou hast commanded us to love thee with all our heart and with all our strength; which commandment none can fulfil without thy help. Help me, then, beloved Son of God, that I may love thee with all my heart and all my strength." And as Brother John was thus praying at the feet of Christ his prayer was granted, and the flame of divine love which he had lost was restored to him, and he felt himself greatly comforted. Then knowing that the gift of divine grace had been restored to him, he began to return thanks to Christ, the blessed one, and devoutly to kiss his feet. Then standing up, and looking on the Saviour's face, Jesus Christ gave him his holy hands to kiss; and having kissed them, Brother John approached the bosom of Christ, and embraced him. Christ, the blessed one, received him in his arms; and as Brother John embraced the Saviour, and was embraced by him, the air was filled with the sweetest perfumes, so sweet that no other perfume in the world could be compared with them. Thus was Brother John consoled, enlightened, and rapt in ecstasy, and this sweet perfume lasted in his soul for many months; and thenceforth from his lips, which had drunk at the fountain of divine wisdom on the sacred bosom of the Saviour, there fell most wonderful and celestial words, which changed the hearts of those who heard them, producing great fruit in souls; and for a long time, whenever Brother John followed the path in the forest where the blessed feet of Christ had passed, he saw the same wonderful light and breathed the same sweet odour. When Brother John came back to himself after this vision, though the corporal presence of Christ had disappeared, his mind was so enlightened and so imbued with divine wisdom, that although he was not a learned man or versed in human studies, he explained most wonderfully

125

the most difficult questions on the Holy Trinity and the profound mysteries of Holy Writ; and when speaking before the Pope, the cardinals, the king, the barons, the masters, and doctors, they were surprised at his sublime discourse, and at the words of wisdom which he pronounced.

CHAPTER L

HOW BROTHER JOHN OF ALVERNIA, WHEN SAYING
MASS ON THE DAY OF ALL SOULS, SAW MANY SOULS
LIBERATED FROM PURGATORY

AS Brother John was saying Mass on the day after All Saints, for the souls of the dead, as the Church has ordered, he offered with such charity and such compassion the holy sacrifice, which the dead desire above all else we can give them, that he seemed to be overwhelmed and consumed by the ardour of the feelings which filled his heart; and when he lifted up the Body of Christ and devoutly offered it to God the Father, entreating him, for the love of his blessed Son Jesus Christ, who had died on the cross for the souls of men, to deliver from the pains of purgatory the souls of the dead which he had created and redeemed, he saw immediately an immense number of souls go out from purgatory, like innumerable sparks of fire coming out of a burning oven; and he saw them go up to heaven, through the merits of the Passion of Christ, who is daily offered for the living and the dead in that most holy sacrifice, which is worthy to be adored for ever and ever.

CHAPTER LI

AT the time when Brother James of Fallerone, a man of great sanctity, was dangerously ill in the Convent of Mogliano, in the custody of Fermo, Brother John of Alvernia, who was then living in the Convent of Massa, hearing of his illness, and loving him as his dear father, began to pray for him, imploring God most devoutly in prayer to restore to Brother James the health of the body, if such were for the good of his soul. As he prayed he was rapt in ecstasy, and he saw in the air a great army of angels and saints above his cell, which was in the forest; they were surrounded by such splendour and glory, that all the country round was illuminated. Among the angels he saw the said Brother James, for whom he was praying, clothed in white and shining raiment; he saw also the holy father St Francis, with the sacred stigmata of Christ on his hands and feet, most glorious; he likewise beheld Brother Lucido the holy, and Brother Matthew of Monte Rubbiano, and many other brothers whom he had neither seen nor known in this life. And as he contemplated with great delight that holy band of saints, it was revealed to him that the sick brother for whom he had been praying would die of the disease whereof he was lying ill, and that his soul would be saved; but that he would not go straight to heaven after death, as it was necessary he should be purified for a time in purgatory. And this revelation made to Brother John filled his heart with such joy that he did not grieve over the death of Brother James, but experienced great sweetness in his soul; and he said within himself: "Brother James, my sweet father; Brother James, my sweet brother; Brother James, faithful servant and friend of God; Brother James, companion of the angels and one of the army of saints!" And as he was thus rejoicing he came to himself; and leaving the convent immediately, he went to visit Brother James at Moliano, and found him so much worse that he could scarcely speak. Then he announced to him the death of his body and the salvation and glory of his soul, of which he was certain through divine revelation; and Brother James received him most joyfully, thanking him for the good news he brought, and praying him devoutly not to forget him. Brother John begged him after death to come to him and tell him where he was and how it fared with him, which Brother James promised to do if it should please the Lord. The moment of his death approaching, Brother James began to repeat with great devotion the verse of the psalm, *In pace in idipsum dormiam et requiescam;* which signifieth, "I will go to sleep in peace, and will rest in life eternal"; and having said these words, he left this world, with a joyful countenance. When he was buried, Brother John returned to the Convent of Massa, and there awaited the accomplishment of the promise of Brother James that he would appear to him after death. As he was in prayer on that same day, Christ, the blessed one, appeared to him surrounded by a multitude of angels and saints; but Brother James was not with them, which thing greatly surprised Brother John, who recommended him most devoutly to Christ the blessed. The following day, as he was again praying in the forest, Brother James appeared in the company of angels, his countenance beaming with joy; and Brother John said to him: "O most dear Father, why didst thou not appear to me on the day thou promised?" Brother James answered: "Because it was necessary that I should be purified in purgatory; but at the same hour that Christ appeared to thee,

128

and in which thou didst recommend me to him, he granted thy prayer and I was freed from all suffering, and I appeared to Brother James of Massa, a holy lay brother, who was serving Mass; and I saw the consecrated Host, when the priest lifted it up, changed into a beautiful living child; and I said to him, 'This day I shall go with him to life eternal, where none can go with-

out him.'" And having said these words, Brother James disappeared, and went up to heaven with the holy company of angels, and Brother John was greatly comforted. The said Brother James of Fallerone died on the Vigil of St James the Apostle, in the month of July, in the above-named Convent of Moliano; and through his merits the divine Goodness wrought many miracles after his death.

129

CHAPTER LII

OF THE VISION OF BROTHER JOHN OF ALVERNIA, BY
WHICH HE BECAME ACQUAINTED WITH ALL THE OR-
DER OF THE HOLY TRINITY

THE said Brother John of Alvernia having renounced all worldly joys and temporal consolations, and having placed all his hope and love in God, the divine bounty granted him many consolations, especially in the days which commemorated some act of Christ, the blessed one. As the Nativity of Christ was approaching, in which he expected some great consolation from God, the Holy Spirit filled his heart with such love to Christ, who had humbled himself so as to take upon him our hu- manity, that it seemed truly as if his soul were a burning furnace; and the great love which consumed his heart agitated him so vio- lently, that he could not resist the ardour of the Holy Spirit, or refrain from crying out. At the same time that he experienced this great fervour he felt such a security of his salvation, that it seemed to him, had he died at that moment, that he would not have suffered in Purgatory; and this state lasted six months, though he felt not always the same degree of fervour, but it in- creased at certain hours of the day. During that time he received many wonderful visitations and consolations from God, and was often rapt in ecstasy, as was seen by the brother who wrote these things. One night especially he was so rapt in God, that he saw in him all things created, both celestial and terrestrial, with all their perfections and their various orders and degrees; and he knew most clearly how every thing created presents itself to its Creator, and how God is above, and within, and around all things created. He was made acquainted likewise with one God in three

130

persons and three persons in one God, and the infinite love which made the Son of God to become man out of obedience to the Father. He was likewise informed in this vision how there is no other way by which the soul can go to God, and have life eternal, but through Christ, the blessed one, who is the way, the truth, and the life of the soul.

CHAPTER LIII

HOW, WHILE HE WAS SAYING MASS, BROTHER JOHN OF ALVERNIA FELL DOWN, AS IF HE HAD BEEN DEAD

A MOST wonderful thing befell the said Brother John in the above-mentioned Convent of Moliano, as is related by the brethren who were present. The first night after the Octave of St Lawrence, and within the Octave of the Assumption of our Lady, having said Matins in the church with the other brethren, the unction of God's grace coming upon him, he went into the garden to meditate on the Passion of Christ, and prepare himself most devoutly to celebrate Mass, which it was his turn to sing that morning. As he was meditating on the words of the Consecration of the Body of Christ and contemplating the boundless charity of Jesus, who not only bought us with his precious Blood, but left his Body and his Blood as food for our souls, the love of sweet Jesus so filled his heart that he could not contain himself, and cried out several times, *Hoc est Corpus meum.* As he said these words Christ, the blessed one, appeared to him, with the Virgin Mary and a multitude of angels, and the Spirit of God made known to him high mysteries of that great sacrament. When day dawned he entered the church, so absorbed by all he had seen that he repeated aloud the above words, with great fervour of spirit, believing that he was not seen or heard by any one (but there was a brother praying in the choir who saw and heard everything), and he remained in this state till the hour came to say Mass. He approached the altar, and began the sacrifice; as he proceeded his heart so overflowed with love to Christ, and the sensation he experienced was so ineffable that he could not express it in words, and he was in doubt whether he ought to leave off the celebration of Mass or to go on. The same thing having happened to him before, and the Lord having mo-derated the sensation, so that he was enabled to finish the sacri-fice, trusting that he would do so again, he proceeded, with great fear and trembling. When he arrived at the Preface of our Lady, the divine illumination and the sensation of ardent love towards God so increased in his heart, that when he reached the *Qui pri-die* he could scarcely resist any longer. When he came to the Consecration, and had pronounced over the Host half of the words, that is to say, *Hoc est*, it was quite impossible for him to go on, but he repeated over and over the same words, *Hoc est enim;* and the reason why he could not proceed was, that he saw before him Christ himself, with a multitude of angels, and he could not endure his Majesty. He saw that Christ would not enter the Host, nor would it be changed into the Body of Christ, un-less he pronounced the other words of the Consecration, namely, *Corpus meum*. Being greatly perplexed and unable to go on, the guardian, with the other brothers, and the people who were in the church to hear Mass, approached the altar and stood amazed, seeing and considering the actions of Brother John; and many were moved to tears by his devotion. At last, after a long time, it pleased God that Brother John should pronounce in a loud voice the words, *enim Corpus meum;* and immediately the form of bread was changed, and Jesus Christ, the blessed one, appear-ed in the Host, in his bodily shape, and in great glory, showing

132

thereby the humility and charity which made him to take flesh of the Virgin Mary, and which now places him daily in the hands of the priest when he consecrates the Host. By this Bro-ther John was raised to a state of contemplation yet sweeter, in-somuch that, when he had elevated the Host and the consecra-ted chalice, he was ravished out of himself, and all corporal sen-sations being suspended, his body fell back. If he had not been supported by the guardian, who was behind him, he would have fallen to the ground; and all the friars with the men and women who were in the church gathering round him, he was carried to the sacristy as if dead, for his body was quite cold, and his fingers so stiffened that they could neither be opened nor moved; and in this state he remained till the third hour, and it was summer. When he came back to himself, I, who was present, feeling a great desire to know what he had experienced, went to him, and begged him, for the love of God, to tell me everything. As he greatly trusted me, he related all that had happened to him; and amongst other things he told me that, as he was consecrating the Body and Blood of Christ, his soul seemed to melt within him like wax, and his body to be without bones, so that he could not lift his arms or his hands, or make the sign of the cross on the Host or on the chalice. He told me likewise that, before he be-came a priest, it had been revealed to him by God that he should faint away when saying Mass; but having said many Masses, and no such thing having yet happened to him, he thought that the revelation did not come from God. Nevertheless, about fifty days before the Assumption of our Lady, when this thing befell him, it had been again revealed to him by God that it should so hap-pen to him about the time of the Feast of the Assumption: but this vision or revelation from our Lord he did not call to mind at the moment.

OF THE SACRED AND HOLY STIGMATA OF ST FRANCIS, AND CERTAIN CONSIDERATIONS THEREON

IN this part we will treat, with sundry devout considerations, of the glorious, sacred, and holy stigmata of our blessed father St Francis, which he received from Christ on the holy mountain of Alvernia. And inasmuch as the said stigmata were five, according to the five wounds of our Lord Jesus Christ, therefore this treatise shall have five considerations.

℄ The first consideration shall be of the manner in which St Francis came to the holy mountain of Alvernia.

℄ The second consideration shall be of his life and conversation with his companions on the same holy mountain.

℄ The third consideration shall be of the seraphical apparition, and the impression of the most sacred stigmata.

℄ The fourth consideration shall be of the descent of St Francis from Mount Alvernia after he had received the sacred stigmata, and of his return to St Mary of the Angels.

℄ The fifth consideration shall be of certain apparitions and divine revelations vouchsafed, after the death of St Francis, to certain holy friars and other devout persons, concerning these sacred and glorious stigmata.

OF THE FIRST CONSIDERATION OF THE SACRED, HOLY STIGMATA

℄ Concerning the first consideration, be it known that in the year 1224, being in his forty-third year, St Francis went, by the inspiration of God, from the Valley of Spoleto into Romagna, taking with him Brother Leo as his companion; and on their way they passed by the Castle of Montefeltro, where was a great concourse of people, and a solemn banquet held, by reason that one of the Counts of Montefeltro was that day to receive his knighthood. And when St Francis heard of this solemnity, and that many gentlemen of various countries were gathered together there, he said to Brother Leo, "Come, let us go up unto this festival; for, by God's help, we shall gather therefrom rich spiritual fruit."

Now, among other men of high degree who had come together to this feast, there was a certain gentleman of Tuscany who was both rich and mighty. He was called Orlando da Chiusi di Casentino; and for the marvellous things which he had heard concerning the holiness and the miracles of St Francis he bore him great devotion, and had an exceeding desire to see him and to hear him preach.

St Francis, then, being come to this castle, entered into the courtyard where all those gentlemen were assembled; and, in fervour of spirit, he mounted on a low wall, and began to preach, choosing for the theme of his discourse these words in the vulgar tongue:

So great is the joy which I expect,
That all pain is joy to me.

And upon this theme, by the direction of the Holy Ghost, he preached so profoundly and so devoutly, proving it by the divers pains and sufferings of the holy apostles and martyrs, and by the manifold tribulations and temptations of holy virgins and all other saints, that all that multitude of men hung upon his words both with their ears and hearts, hearkening to him as to an angel of God. Among whom the said Orlando, being touched in heart by God through the marvellous preaching of St Francis, was led to speak to him after the sermon touching the state of his soul. So taking him aside, he said to him, "O Father, I would fain take counsel with thee concerning the salvation of my soul." St Francis answered him, "It pleaseth me well: but go now and pay respect to thy friends, who have bidden thee to this feast, and dine with them; and after dinner we will speak together as much as it shall please thee."

135

Orlando, therefore, went to dine, and after dinner returning again to St Francis, he discoursed with him at length concerning the state of his soul, and in the end he said to him, "I have a mountain in Tuscany, a devout and solitary place, called Mount Alvernia, far from all discourse of men, well fitted for one who would do penance for his sins, or who desires to lead a solitary life; if it please thee, I will freely give it to thee and thy companions for the welfare of my soul."

When St Francis heard of this bountiful offer of a thing which he had greatly desired, he was exceeding glad, and thanking and praising God in the first place, and after him Orlando, he thus replied: "Orlando, as soon as thou shalt have returned to thy home, I will send to thee some of our brethren, to whom thou shalt show this place; and if it shall seem to them well fitted for prayer and penance, I will at once accept thy charitable offer."

Having said thus, St Francis departed, returning to St Mary of the Angels; and Orlando likewise returned to his castle, which was called Chiusi, and was about a mile distant from Mount Alvernia. St Francis then sent two of his companions to the said Orlando, who received them with much charity and gladness; and he sent with them to Mount Alvernia full fifty men-at-arms, to be their defence against wild beasts. And these brethren, being thus accompanied, ascended the mount, and searched diligently, until at last they came to a spot well fitted for devout contemplation; and this they chose for the habitation of St Francis, and, with the help of the men-at-arms in their company, they made some little cells with branches of trees; and thus they accepted Mount Alvernia, taking possession of it in the name of God, and forthwith returned again unto St Francis, who rejoiced greatly at what they told him, and, thanking and praising God, spoke with a joyful countenance to these friars, saying, "My children, we draw near to our Lent of St Michael the Archangel. I firmly believe it to be the will of God that we keep this Lent upon Mount Alvernia, which, by divine dispensation, has been prepared for us, that we by penance may merit from our Lord the consolation of consecrating this blessed mount to the honour and glory of God, of his glorious Mother the Virgin Mary, and of the holy angels."

And having said this, St Francis took with him Brother Masseo da Marignano of Assisi; and Brother Angelo Tancredi of Rieti, who, in the world, had been a noble knight, and was still noted for his gentle courtesy; and Brother Leo, who was a man of the greatest simplicity and purity, for the which cause St Francis loved him greatly.

And with these three brethren St Francis betook himself to prayer, then, having recommended himself and his companions to the prayers of the brethren who were left behind, he set forth with these three, in the name of Jesus Christ crucified, to go to Mount Alvernia. And on the way he called Brother Masseo to him, and said: "Thou, Brother Masseo, shalt be our guardian and our superior on this journey, both in the way and while we sojourn together on the mount; and we will observe our wonted custom, which is, that one while we will say Office, one while we will speak of God, one while we will keep silence; and we will take no thought beforehand of eating, or drinking, or sleeping, but when the evening comes we will beg a little bread, and stay and rest ourselves in that place which God shall prepare for us."

Then these three comrades bowed their heads, and making the sign of the cross went on their way; and the first evening they came to a house of the brethren, and there abode. The second evening, because the weather was bad and they were weary, they could not reach any house of friars, neither any town nor castle; wherefore, when night came on, they took shelter in a ruined and deserted church, and there laid them down to rest. Now, while his companions slept, St Francis betook himself to prayer;

and, behold, in the first watch of the night there came to him a multitude of most fierce demons who, with great noise and frenzy, began to attack him on all sides, in order to disturb him in his prayer; but this they could not do, because God was with him. When, therefore, St Francis had endured that conflict a long time, he began to cry aloud: "O accursed spirits, you can do nothing save by the divine permission; wherefore I bid you, on the behalf of the omnipotent God, to do with my body whatso‹ ever he shall permit you to do, and most willingly will I endure it; because I have no greater enemy than my body, and therefore if you will avenge me upon it you shall do me good service." Then did the devils begin to torment him worse than ever. But he cried out, and said: "O my Lord Jesus Christ, I thank thee for this thy great love and charity towards me; for it is a token of great love when the Lord punisheth his servant well in this life, that so he may not be punished in the other. And I am ready gladly to endure every pain and suffering which thou, my God, art pleased to send me for my sins." Then the devils dispersed and left him, being vanquished and confounded by his patience and constancy. And St Francis in great fervour of spirit left the church and went into a wood hard by, and there, beating his breast, with sighs and tears, sought after Jesus, the beloved of his soul. And having found him at last, in the secret of his heart, now he spoke to him reverently as his Lord, now he made answer to him as his judge, now he besought him as his father, now he con‹ versed with him as his friend. On that night and in that wood, his companions, being awake and listening to him, heard him with many tears and cries implore the divine mercy on behalf of sinners. He was heard to weep aloud for the Passion of Christ as if he had beheld it with his bodily eyes. On that same night also he was seen praying with arms outstretched in the form of a cross, and thus was he lifted up and suspended for a long time in the air, surrounded with a dazzling glory. And so, in these holy exercises, he passed all that night without sleeping.

And the next morning, his companions, knowing that he was too weak to walk, went to a poor labouring man of the country, and prayed him, for the love of God, to lend his ass to Brother Francis their father, for he was not able to travel on foot. When the poor man heard them speak of Brother Francis, he asked them: "Are you, then, of the brethren of that friar of Assisi of whom men speak so much good?" Then the friars made answer that it was even he for whom they would borrow the ass. Then that good man made ready the ass with great care and devotion, and brought it to St Francis, and with great reverence caused him to mount thereon. So the brethren set forth again, the poor man following behind his ass.

Now when they had gone forward a little, the peasant said to St Francis: "Tell me, art thou Brother Francis of Assisi?" And St Francis answered, "Yes." "Take heed, then," said the peasant, "that thou be in truth as good as all men account thee; for many have great faith in thee, and therefore I admonish thee to be no other than what the people take thee for."

When St Francis heard these words, he was not angry at being thus admonished by a peasant, neither did he say within himself, as many a proud friar who in our days wears his habit would say: "What right has such a creature as this to admonish me?" But instantly dismounting from the ass, he knelt down upon the ground before that poor man; and kissing his feet, humbly thanked him for that his charitable admonition. Then the peasant, together with the companions of St Francis, with great devotion raised him from the ground, and placed him again upon the ass, and so went on their way.

And when they were come to about the midst of the ascent of the mount, because the way was toilsome, and the heat exceeding great, the peasant was overcome with thirst, insomuch that he began to cry after St Francis saying: "Alas! alas! I am dying of thirst; unless I have something to drink, I shall presently faint."

Then St Francis dismounted from the ass, and betook himself to prayer, remaining upon his knees, with hands uplifted up to heaven, until he knew by revelation that his prayer was heard. Then said he to the peasant: "Run quickly to yonder rock, and there thou shalt find a stream of living water, which Jesus Christ of his mercy has caused to flow out from the stone." Then went he to the place which St Francis had shown to him, and found a beautiful fountain, issuing by virtue of the prayer of St Francis, from that hard rock; and he drank of it plentifully, and was refreshed. And certain it is that this spring of water flowed forth miraculously at the prayer of St Francis, for neither before nor after was a spring to be found at that spot, nor any running water save at a great distance therefrom. This done, St Francis, with his companions and the peasant, returned thanks to God for the miracle thus vouchsafed, and went on their way; and when they drew near to the rock of Alvernia, it pleased St Francis to rest awhile under an oak, which grew by the way, and is still to be seen there, and from thence he began to consider the position of the place and the country. And while he was thus considering, behold there came a great multitude of birds from divers regions, which, by singing and clapping their wings, testified great joy and gladness, and surrounded St Francis in such wise, that some perched upon his shoulders, some on his arms, some on his bosom, and others at his feet, which when his companions and the peasant saw, they marvelled greatly; but St Francis, being joyful at heart, said to them: "I believe, dearest brethren, that our Lord Jesus Christ is pleased that we should dwell on this solitary mount, inasmuch as our little brothers and sisters, the birds, show such joy at our coming." And having said these words, he arose and proceeded to the place which had been fixed upon by his companions; and so did St Francis come to the holy mount of Alvernia.

OF THE SECOND CONSIDERATION OF THE SACRED, HOLY STIGMATA

ℂ The second consideration is of the conversation of St Francis and his companions upon Mount Alvernia. Be it known, then, that when Orlando heard that St Francis with three companions was come to dwell on Mount Alvernia, he was filled with exceeding joy, and on the morrow he came with many others from his castle to visit St Francis, bringing with him bread and wine, and other things necessary for him and his companions; and when he came thither, he found them in prayer, and drawing near he saluted them. Then St Francis arose, and with great joy and charity received Orlando and his company; and so they began to converse together. And after they had spoken together for some time, and St Francis had thanked him for the devout solitude which he had bestowed upon them and for his coming to visit them there, he prayed Orlando to cause a little cell to be made for him at the foot of a beautiful beech-tree, which was about a stone's-throw from the place where they now were; and this Orlando immediately caused to be done. Then, because evening was drawing on, and it was now time for them to depart, St Francis preached to them for a little space; and when he had finished preaching, and had given them his blessing, Orlando called St Francis and his companions aside, and said to them: "My dearest brothers, never was it my intention that you should be exposed on this savage mountain to any corporal necessity, which might hinder you from attending perfectly to things spiritual; wherefore it is my desire — and I say it to you now once for all — that you send freely to my house for everything you want, and if you fail to do so I shall take it very ill at your hands." And so saying, he departed with his company and returned to his castle.

Then St Francis caused his companions to sit down, and taught them the manner of life they were to keep, that they might live religiously in their solitude; and among other things, most earnestly did he enjoin on them the strict observance of holy poverty, saying: "Let not Orlando's charitable offer cause you in any way to offend against our lady and mistress, holy poverty. Hold it for certain that, the more we keep aloof from her, the more will the world keep aloof from us, and the greater want shall we endure: but if we closely embrace holy poverty, the world will come after us, and will minister to us abundantly. God has called us into this holy religion for the salvation of the world, and has made this compact between the world and us—that we should give it good example, and that it should provide for our necessities. Let us, then, persevere in holy poverty; for it is the way of perfection, and the pledge of eternal riches." And after many devout and holy words, he thus concluded: "This is the manner of life which I impose upon you and upon myself; and because I behold my death approaching, I purpose to remain in solitude to recollect myself in God, and to weep over my sins in his sight. Therefore, when it shall so please him, let Brother Leo bring me a little bread and water, and on no account suffer any secular to come near me; but do you answer for me to them." And having thus said, he gave them his blessing, and went his way to his cell under the beech-tree; and his companions remained behind, fully purposed to obey his commands.

Now a few days afterwards, as St Francis was considering the formation of the mountain, and marvelling at the great fissures and openings in the solid rock, it was revealed to him by God in prayer that these strange caverns had been made miraculously at the hour of the Passion of Christ, when, according to the Evangelist's words, the rocks were rent; and this was by the will of God, who manifested himself thus wonderfully upon Mount Alvernia, because there the Passion of our Lord Jesus Christ was to be renewed in the soul of his servant by love and compassion, and in his body by the impression of the sacred, holy stigmata.

When St Francis had received this revelation, he forthwith shut himself up in his cell, and, in great recollection of soul, prepared himself for the mystery which was to be revealed to him; and from that time forth he began to taste more frequently the sweetness of divine contemplation, by which he was sometimes so absorbed in God, that he was seen by his companions to be raised corporally above the ground, and rapt in prayer; and in these raptures were revealed to St Francis not only things present and future, but even the secret thoughts and desires of the brethren, as was experienced by Brother Leo, his companion in those days.

For this same Brother Leo, being beset by a most grievous spiritual temptation, felt a great longing to have some devout thing written by the hand of St Francis, feeling assured that, if he had it, the temptation would leave him, either wholly or in part. But, either out of shame or reverence, he dared not speak of his desire to St Francis, to whom nevertheless it was revealed by the Holy Ghost; whereupon he called the brother to him, and bade him bring him wherewithal to write, and with his own hand he wrote a verse in honour of Christ, drawing at the foot thereof the sign of a cross *Tau:* and according to Brother Leo's desire, he gave it to him, saying, "Take this writing, dearest brother, and keep it most diligently till the day of thy death. May God bless thee, and guard thee from all temptation! But if temptation come unto thee, be not afraid, for I hold thee to be more truly the servant of God, and more worthy of love the harder thou art oppressed by temptation. And I tell thee in all since-

143

rity, that no man should account himself to be a perfect friend of God until he has passed through manifold temptations and tribulations."

Now when Brother Leo had received this writing with great faith and devotion, at once all the temptation departed from him; and returning to his companions, he told them with great joy of the grace which he had received from God through that writing of St Francis; and the brethren laid it up and kept it diligently, and by it they were enabled to work many miracles.

And from that day forward Brother Leo set himself with a good and pure intention to scrutinise and attentively consider the life of St Francis; and in reward of his purity he was permitted many times to behold him rapt in God and suspended above the earth, sometimes at the height of three feet above the ground, sometimes four, sometimes raised as high as the top of the beech-trees, and sometimes exalted so high in the air, and surrounded with so dazzling a glory, that he could scarce endure to look upon him.

And what did this simple friar when St Francis, in his raptures, was thus raised above his reach? He would go softly behind him, and, with tears, embrace and kiss his feet, saying: "My God, have mercy upon me, a sinner, and by the merits of this holy man let me find grace in thy sight." And once when he was standing beneath the feet of St Francis, who was raised so high that he could not touch him, he saw a scroll descend from heaven and rest upon his head, whereon were these words, written in letters of gold: *Here abideth the grace of God!* And when he had read the scroll, he saw it return again to heaven.

By the gift of the grace of God which dwelt in him, St Francis was not only absorbed in God by ecstatic contemplation, but was comforted often by angelical visitations. One day when he was meditating upon his death, and upon what might hereafter befall his Order, he said: "O Lord God, when I am dead, what will

144

become of this thy poor family, which in thy goodness thou hast committed to me, a sinner? Who will comfort, who will correct, who will pray to thee for it?"

Then did an angel of God appear to him, and comfort him with these words: "I declare to thee, on behalf of God, that thine Order shall never fail until the day of judgement; and no sinner, be he ever so great, who shall bear a hearty love to this thine Order, but shall find mercy with God; and no man shall live long who shall maliciously persecute it. Nor shall any evil-doer, who shall refuse to amend his life, long persevere in thine Order. And be not thou troubled if thou perceive some brethren who are not good, and observe not the rule as they ought to do, and fear not lest on that account this religion will fail; for there shall always be many and many a one who will observe with great per⸗ fection the life of Christ's Gospel, and the purity of the rule; and all these, after their bodily life is ended, shall enter into life eternal, without passing through Purgatory. Others will observe it, but not perfectly; and these, before they reach Paradise, shall remain for a while in Purgatory; but the time of their purifica⸗ tion God will commit unto thee. 'But of those who in no way observe the rule, take thou no care,' saith the Lord; for neither doth he care for them." And when the angel had said these words, he departed, leaving St Francis greatly strengthened and consoled.

And now the Feast of our Lady's Assumption drew near, and St Francis sought for a more secret and solitary place in which he might spend alone the Lent of St Michael the Archangel, which begins on the Feast of the Assumption. Wherefore he call⸗ ed Brother Leo, and said thus to him: "Go and stand at the door of the brethren's oratory, and when I shall call thee, turn to me." And Brother Leo went and stood at the door, and St Francis went away a space, and called aloud, and Brother Leo heard and

145

turned towards him. Then St Francis said: "My son, let us seek for some more secret place, where thou wilt not hear me when I call thus to thee." And when they had searched the mount, they found a place on the northern side most secret and well fitted for the purpose, but they could not reach it because of a frightful chasm in the rock; across this chasm they cast a tree to serve for a bridge, and so passed over. Then St Francis sent for the other friars, and told them that he purposed to spend the Lent of St Michael in that solitary place, and prayed them, therefore, to make for him a little cell, so that, though he should cry aloud, he might not be heard by them. And when the cell was made, he said to them: "Return now to your place, and leave me here alone; for, by the help of God, I intend to pass this Lent here, without any disturbance or perturbation of mind; therefore let none of you come unto me, nor suffer any secular person to come near the cell. But thou only, Brother Leo, once a day shalt come to me with a little bread and water, and once at night at the hour of Matins, and thou shalt come in silence; and when thou art upon the bridge thou shalt say, *Domine labia mea aperies;* and if I answer thee, thou shalt come to the cell, and we will say Matins together; and if I do not answer thee, thou shalt depart forthwith." And this St Francis said because he was sometimes so absorbed in God that he heard nothing, nor felt anything by his bodily senses. And having thus spoken, he gave them his blessing, and they returned to their place.

Thus, on the Feast of the Assumption, St Francis began the holy Lent, with great abstinence and austerity, macerating his body and invigorating his soul by fervent prayers, vigils, and disciplines; and thus increasing more and more, and going from virtue to virtue, he prepared his soul to receive divine mysteries and illuminations, and his body to sustain the cruel conflicts with the demons, who often attacked him sensibly. And among other

146

times it befell one day in this Lent that St Francis, going forth from his cell in great fervour of spirit, went to pray in a cave hollowed out of a rock at the top of a steep and frightful preci﹣ pice, when the devil suddenly appeared before him in a terrible form, and sought to hurl him to the bottom. St Francis, being unable to fly or to endure the horrible aspect of the devil, turned his face, hands, and whole body towards the rock, and recom﹣ mended himself to God, groping with his hands, yet finding no﹣ thing to which he might cling. But, as it pleased God, who never suffers his servants to be tempted beyond what they are able to bear, the rock suddenly opened and received his body within it; and, as if he had placed his hands and face in liquid wax, the form of the hands and face of St Francis remained impressed upon the stone; and thus, by the help of God, he escaped out of the hands of the devil. But the injury which the devil could not then do to St Francis by casting him down the precipice, he in﹣ flicted long after his death upon one of his beloved and devoted brethren, who was standing in the same spot preparing some planks of wood for the safe passage of those who should come to the place out of devotion to St Francis and the miracle which had been wrought there. For one day, when he had a heavy piece of wood on his shoulder, the devil cast him down thus laden to the bottom of the rock. But God, who had preserved St Francis from falling, by his merits delivered the devout friar from all injury in his fall; for as he fell, with a loud voice and great devotion he recommended himself to St Francis, who immediately appeared to him, and taking him in his arms, set him down at the bottom of the rock without suffering any injury whatsoever. The breth﹣ ren, who had heard his cry when he fell, believing that he was assuredly dead, and that he had been dashed to pieces by his fall from so great a height upon those pointed rocks, taking a bier went round the mountain by another way, with great weeping and lamentation, to collect his mangled remains and give them burial. Having, then, descended the mountain, behold, the brother who had fallen met them with the wood on his shoulder with which he fell, singing the *Te Deum* with a loud voice. And the brethren marvelling greatly thereat, he related to them in order the manner of his fall, and how St Francis had delivered him from all danger. Then all the brethren came with him to the place, devoutly chanting the *Te Deum,* and praising and thanking God and St Francis for the miracle that had been wrought in their brother.

St Francis, then, passing this Lent, as has been said, in the midst of these conflicts with the devil, received many consolations from God, not only by angelic visitations, but through the ministry of the wild mountain-birds. For, through all that Lent, a falcon, whose nest was hard by his cell, awakened him every night a little before the hour of Matins by her cry and the flapping of her wings, and would not leave him till he had risen to say Matins; and if at any time St Francis was more sick than usual, or weak, or weary, this falcon, like a discreet and charitable Christian, would call him somewhat later than was her wont. Now St Francis took great delight in this clock of his, because the great carefulness of the falcon drove away all sloth and summoned him to prayer; and moreover during the daytime she would often abide familiarly with him.

To conclude this second consideration, St Francis, being much weakened in body both by his great abstinence and by his conflicts with the devil, and desiring to strengthen his body by the spiritual food of the soul, began to meditate upon the unbounded joy and glory of the blessed in heaven; and he besought of God to grant him some little foretaste of their bliss. Now while this thought was in his mind, suddenly an angel appeared to him in surpassing glory, having a viol in his left hand and a bow in his

148

right. And as St Francis stood in amazement at the sight, the angel drew the bow once across the strings of the viol, when the soul of St Francis was instantly so ravished by the sweetness of the melody, that all his bodily senses were suspended, and he believed, as he afterwards told his companions, that, if the strain had been continued, the intolerable sweetness would have drawn his soul from his body. And so much for the second consideration.

OF THE THIRD CONSIDERATION OF THE SACRED, HOLY STIGMATA

℃ We are come now to the third consideration, namely, of the seraphical apparition, and the impression of the sacred, holy stigmata.

As the Feast of the Holy Cross then drew nigh, in the month of September, Brother Leo went one night at his accustomed hour to say Matins with St Francis. When he came to the bridge, he said, as he was wont to do, *Domine labia mea aperies;* but St Francis made no answer. Yet Brother Leo turned not back as he had been commanded to do, but with a good and holy intention he passed the bridge and went straight into the cell; but there he found not St Francis. Thinking, therefore, that he was gone to pray in some solitary place, he went softly through the wood, seeking him in the moonlight. At last he heard his voice, and drawing near, beheld him kneeling in prayer with his face and hands lifted up towards heaven, and crying, in fervour of spirit: "Who art thou, my dearest Lord? and who am I, a most vile worm and thy most unprofitable servant?" and these words he repeated over and over again, adding nothing more. At this Brother Leo, greatly marvelling, lifted up his eyes to heaven, and beheld a torch of most intense and glorious fire, which seemed to descend and alight upon the head of St Francis; and from the flame there seemed to issue forth a voice which spake with him,

149

but Brother Leo knew not the words which were spoken. Hear‐
ing this, and accounting himself unworthy to stand in that holy
place, and fearing also to offend St Francis and to disturb him
by his presence, he went away silently, and stood afar off to be‐
hold what would follow; and looking earnestly upon St Francis,
he saw him thrice spread forth his hands to the flame, and after
a long time he beheld it mount again to heaven. Then he turned
joyfully to go back to his cell, being greatly consoled by the vis‐
ion. But, as he turned, St Francis heard the rustling of the leaves
under his feet, and commanded him not to stir, but to await his
coming. And Brother Leo in obedience stood still, and waited in
so great fear that, as he afterwards told his companions, he would
have wished that the earth might swallow him up rather than
wait for St Francis, whose anger he feared exceedingly; for he
took great heed always not to offend him, lest he should be de‐
prived of his company.

When St Francis, then, came up to him, he said: "Who art
thou?" and Brother Leo, in fear and trembling, answered: "Fa‐
ther, I am Brother Leo." And St Francis said to him: "Where‐
fore hast thou come hither, dear brother? did I not forbid thee
to observe me? Tell me now, by holy obedience, whether thou
hast seen or heard anything?" And Brother Leo replied: "Fa‐
ther, I heard thee speak and say many times, 'Who art thou, my
dearest Lord? and who am I, a most vile worm and thy most un‐
profitable servant?'" And then, kneeling before St Francis, Bro‐
ther Leo accused himself of disobedience to his command, and
besought his pardon with many tears. After which, he devoutly
prayed him to expound to him the meaning of the words which
he had heard, and to tell him also those which he had not heard.
Then St Francis, seeing that, for his simplicity and purity, God
had revealed so much to Brother Leo, condescended to reveal
and expound also that which he desired further to know; and

thus he spake to him: "Know, dearest brother, that when I said those words which thou didst hear, two great lights were before my soul, the one the knowledge of myself, the other the knowledge of the Creator. When I said: 'Who art thou, my dearest Lord?' I was in a light of contemplation, in which I beheld the abyss of the infinite goodness and wisdom and power of God; and when I said: 'Who am I?' I was in a light of contemplation, wherein I saw the lamentable abyss of my own vileness and misery: wherefore I said: 'Who art thou, the Lord of infinite wisdom and goodness, who dost vouchsafe to visit me, a vile worm and abominable?' And in that flame which thou didst behold was God, who under that appearance spake to me, as of old he spake to Moses. And among other things which he said to me, he asked of me three gifts; and I made answer: 'O Lord, I am all thine; thou knowest full well that I have nothing else but my cord and my tunic, and even these are thine; what, then, can I offer or give to thy Majesty?' Then he said to me: 'Search in thy bosom, and offer me what thou shalt find there.' And searching, I found there a golden ball, and I offered it to God; and the like I did three times, even as God commanded me; and then I knelt down thrice, and blessed and gave thanks to God, who had thus given me something to offer him. And immediately it was given me to understand that these three offerings signified holy obedience, most entire poverty, and most pure chastity, which God by his grace has enabled me so perfectly to observe that I have nothing to reproach myself thereupon. And whereas thou didst see me put my hand into my bosom and offer to God those three virtues, signified by these three golden balls which God had placed in my bosom, so God has infused such virtue into my soul, that for all the gifts and graces which of his sovereign bounty he has bestowed upon me, I should always with heart and voice praise and magnify him. These are the words which thou didst hear when thou didst see me thrice lift up my hands. But take heed, brother little lamb, that thou observe me no more, but return to thy cell with the blessing of God; and take heed to my words, for yet a few days, and God will work such strange and marvellous things upon this mountain as shall astonish the whole world; for he will do a new thing which he hath never done before to any creature upon this earth."

And when he had said these words, he bade him bring the book of the Gospels, because God had put it into his mind that, by thrice opening that book, he should learn what God would be pleased to do with him. And when the book was brought to him, St Francis went to prayer; and when he had prayed, he caused Brother Leo to open the book three times in the name of the most holy Trinity; and, by the divine disposal, it opened each time at the Passion of Christ. And by this it was given him to understand that, even as he had followed Christ in the actions of his life, so should he follow and be confirmed to him in the sufferings and afflictions of his Passion, before he should pass out of this life. And from that day forward St Francis began to taste more abundantly the sweetness of divine contemplation, and of divine visitations, among which he had one, preparatory to the impression of the sacred, holy stigmata, after the following manner. The day before the Feast of the most Holy Cross, as St Francis was praying secretly in his cell, an angel of God appeared to him, and spake to him thus from God: "I am come to admonish and encourage thee, that thou prepare thyself to receive in all patience and humility that which God will give and do to thee."

St Francis replied: "I am ready to bear patiently whatsoever my Lord shall be pleased to do to me"; and so the angel departed. On the following day — being the Feast of the Holy Cross — St Francis was praying before daybreak at the entrance of his cell, and turning his face towards the east, he prayed in these words: "O Lord Jesu Christ, two graces do I ask of thee before I die; the first, that in my lifetime I may feel, as far as possible, both in my soul and body, that pain which thou, sweet Lord, didst endure in the hour of thy most bitter Passion; the second, that I may feel in my heart as much as possible of that excess of love by which thou, O Son of God, wast inflamed to suffer so cruel a Passion for us sinners." And continuing a long time in that prayer, he understood that God had heard him, and that, so far as is possible for a mere creature, he should be permitted to feel these things.

Having then received this promise, St Francis began to contemplate most devoutly the Passion of Jesus Christ and his infinite charity; and so greatly did the fervour of devotion increase within him, that he was all transformed into Jesus by love and compassion.

And being thus inflamed in that contemplation, on that same morning he beheld a seraph descending from heaven with six fiery and resplendent wings; and this seraph with rapid flight drew nigh unto St Francis, so that he could plainly discern him, and perceive that he bore the image of one crucified; and the wings were so disposed, that two were spread over the head, two were outstretched in flight, and the other two covered the whole body. And when St Francis beheld it, he was much afraid, and filled at once with joy and grief and wonder. He felt great joy at the gracious presence of Christ, who appeared to him thus familiarly, and looked upon him thus lovingly, but, on the other hand, beholding him thus crucified, he felt exceeding grief and compassion. He marvelled much at so stupendous and unwonted a vision, knowing well that the infirmity of the Passion accorded ill with the immortality of the seraphic spirit. And in that perplexity of mind it was revealed to him by him who thus appeared, that by divine providence this vision had been thus shown

153

to him that he might understand that, not by martyrdom of the body, but by a consuming fire of the soul, he was to be transfor‐ med into the express image of Christ crucified in that wonderful apparition. Then did all the Mount Alvernia appear wrapped in intense fire, which illumined all the mountains and valleys around, as it were the sun shining in his strength upon the earth, for which cause the shepherds who were watching their flocks in that country were filled with fear, as they themselves afterwards told the brethren, affirming that this light had been visible on Mount Alvernia for upwards of an hour. And because of the brightness of that light, which shone through the windows of the inn where they were tarrying, some muleteers who were tra‐ velling in Romagna arose in haste, supposing that the sun had risen, and saddled and loaded their beasts; but as they jour‐ neyed on, they saw that light disappear, and the visible sun arise.

In this seraphical apparition, Christ, who appeared under that form to St Francis, spoke to him certain high and secret things, which in his lifetime he would never reveal to any person, but after his death he made them known to one of the brethren, and the words were these: "Knowest thou," said Christ, "what I have done to thee? I have given thee the stigmata which are the insig‐ nia of my Passion, that thou mayst be my standard-bearer; and as on the day of my death I descended into limbo, and by virtue of these my stigmata delivered thence all the souls whom I found there, so do I grant to thee that every year on the anniversary of thy death thou mayst go to Purgatory, and take with thee to the glory of Paradise all the souls of thy three Orders, the Friars Mi‐ nor, the Sisters, and the Penitents, and likewise all others whom thou shalt find there, who have been especially devout to thee; that so thou mayst be conformed to me in death, as thou hast been like to me in life." Then, after long and secret conference together, that marvellous vision disappeared, leaving in the heart of St Francis an excessive fire and ardour of divine love, and on his flesh a wonderful trace and image of the Passion of Christ. For upon his hands and feet began immediately to appear the figures of the nails, as he had seen them on the Body of Christ crucified, who had appeared to him in the likeness of a seraph. And thus the hands and feet appeared pierced through the midst by the nails, the heads whereof were seen outside the flesh in the palms of the hands and the soles of the feet, and the points of the nails stood out at the back of the hands and the feet in such wise that they appeared to be twisted and bent back upon them-selves, and the portion thereof that was bent back or twisted stood out free from the flesh, so that one could put a finger through the same as through a ring; and the heads of the nails were round and black. In like manner, on the right side appeared the image of an unhealed wound, as if made by a lance, and still red and bleeding, from which drops of blood often flowed from the holy breast of St Francis, staining his tunic and his drawers.

And because of this his companions, before they knew the truth from himself, perceiving that he would not uncover his hands and his feet, and that he could not set the soles of his feet upon the ground, and finding traces of blood upon his tunic when they washed it, understood of a certainty that he bore in his hands and feet and side the image and similitude of our Lord Jesus Christ crucified. And although he laboured hard to conceal these sacred stigmata holy and glorious, thus clearly impressed upon his flesh, yet finding that he could with difficulty hide them from his familiar companions, and fearing at the same time to reveal the secrets of God, he was in great doubt and trouble of mind whether or not he should make known the seraphical vision and the impression of the sacred, holy stigmata. At last, being prick-ed in conscience, he called together certain of the brethren, in whom he placed the greatest confidence, and proposing to them his doubt in general terms, asked their counsel on the matter. Now among these friars there was one of great sanctity, called Brother Illuminato; and he, being truly illuminated by God, understood that St Francis must have seen something miraculous, and said thus to him: "Know, Brother Francis, that not for thyself alone, but for others, doth God reveal to thee his secrets, and therefore thou hast cause for fear lest thou be worthy of censure if thou conceal that which, for the good of others, has been made known to thee."

Then St Francis, being moved by these words, with great fear and reverence told them the manner of the aforesaid vision, adding that Christ, who had thus appeared to him, had said to him certain things which he might never make known so long as he should live.

Now although these sacred wounds, which had been impressed upon him by Christ, gave great joy to his heart, yet they caused unspeakable pain to his body; so that, being constrained by necessity, he made choice of Brother Leo, for his great purity and simplicity, to whom he revealed the whole matter, suffering him to touch and dress his wounds on all days except during the time from Thursday evening till Saturday morning, for then he would not by any human remedy mitigate the pain of Christ's Passion, which he bore in his body, because at that time our Saviour Jesus Christ was taken and crucified, died and was buried for us. And it came to pass sometimes that when Brother Leo was removing the bandage from the wound in the side, St Francis, because of the pain caused thereby, would lay his hand on Brother Leo's breast, and at the touch of that holy hand Brother Leo felt such sweetness of devotion as well-nigh made him to fall fainting to the ground.

To conclude, so far as concerns this third consideration, St Francis, having completed the Lent of St Michael the Archangel,

156

prepared himself by divine revelation to return with Brother Leo to St Mary of the Angels; and calling to him Brother Masseo and Brother Angelo, he commended that holy mount unto their care, and blessing them in the name of Jesus crucified, he suffered them, at their earnest prayer, to see, touch, and kiss his sacred hands adorned with those holy, glorious, and sacred stigmata; and so leaving them in great joy and consolation, he parted from them and came down from the holy mountain.

OF THE FOURTH CONSIDERATION OF THE SACRED, HOLY STIGMATA

℃ As to the fourth consideration, be it known, that after the true love of Christ had perfectly transformed St Francis into God, and into the true image of Christ crucified, that angelical man, having fulfilled the Lent of forty days in honour of St Michael the Archangel on the holy mountain of Alvernia, came down from the mount with Brother Leo and a devout peasant, on whose ass he rode, because, by reason of the nails in his feet, he could hardly go on foot. And the fame of his sanctity being already spread abroad through the country by the shepherds who had seen Mount Alvernia all on fire, and who took it to be a token of some great miracle wrought by God in his person, no sooner had he descended from the mountain than all the people of the country through which he passed, men and women, great and small, pressed round him, eagerly desiring to touch and kiss his hands; and though he could not altogether repress their devotion, yet, in order to conceal the sacred, holy stigmata, he wrapped bandages round his hands, and covered them with his sleeves, giving them only the fingers to kiss. But though he thus strove to conceal the secret of the sacred stigmata, in order to shun all occasion of worldly glory, it pleased God for his own glory to work many miracles by virtue of the same holy stigmata, and especially in this journey from Mount Alvernia to St Mary of the Angels. And the same hath he since renewed in many and divers parts of the world, both during the lifetime of St Francis and after his glorious death, that their mysterious and marvellous virtue, and the exceeding charity and mercy of Christ towards him, might be made manifest to the world by clear and evident miracles, such as these which follow.

As St Francis drew near to a city on the confines of Arezzo, a woman came to him weeping bitterly, and carrying in her arms her son, a boy of eight years old, so greatly swollen with dropsy that he could not stand upright upon his feet; and laying him down before St Francis she besought him to pray to God for him. St Francis first betook himself to prayer, and then laying his holy hands upon the child, the swelling subsided at once, and he restored him completely cured to his mother, who received him with great joy, and took him home, thanking God and St Francis, and taking delight in showing her restored child to all her neighbours who came to her house to witness the cure.

On the same day St Francis passed on through Borgo San Sepolcro; and as soon as he approached the castle, a multitude of people poured forth from the castle and the neighbouring villages to meet him, many of them bearing olive-branches in their hands, and crying aloud: "Behold the saint; behold the saint!" And in their devotion and eager desire to touch him, the people pressed mightily upon him; but he, being rapt in contemplation, and his mind wholly fixed on God, although thus pressed upon and dragged hither and thither by the multitude, was insensible of all that passed around, and knew nothing of all that was said or done, or even that he had passed by that castle or through that country. When, therefore, the multitude had returned to their own houses, and he had reached a house of lepers about a mile on the other side of the town, coming to himself as

if just returned from the other world, the heavenly contempla‑
tive asked his companion: "When shall we come to the town?"
For his soul, fixed and rapt in the contemplation of heaven, had
been unconscious of all things earthly, and perceived neither
lapse of time, nor change of place, nor persons passing by. And
the like befell him many different times, as his companions often
experienced.

That evening St Francis arrived at the house of the brethren
of Monte Casale, where was a friar so grievously ill, and so cruelly
afflicted by his sickness, that it seemed to be rather an infliction
and torment of the devil than any natural infirmity; for some‑
times he would cast himself down on the ground, trembling fear‑
fully, and foaming at the mouth. At other times every nerve in
his body seemed to be distended, or contracted, or distorted, and
he would spring convulsively from the ground, and immediately
fall prostrate again. St Francis, then, being seated at table, and
hearing from the brethren the miserable condition of this friar,
which seemed past remedy, took compassion on him, and taking
a morsel of the bread which he was eating, he made the sign of
the cross upon it with those holy hands that bore the stigmata of
Christ, and sent it to the sick brother, who had no sooner eaten
it than he was perfectly cured, and never more felt any return of
his infirmity.

On the following morning St Francis sent two of the brethren
from that place to abide at Alvernia, and with them the peasant
who had lent him the ass, desiring him to return to his house.
And having remained a few days in that place, St Francis depart‑
ed and went to the city of Castello. And behold many of the cit‑
izens came to meet him, bringing with them a woman who for
a long time past had been possessed by a devil; and they humbly
besought him to deliver her, because she troubled all the coun‑
try round by howling fearfully, or shrieking piteously, or at times

by barking like a dog. Then St Francis, having first prayed and made the sign of the most holy cross over her, commanded the devil to depart out of her; and forthwith he departed, leaving her whole both in mind and body. And as the news of the miracle spread among the people, another woman full of faith brought a child sick of a grievous ulcer, and devoutly besought him to bless it with his hand. Then St Francis, accepting her devotion, took the child, and removing the bandage, made the sign of the most holy cross thrice over the wound; and then, having bound it up again with his own hands, he delivered the child to his mother, who, as it was evening, laid him down immediately on his bed to sleep. In the morning, when she went to take him out of his bed, she found the wound unbandaged and perfectly healed, no trace remaining of it, save that in the place where it had been there was impressed the likeness of a red rose in testimony of the miracle, which remained until his death, and many a time excited him to devotion to St Francis, by whom he had been healed.

In that city, at the desire of the devout inhabitants, St Francis abode a month, during which time he wrought many miracles, and then departed thence to go to St Mary of the Angels with Brother Leo and a good man who had lent him an ass on which he rode. It so happened that, as they travelled night and day, finding no place where they could lodge for the night, they took shelter from the cold and the snow, which was falling fast, in the cavity of a hollow rock. And night coming upon them as they remained under this miserable shelter, which scarcely protected them from the inclemency of the weather, the poor man to whom the ass belonged, being unable to sleep for the cold, and having no means of kindling a fire, began to complain bitterly, and to weep and almost to murmur at St Francis for having brought him into such a place. Then St Francis, hearing him, had compassion on him, and in fervour of spirit stretched out his hand and touched him, when — wonderful to say — no sooner did the poor man feel the touch of that hand which had been pierced and enkindled by the seraph's fire than all sensation of cold departed from him, and such glowing heat inflamed him within and without, as if he had been placed near the mouth of a fiery furnace, that, being instantly relieved and comforted both in body and soul, he fell asleep, and slept — as he said himself — all night through till morning, more sweetly amid the rocks and snow than he had ever slept in his own bed.

Now when they had journeyed for another day, they came to St Mary of the Angels, and as they drew nigh to it, Brother Leo lifted up his eyes and beheld a most beautiful cross, and upon it the image of the Crucified, going before St Francis, who followed after it; so that when he stood still, the cross stood still; and when he went forward, the cross went ever before him; and such was the splendour of that cross, that it not only illumined the face of St Francis, but made all the way bright around him, and so continued shining till he entered the convent of St Mary of the Angels. St Francis, then, coming with Brother Leo, was received by the brethren with great charity and joy, and from that day forward St Francis dwelt for the most of his time at St Mary of the Angels until the day of his death. And as the fame of his sanctity and of his miracles went forth more and more through the Order and through the whole world, so much the more out of the depth of his humility did he conceal the gifts and graces of God as far as he could, calling himself the greatest of sinners.

On occasion of this Brother Leo marvelling, on a certain day, considered foolishly within himself: "See now, how he calleth himself the greatest of sinners, and that before all men, when he has become great in the Order and is so much honoured of God; while yet in secret he never confesses himself to be guilty of carnal sin: is it then that he is still a virgin?" And thenceforth there took him a great longing to know the truth in this matter, yet did he not dare to ask St Francis. Wherefore he turned himself to God, praying earnestly that he would reveal to him the truth he so much wished to know; and by his many prayers and through the merit of St Francis he was heard, and it was answered to him that St Francis was, in very truth, a virgin in his body, by means of the vision that followeth. For in his vision he beheld St Francis standing in a high place and an honourable, whereto none other could attain to stand beside him; and it was said unto him in the spirit that this place, so lofty and so excellent, signified the most high virginal chastity of St Francis, which was wholly reasonable in that flesh of his that was to be adorned with the sacred, holy stigmata of Christ.

St Francis finding that, by reason of the stigmata of Christ, his bodily strength was gradually wasting away, and that he could no longer rule over the Order, hastened to assemble a general chapter; and the brethren being all met together, he humbly laid before them his incapacity, by reason of his infirmities, any longer to fill the office of general, although he might not resign the generalate, to which he had been appointed by the Pope, nor name a successor without his express sanction; but he nominated Brother Peter Cattani his vicar, affectionately and with all his heart recommending the Order to him and to the ministers provincial. And having done this, St Francis, being strengthened in spirit, raised his eyes and hands to heaven, saying thus: "To thee, O Lord my God, — to thee do I commend thy family, which till now thou hast committed to me, and of which, by reason of my infirmities, as thou knowest, O my sweetest Lord, I can now no longer take care. I commend it also to the ministers provincial, who shall render an account to thee at the day of judgement if any brother perish by their negligence, or evil exam-

ple, or over-sharp correction." And by these words, as it pleased God, all the brethren understood that he spoke of the sacred
stigmata — which he called his infirmities — and none of them
could refrain from weeping for devotion. And thenceforth he
left all the care and government of the Order in the hands of his
vicar and of the ministers provincial; and he said: "Now that for
my infirmities I have given over the care of the Order, I have
nothing to do henceforth but to pray to God for this our Religion, and to give a good example to the brethren. And I know
moreover that, even were I freed from my infirmities, the greatest good which I could do to the Order would be to pray to God
for it continually, that he would be pleased to defend and rule
and preserve it."

Now, as we have said before, St Francis did all in his power to
conceal the sacred, holy stigmata, for after he received them he
kept always his hands and feet covered; yet could he not hinder
that many times several of the brethren contrived to see and
touch them, and especially the wound of the side, which with the
greatest diligence he sought to conceal. Thus a brother who waited on him, having one day persuaded him to take off his tunic
in his presence that he might shake the dust out of it, clearly
saw the wound in the side; and thrusting his hand suddenly into
the bosom of St Francis, he touched it with three fingers, ascer-
taining its length and breadth: and in like manner it was discovered at another time by his vicar. But it was attested still more
clearly by Brother Ruffino, a man of most sublime contemplation, of whom St Francis was wont to say that in all the world he
knew not a holier man; so that for his great sanctity he loved him
most heartily and granted to him all that he desired. In three several ways did this Brother Ruffino certify both himself and others
of the reality of the sacred, holy stigmata, and especially of that
in the side. The first was that, having obtained permission to

163

wash his undergarment, which St Francis wore very loose, that by wrapping it well around him he might conceal the wound in his pierced side, the said Brother Ruffino examined it diligently and continually found traces of blood on the right side of the garment, by which he knew for certain that the blood came from the wound aforesaid; whereupon St Francis reproved him for spreading out the garment in order to discover the mark of the wound. The second way was that the said Brother Ruffino once purposely put his finger into the wound in the side; when St Francis, for the pain he felt, cried aloud: "God forgive thee, Brother Ruffino, for what thou hast done." The third way was that this brother once besought St Francis of his charity to change habits with him, to which the charitable father having consented, although unwillingly, in the exchange of the garments he clearly saw the wound in the right side. Brother Leo likewise, and many others of the brethren, saw the sacred, holy stigmata during the lifetime of St Francis; and although for their sanctity these brethren were worthy of all faith upon their simple word, nevertheless, to remove all doubt did they swear upon the sacred Scriptures that they had seen them plainly. Certain of the Cardinals, also, who enjoyed great familiarity with St Francis, composed devout and beautiful hymns, antiphons, and proses in honour of the said sacred, holy stigmata. The Sovereign Pontiff also, Pope Alexander, when preaching to the people in the presence of the Cardinals, among whom was the holy Brother Bonaventure, himself a Cardinal, affirmed that with his own eyes he had seen the sacred, holy stigmata of St Francis during his lifetime. And the Lady Jacopa di Settesoli, who was the greatest lady in Rome of her time, and most devout to St Francis, before and after his death saw and kissed them with great reverence; for she came from Rome to Assisi by divine revelation, at the death of St Francis; and thus it came to pass. A few days before his death, St Francis lay sick

164

in the bishop's palace at Assisi with certain of his companions, and notwithstanding his infirmity he oftentimes sang canticles in honour of Jesus Christ. One of his companions, therefore, said to him one day: "Father, thou knowest that the citizens of this place have great faith in thee, and account thee to be a holy man, perhaps therefore they may think that, if thou be what they take thee for, being so grievously sick, thou shouldst think upon death in this thine infirmity, and weep rather than sing. And know that this singing of thine, and of ours whom thou wilt have to sing with thee, is heard by many in the palace and without, forasmuch as this palace is guarded on thine account by many men-at-arms, who may perhaps take scandal thereat. Therefore I think," said this friar, "that thou wilt do well to depart hence, and to return to St Mary of the Angels; for we are not well here among seculars." Then St Francis answered him: "Thou knowest, dearest brother, that two years ago, when we were at Foligno, God revealed the end of my life to thee, and he revealed it to me also — that in this sickness, and in a few days, this my life shall come to an end. And in this revelation God assured me of the remission of all my sins, and of the bliss of Paradise. Until I received that revelation, I wept over my sins and at the thought of death; but since I have received it, I have been so full of joy that I can weep no longer; and therefore I sing, and will sing to God, who hath bestowed on me the gift of his grace, and hath certainly promised me the gift of heavenly glory. For our departure hence, it pleaseth me well, and I willingly consent thereto; but find you a way to carry me, for because of my infirmity I cannot walk." Then the brethren took him up and bore him on their shoulders, and many of the citizens went with them. And coming to a hostel which was on the way, St Francis said to those who bore him: "Set me down upon the ground, and turn my face towards the city"; and when he was thus turned towards Assisi, he blessed the city with many blessings, saying: "Blessed be thou of God, O holy city, forasmuch as by means of thee many souls shall be saved, and in thee many servants of God shall dwell, and of thy children many shall be elected to eternal life." And when he had said these words, he caused himself to be borne onwards to St Mary of the Angels; and they carried him to the infirmary, and there laid him down to rest. Then St Francis called to him one of his companions, and said to him: "Dearest brother, God has revealed to me that by this sickness, a few days hence, I am to pass from this life; and thou knowest that the devout Lady Jacopa di Settesoli, who is so dear to our Order, would be deeply grieved, should she hear of my death, not to have been present at it; therefore signify to her that, if she desire to see me again in life, she must come hither with all speed." And the brother made answer: "Too true, Father; for indeed, because of the great devotion she bears thee, most unmeet were it that she should not be present at thy death." "Go, then," said St Francis; "bring pen and paper, and write as I shall bid thee." And when he had brought them, St Francis dictated the letter in the following form: "To the Lady Jacopa, the handmaid of the Lord, Brother Francis, the poor little one of Christ, wisheth health and the fellowship of the Holy Ghost in our Lord Jesus Christ. Be it known to thee, most beloved, that Christ our Lord hath by his grace revealed to me the day of my death, which is near at hand. Wherefore, if thou wouldst find me alive, as soon as thou shalt receive this letter, do thou set forth immediately, and come to St Mary of the Angels; for if thou come not forthwith, thou shalt not find me alive. And bring with thee hair-cloth wherein to wrap my body, and the cerecloth that will be needed for my burial. I pray thee that thou wouldst bring me also some of the food such as thou gavest to me when I was sick at Rome." Now, while this letter was being written, it was revealed to St Francis that the

166

Lady Jacopa was coming to him, and was already near at hand, and that she had brought with her all the things which were asked for in the letter. Having, then, received this revelation, St Francis bade the brother who was writing to write no more, for it was not needed, but to lay the letter aside; whereupon the brethren greatly marvelled why he would not have it finished or sent. But a short space afterwards, there came a loud knocking at the door, and St Francis bade the porter open it; which, when he had done, he saw the Lady Jacopa, the most noble of all the ladies of Rome, with two of her sons, who were senators of Rome, and a great company of horsemen, and they entered the house; and the Lady Jacopa went straight to the infirmary to St Francis. And St Francis felt great consolation at her coming, and she also rejoiced exceedingly to find him alive, and to speak with him. Then she declared to him how, being at Rome in prayer, God had revealed to her that his life would shortly come to an end, and that he would send for her and ask those things of her which she had now brought. Then she brought them to St Francis and gave him to eat; and when he had eaten, and was now much strengthened thereby, the Lady Jacopa knelt at the feet of St Francis, and with such exceeding devotion kissed and bathed with her tears those feet, marked and adorned with the wounds of Christ, that the brethren who were standing round thought they beheld the Magdalen at the feet of Jesus Christ, and could in no way remove her from him. At length, after a long space of time they raised her up, and, taking her aside, they asked her how it was she had come thus opportunely, and thus well provided with all things needful for St Francis, both in his life and for his burial. To this the Lady Jacopa answered, that as she was praying one night in Rome she heard a voice from heaven, which said: "If thou wouldst find St Francis alive, go without delay to Assisi, and take with thee those things which thou hast been

167

accustomed to prepare for him in sickness, and those which shall be needed for his burial." And, continued the Lady, "As the voice bade me do, so have I done." So the Lady Jacopa abode at Assisi until St Francis passed from this life and was buried; and she and all her company paid great honour to his burial, and bore all the cost of it. Then returning to Rome, that noble lady soon afterwards died a holy death, desiring, out of devotion to St Francis, to be carried to St Mary of the Angels, and there to be buried; which was done according to her will.

HOW JEROME, WHO AT FIRST BELIEVED NOT, SAW AND TOUCHED THE SACRED, HOLY STIGMATA OF ST FRANCIS

⁑ On the death of St Francis his glorious, sacred stigmata were seen and kissed, not only by the said Lady Jacopa and her company, but by many citizens of Assisi; among others by a knight of great renown, named Jerome, who had doubted much, and disbelieved them; as St Thomas disbelieved the wounds of Christ. And to assure himself and others, he boldly, in the presence both of the brethren and of seculars, moved the nails in the hands and feet, and strongly pressed the wound in the side. By which means he was enabled to bear constant witness to the truth of the miracle, swearing on the Gospels that he had seen and touched the glorious, holy stigmata of St Francis, the which were seen and touched also by St Clare and her religious, who were present at his burial.

OF THE DAY AND YEAR OF THE DEATH OF ST FRANCIS

⁑ St Francis, the glorious confessor of Christ, passed from this life in the year of our Lord 1226, on Saturday, October 4, and was buried on the Sunday following. He died in the twentieth year of his conversion — that is, from the time when he began to do penance — the second year after the impression of the sacred, holy stigmata, and the forty-fifth of his age.

OF THE CANONISATION OF ST FRANCIS

❡ St Francis was canonised in the year 1228 by Pope Gregory IX, who came in person to Assisi for his canonisation. And this shall suffice for the fourth consideration.

OF THE FIFTH AND LAST CONSIDERATION OF THE SACRED, HOLY STIGMATA

❡ The fifth and last consideration is of certain apparitions, revelations, and miracles, which God vouchsafed after the death of St Francis, in confirmation of the truth of his sacred stigmata, and to certify the day and hour on which Christ gave them to him. In the year of our Lord, then, 1282, in the month of October, Brother Philip, the minister of Tuscany, by the command of Brother John Buonagrazia, the minister general, required under holy obedience Brother Matthew da Castiglione of Arezzo, a man of great devotion and sanctity, to tell him what he knew of the day and hour in which the sacred, holy stigmata were impressed by Christ on the body of St Francis, because he had heard that it had been revealed to him. And Brother Matthew, being constrained by holy obedience, made answer thus: "Being one of the community of Alvernia, last May I was praying in my cell, which is on the spot where the seraph is believed to have appeared. And in my prayer I besought God most devoutly that he would be pleased to make known to some person the day, the hour, and the place in which the sacred, holy stigmata were impressed on the body of St Francis. And persevering thus for a long time in this prayer, St Francis appeared to me in great glory, and said to me: 'My son, what prayer art thou making to God?' And I said to him: 'Father, I am praying such and such things.'

169

And he said to me: 'I am thy Father Francis. Dost thou know me?' 'Yes, Father,' said I. Then he showed me the sacred, holy stigmata in his hands and feet and side, saying: 'The time is now come when God wills that to be manifested for his glory, which the brethren have not hitherto sought to know. Know, then, that he who appeared to me was no angel, but Jesus Christ himself under the appearance of a seraph, who, with his own hands, impressed those wounds upon my body, as he himself received them in his body on the cross: and it was thus. On the day before the Exaltation of the Holy Cross, an angel came to me, and bade me, on the part of God, to prepare to receive with patience whatsoever he should be pleased to send me. And I made answer that I was prepared to receive and endure whatever God should be pleased to appoint for me. And on the following morning, being the morning of Holy Cross day, which in that year fell on a Friday, I left my cell at daybreak in great fervour of spirit, and went to pray in that very spot where thou now dwellest, where I was often accustomed to pray. And as I was praying, there descended through the air with great rapidity the figure of a young man crucified, in the guise of a seraph with six wings. At which marvellous sight I knelt down humbly, and began devoutly to contemplate the unbounded love of Jesus Christ crucified, and the unbounded anguish of his Passion. And such compassion did this spectacle excite within me, that it seemed to me as if I felt that Passion in my own body, and the whole mountain shone like the sun in his presence: and, thus descending, he came close to me. And standing before me, he spoke to me certain secret words, which I have never yet revealed to any one, but the time is now at hand when they shall be revealed. Then after a little space, Christ departed and returned to heaven, and I found myself thus signed with these wounds. Go, then,' said St Francis, 'and assure thy minister of these things; for this is the work of

God and not of man.' Having said these words, St Francis blessed me and returned to heaven, accompanied by a great multitude of glorious spirits." All these things the said Brother Matthew declared that he had seen, not sleeping, but waking. And he made oath that he had thus related them to the said minister in his cell at Florence, when so enjoined by him to do under holy obedience.

CHAPTER LIV

HOW A HOLY FRIAR, HAVING READ IN THE LEGEND
OF ST FRANCIS OF THE SECRET WORDS SPOKEN TO HIM
BY THE SERAPH, PRAYED SO EARNESTLY TO GOD THAT
ST FRANCIS REVEALED THEM TO HIM

IT happened as a devout and holy friar was reading in the legend of St Francis the chapter concerning the sacred, holy stigmata, that he began in great anxiety of mind to ponder what those most secret words could be, spoken by the seraph to St Francis, which he would never reveal to any one in his lifetime. And he said thus to himself: "St Francis would never tell these words to any one while he was alive; but now since his corporal death he would perhaps reveal them, were he devoutly besought to do so." And from that day forth the fervent friar betook himself to prayer, beseeching God and St Francis to reveal these words to him; and after persevering for eight years in this prayer, it was at last granted in the following manner: One day after dinner as he was making his thanksgiving in the church, and remained there praying to this end with greater devotion than usual, and with many tears, he was presently summoned by another friar, by order of the Father Guardian, to go with him to the city on the business of the convent. Not doubting, therefore, that obedience is more meritorious than prayer, he no sooner heard the command of his Superior than he left the church, and went humbly with the brother who called him. And this act of obedience was so pleasing to God, that by it he merited what he had not obtained by all his long years of prayer; for as soon as they had passed through the gate, they met two stranger friars, who seemed as if they had come from a far land, one of whom appeared young, and the other lean and old; and by reason of the bad weather they were both wet and muddy. On which the obedient friar spoke thus to his companion: "Oh, dearest Brother, if the business on which we are going may brook some little delay, seeing that these stranger brethren have great need of a charitable reception, I pray thee let me first go and wash their feet,—and specially those of this ancient brother, and thou mayst wash the feet of the younger, — and then we will go upon the business of the convent." Then the other friar yielding to the charity of his companion, they returned to the house, and most charitably received those stranger brethren, bringing them into the kitchen to warm and dry themselves at the fire, at which eight other brethren of the place were already warming themselves. And after they had been awhile at the fire, they took them aside to wash their feet, as they had agreed together to do. Now as the obedient brother was washing the feet of the ancient friar, he beheld on them the marks of the sacred, holy stigmata, and immediately embracing them in joy and wonder, he began to cry: "Either thou art Christ, or thou art St Francis!" At that cry, and at these words, the brethren who were at the fire rose up, and drawing near, beheld with great fear and reverence those glorious stigmata. Then the ancient friar suffered them at their earnest desire to behold them clearly, and also to touch and kiss them. And as they wondered more and more, and scarce believed for joy, he said to them: "Doubt not and fear not, beloved

172

brethren and children; I am your father, Brother Francis, who by the will of God founded three Orders. And inasmuch as this brother, who but now has washed my feet, has been beseeching me these eight years past, and to-day more fervently than ever, to reveal to him the secret words spoken to me by the seraph when he gave me the stigmata, which words I would never reveal during my lifetime, now by the command of God, for his perseverance and for his prompt obedience by which he left the sweetness of contemplation, I am sent to reveal to him, before you, that which he has asked to know."

Then St Francis, turning to the friar, said thus: "Know, dearrest brother, that when I was on Mount Alvernia, wholly absorbed in the remembrance of the Passion of Christ, in that seraphical apparition I was thus stigmatised by Christ in my body, and then he spoke to me thus: 'Knowest thou what I have done to thee? I have given thee the signs of my Passion that thou mayest be my standard-bearer. And as on the day of my death I descended into Limbo, and by virtue of my stigmata drew forth and took with me to Paradise all the souls whom I found there, so do I now grant to thee, in order that thou mayest be conformed to me in death as thou hast been in life, that when thou shalt have passed out of this life, thou shalt descend into Purgatory every year on the anniversary of thy death, and by the virtue of thy stigmata which I have given thee shalt deliver thence and take with thee to Paradise all the souls which thou shalt find there of thy three Orders — Minors, Sisters, and Penitents, — with all others soever who shall have been devout to thee.' And these words I never told to any one while I was in life." Having said these words, St Francis and his companion immediately disappeared. Many brethren heard this related by the eight friars who witnessed the vision, and heard the words of St Francis.

CHAPTER LV

ST FRANCIS once appeared on Mount Alvernia to Brother John of Alvernia, a man of great sanctity, while he was in prayer, and spoke with him for a long space of time; and before he departed he said to him: "Ask of me what thou wilt." Then Brother John made answer: "Father, I pray thee, tell me that which I have long desired to know, — what thou wast doing, and where thou wast, when the seraph appeared to thee." And St Francis replied: "I was praying in that place whereon the chapel of Count Simon da Battifolle now stands, and I asked two favours of my Lord Jesus Christ. The first was that he would grant to me in my lifetime to feel, as far as might be possible, both in my soul and body, all that he had suffered in his most bitter Passion. The second favour which I asked was, that I might feel in my heart that exceeding love which enkindled his, and moved him to endure so great a Passion for us sinners. And then God put it into my heart that it was granted to me to feel both, as far as is possible for a mere creature; and this promise was well fulfilled to me by the impression of the stigmata." Then Brother John asked him whether those sacred words spoken to him by the seraph had been truly related by the brother who affirmed that he had heard them from the mouth of St Francis, in the presence of eight friars. And St Francis made answer, that they were even so as that brother had said. Then Brother John, emboldened to ask by the saint's liberality in granting his requests, said thus: "O Father, I beseech thee most earnestly that thou wilt

174

suffer me to see and kiss thy glorious, sacred stigmata; not that
I have any doubt upon the matter, but because such has always
been my most earnest desire." And St Francis graciously showing them to him, Brother John plainly saw and touched and kissed them. Lastly he said to him: "Father, grant me, if it be the
will of God, to feel in some small measure the consolation which
thou didst experience when thou didst behold our dear Lord
come down to thee to give thee the stigmata of his most holy
Passion." Then St Francis replied: "Dost thou see these nails?"
"Yes, Father," said Brother John. "Touch once more," said St
Francis, "this nail which is in my hand." Then Brother John,
with great fear and reverence, touched that nail, and as he touched it there issued forth from it a perfume, with as it were a little
cloud of incense, which, entering the nostrils of Brother John,
filled both his soul and body with such overpowering sweetness
that he was immediately rapt in God: and in that ecstasy he remained insensible from that hour, which was the hour of Tierce,
until Vespers. And of that vision and familiar converse with
St Francis Brother John never spoke to any save to his confessor
till the day of his death; but on his deathbed he revealed it to
several of the brethren.

CHAPTER LVI

OF A HOLY FRIAR WHO SAW A WONDERFUL
VISION OF A COMPANION WHO WAS DEAD

IN the province of Rome a very devout and holy friar saw this wonderful vision. A brother, who was exceedingly beloved by him, died one night, and was buried in the morning at the entrance of the chapter-house. On the same day the friar withdrew after dinner into a corner of the chapter-house, and there prayed most fervently to God and St Francis for the soul of this his beloved companion. And persevering in prayer with many tears till midday, when all the rest lay down to sleep, on a sudden he heard a loud noise in the cloister. Being seized with great terror, he cast his eyes on the grave of his companion, and beheld St Francis standing at the entrance of the chapter-house, and behind him a great multitude of friars surrounding the grave. And looking farther, he saw in the midst of the cloister a great and intense fire burning, and in it the soul of his deceased companion; and looking round the cloister, he beheld our Lord Jesus Christ going round it, with a great company of angels and saints. And as he beheld these things in great amazement, he saw that when Christ passed by the chapter-house, St Francis with all those friars knelt down, and said thus to him: "I beseech thee, my dearest Lord and Father, by that inestimable charity which thou didst show to the human race in thine Incarnation, to have mercy upon the soul of this my brother, which is burning in that fire"; yet Christ answered nothing, but passed on. And returning again the second time, and passing by the chapter-house, St Francis knelt down again with his friars, and besought him in these words: "I beseech thee, most pitiful Father and Lord, by the unbounded charity which thou didst show to the human race when thou didst die for it on the wood of the cross, to have mercy on the soul of this my brother"; but Christ again passed by, and heeded him not. And going again round the cloister, he passed the third time by the chapter-house, and then St Francis, kneeling down as before, showed him his hands and his feet and his side, saying: "I pray thee, merciful Lord and Father, by that great anguish and great consolation which I experienced when thou didst impress these stigmata upon my flesh, to have mercy on the soul of this my brother, which is in the flames of Purga-tory." Wonderful to tell, Christ being thus besought for the third time by St Francis, in the name of his stigmata, immediately stood still, and, looking upon them, he granted his prayer, saying: "I grant to thee, Francis, the soul of thy brother." And hereby assuredly he intended to honour and confirm the glorious stigmata of St Francis, and openly to testify that the souls of his brethren which go to Purgatory have no easier way of deliverance than by virtue of his stigmata, by which they are freed from pain, and brought to the glory of Paradise, according to the words which Christ said to St Francis when he imprinted them upon his body.

No sooner had our Lord spoken these words than the fire in the cloister vanished, and the dead friar came to St Francis, and, together with him and with Christ, all that blessed company, with their glorious King, ascended into heaven. For which cause the friar his companion, who had prayed for him, seeing him delivered from suffering and received into Paradise, was filled with exceeding joy. And then he related the whole vision in or-der to the other friars, and all together they praised and gave thanks to God.

CHAPTER LVII

HOW A NOBLE KNIGHT WHO WAS DEVOUT TO ST FRANCIS WAS ASSURED OF HIS DEATH AND OF THE SACRED STIGMATA

A NOBLE knight of Massa di San Pietro, named Landulph, who was most devout to St Francis, and had received the habit of the Third Order from his hand, was thus certified of his death and of the truth of his sacred, holy and glorious stig-mata. When St Francis lay on his deathbed, the devil entered into a woman of that place, and cruelly tormented her, and with-al made her to speak with such learning and subtlety, that she overcame all the clerks and learned men who came to dispute with her. Now it came to pass that the devil, departing from her, left her free for the space of two days, after which he returned again, and afflicted her more cruelly than before. Which when Landulph heard he went to the woman, and asked the devil which dwelt within her wherefore he had departed from her for those days, and why he had since returned to torment her worse than before. And the devil answered thus: "When I left her, I went with all my companions in these parts, being gathered to-gether in great force, to the deathbed of Francis the beggar, to dispute with him, and carry away his soul; but, because it was sur-rounded and defended by a multitude of angels, far more numer-ous than we, who carried it straight to heaven, we were forced to retire discomfited; and therefore have I returned to make up to this wretched woman for the peace in which I left her for those days."

Then Landulph conjured him in the name of God to tell him what was the truth regarding the holiness of St Francis, whom he affirmed to be dead, and of St Clare, who was still alive. And the devil answered him: "I must tell thee the truth whether I will or not. The anger of God the Father was so enkindled against the sins of the world, that he was ready to pass sentence upon it, and to destroy all men and women from the face of the earth, unless they would repent. But Christ his Son, praying for sinners, promised to renew his life and Passion in the person of a man, namely, in Francis, a poor mendicant: through whose life and doctrine many throughout the world should be brought back into the way of truth, and many also to penance. And now, to show to the world what he had wrought in St Francis, he has been pleased that the stigmata of his Passion, which he had imprinted on his body during life, should be seen and touched by many since his death. In like manner did the Mother of Christ promise to renew her virginal purity and her humility in the person of a woman, to wit in Sister Clare, that by her example many wo; men might be delivered out of my hands. And the eternal Fa; ther, being appeased by these promises, deferred his final sen; tence." Then Landulph, wishing to know for certain whether the devil, who is the abode and father of lies, spoke truth in these matters, and especially with regard to the death of St Francis, sent a faithful servant of his to Assisi, to St Mary of the Angels, to inquire whether St Francis were alive or dead; whither, when the messenger had arrived, he found that he was indeed dead, and brought certain information to his lord that St Francis had passed from this life on the very day and hour of which the devil had spoken.

179

CHAPTER LVIII

HOW POPE GREGORY IX, WHO HAD DOUBTED OF THE STIGMATA OF ST FRANCIS, WAS ASSURED OF THEIR TRUTH

PASSING over all the miracles of the sacred, holy stigmata of St Francis, it shall suffice in conclusion of this fifth consideration to relate the following: Pope Gregory IX having some little doubt, as he afterwards related, concerning the wound in the side of St Francis, the saint one night appeared to him, and raising his right arm a little, discovered to him the wound in his side. He then bade him bring a flask and place it beneath the wound, and when the Pope had done so, he saw it filled to the brim with blood mingled with water, which flowed from the wound; and thereupon all doubt immediately departed from him. After this, with the concurrence of all the Cardinals, he approved the sacred, holy stigmata of St Francis by a special bull granted to the friars at Viterbo in the eleventh year of his papacy; and in the following year he issued another, with still more copious privileges. Pope Nicholas III and Pope Alexander also confirmed the same, with fuller privileges, decreeing that whosoever should deny the sacred, holy stigmata might be proceeded against as a heretic. And this shall suffice concerning the fifth consideration of the glorious, holy, and sacred stigmata of our father St Francis, whose life may God give us grace to follow in this world, that by virtue of his glorious stigmata we may deserve to be saved with him in Paradise! To the praise of Jesus Christ and his poor servant St Francis! Amen.

PART TWO

HERE BEGINNETH THE LIFE OF
BROTHER JUNIPER

CHAPTER I

HOW BROTHER JUNIPER CUT OFF THE FOOT OF A PIG TO GIVE IT TO A SICK BROTHER

ONE of the most chosen disciples and first companions of St Francis was Brother Juniper, a man of profound humility and of great fervour and charity, of whom St Francis once said, when speaking of him to some of his companions: "He would be a good Friar Minor who had overcome the world as perfectly as Brother Juniper." Once when he was visiting a sick brother at St Mary of the Angels, he said to him, as if all on fire with the charity of God: "Can I do thee any service?" And the sick man answered: "Thou wouldst give me great consolation if thou couldst get me a pig's foot to eat." Brother Juniper answered immediately: "Leave it to me; thou shalt have one at once." So he went and took a knife from the kitchen, and in fervour of spirit went into the forest, where many swine were feeding, and having caught one, he cut off one of its feet and ran off with it, leaving the swine with its foot cut off; and coming back to the convent, he carefully washed the foot, and diligently prepared and cooked it. Then he brought it with great charity to the sick man, who ate it with avidity; and Brother Juniper was filled with joy and consolation, and related the history of his assault upon the swine for his diversion. Meanwhile, the swineherd who had seen the brother cut off the foot, went and told the tale in order, and with great bitterness, to his lord, who, being informed of the fact, came to the convent and abused the friars, calling them hypocrites, deceivers, robbers, and evil men. "Why," said he, "have you cut off the foot of my swine?" At the noise which he made, St Francis and all the friars came together, and with all humility made excuses for their brother, and, as ignorant of the fact, promised, in order to appease the angry man, to make amends for the wrong which had been done to him. But he was not to be appeased, and left St Francis with many threats and reproaches, repeating over and over again that they had maliciously cut the foot off his swine, refusing to accept any excuse or promise of repayment; and so departed in great wrath. And as all the other friars wondered, St Francis, being full of prudence, thought within himself: "Can Brother Juniper indeed have done this through indiscreet zeal?" So he sent for him, and asked him privately: "Hast thou cut off the foot of a swine in the forest?" To which Father Juniper answered quite joyfully, not as one who has committed a fault, but believing he had done a great act of charity: "It is true, sweet Father, that I did cut off that swine's foot; and if thou wilt listen compassionately, I will tell thee the reason. I went out of charity to visit the brother who is sick." And so he related the matter in order, adding: "I tell thee, dear father, that this foot did the sick brother so much good, that if I had cut off the feet of a hundred swine instead of one, I verily believe that God would have been pleased therewith." To whom St Francis, in great zeal for justice, and in much bitterness of heart, made answer: "O Brother Juniper, wherefore hast thou given this great scandal? Not without reason doth this man complain, and thus rage against us; perhaps even now he is going about the city spreading this evil report of us, and with good cause. Therefore I command thee by holy obedience, that thou go after him until thou find him, and cast thyself prostrate before him, confessing thy fault, and promising to make such full satisfaction that he shall have no more reason to complain of us, for this is indeed a most grievous offence." At these words Brother Juniper was much amazed, wondering that any one should have been angered at so charitable an action; for all temporal things appeared to him of no value, save in so far as they could be charitably applied to the service of our neighbour. So he made answer: "Doubt not, Father, but that I shall soon content and satisfy him. And why should there be all this disturbance, seeing that the swine was rather God's than his, and that it furnished the means for an act of charity?" And so he went his way, and coming to the man, who was still chafing and past all patience, he told him for what reason he had cut off the pig's foot, and all with such fervour, exultation and joy, as if he were telling him of some great benefit he had done him which deserved to be highly rewarded. The man grew more and more furious at his discourse, and loaded him with much abuse, calling him a fantastical fool and a wicked thief. Brother Juniper, who delighted in insults, cared nothing for all this abuse, but marvelling that any one should be wrath at what seemed to him only a matter of rejoicing, he thought he had not made himself well understood, and so repeated the story all over again, and then flung himself on the man's neck and embraced him, telling him that all had been done out of charity, and inciting and begging him for the same motive to give the rest of the swine also; and all this with so much charity, simplicity, and humility, that the man's heart was changed within him, and he threw himself at Brother Juniper's feet, acknowledging with many tears the injuries which by word and deed he had done to him and his brethren. Then he went and killed the swine, and having cut it up, he brought it, with many tears and great devotion, to St Mary of the Angels, and gave it to those holy friars in compensation for the injury he had done them. Then St Francis, considering the simplicity and patience under adversity of this good Brother Juniper, said to his companions and those who stood by: "Would to God, my brethren, that I had a forest of such Junipers!"

CHAPTER II

AN INSTANCE OF BROTHER JUNIPER'S GREAT POWER
AGAINST THE DEVIL

THE devils could not endure the purity of Brother Juniper's innocence and his profound humility, as appears in the following example: A certain demoniac one day fled in an unaccustomed manner, and through devious paths, seven miles from his home. When his parents, who had followed him in great distress of mind, at last overtook him, they asked him why he had fled in this strange way. The demoniac answered: "Because that fool Juniper was coming this way. I could not endure his presence, and therefore, rather than wait his coming, I fled away through these woods." And on inquiring into the truth of these words, they found that Brother Juniper had indeed arrived at the time the devil had said. Therefore when demoniacs were brought to St Francis to be healed, if the evil spirit did not immediately depart at his command, he was wont to say: "Unless thou dost instantly leave this creature, I will bring Brother Juniper to thee." Then the devil, fearing the presence of Brother Juniper, and being unable to endure the virtue and humility of St Francis, would forthwith depart.

CHAPTER III

ONCE upon a time the devil, desiring to terrify Brother Juniper, and to raise up scandal and tribulation against him, betook himself to a most cruel tyrant, named Nicholas, who was then at war with the city of Viterbo, and said to him: "My lord, take heed to watch your castle well, for a vile traitor will come here shortly from Viterbo to kill you and set fire to your castle. And by this sign you shall know him: he will come in the guise of a poor beggar, with his clothes all tattered and patched, and with a torn hood falling on his shoulders, and he will carry with him an awl, wherewith to kill you, and a flint and steel wherewith to set fire to the castle; and if you find not my words to be true, punish me as you will." At these words Nicholas was seized with great terror, believing the speaker to be a person worthy of credit; and he commanded a strict watch to be kept, and that if such a person should present himself he should be brought before him forthwith. Presently Brother Juniper arrived alone; for, because of his great perfection, he was allowed to travel without a companion as he pleased.

On this there went to meet him certain wild young men, who began to mock him, treating him with great contempt and indignity. And Brother Juniper was no way troubled thereat, but rather incited them to ill-treat him more and more. And as they came to the castle-gate, the guards seeing him thus disfigured, with his scanty habit torn in two — for he had given half of it on the way to a beggar, for the love of God, so that he had no longer the appearance of a Friar Minor — recognising the signs given of the expected murderer, they dragged him with great fury before the tyrant Nicholas. They searched him to find whether he had any offensive weapons, and found in his sleeve an awl, which he used to mend his sandals, and also a flint and steel which he carried with him to strike a light when he abode, as he often did, in the woods or in desert places. Nicholas, seeing the signs given by the devil, commanded that a cord should be fastened round his neck, which was done with so great cruelty that it entered into the flesh. He was then most cruelly scourged; and being asked who he was, he replied: "I am a great sinner." When asked whether he wanted to betray the castle to the men of Viterbo, he answered: "I am a great traitor, and unworthy of any mercy." Being questioned whether he intended to kill the tyrant Nicholas with that awl, and to burn the castle, he replied that he should do greater things than these, should God permit him. This Nicholas then, being wholly mastered by his fury, would examine no further, but without delay condemned Brother Juniper, as a traitor and murderer, to be fastened to a horse's tail, and so dragged on the ground to the gallows, there to be forthwith hanged by the neck. And Brother Juniper made no excuse for himself, but, as one who joys to suffer for the love of God, he was full of contentment and rejoicing. So the command of the tyrant was carried into effect. Brother Juniper was tied by the feet to the horse's tail, and dragged along the ground, making no complaint, but, like a meek lamb led to the slaughter, he submitted with all humility. At this spectacle of prompt justice, all the people ran together to behold the execution of so hasty and cruel a judgement, but no one knew the culprit. Nevertheless it befell, by the will of God, that a good man, who had seen Brother Juniper taken and sentenced forthwith, ran to the house of the Friars Minor, and said: "I pray you, for the love of God,

to come with me at once, for a poor man has been seized and im‹
mediately condemned and led to death. Come, that he may at
least place his soul in your hands, for he seems to me a good man,
and he has had no time to make his confession; even now they
are leading him to the gallows, yet he seems to have no fear of
death nor care of his soul. Oh, be pleased to come quickly!"
Then the guardian, who was a compassionate man, went at once
to provide for the salvation of this soul; and when he came to
the place of execution, he could not get near for the crowd; but,
as he stood watching for an opening, he heard a voice say: "Do
not so, do not so, cruel men; you are hurting my legs!" And as
he recognised the voice of Brother Juniper, the guardian, in fer‹
vour of spirit, forced his way through the crowd, and tearing the
bandage from the face of the condemned, he saw that it was in‹
deed Brother Juniper, who looked upon him with a cheerful and
smiling countenance. Then the guardian with many tears be‹
sought the executioners and all the people for pity to wait a lit‹
tle space, till he should go and beseech the tyrant to have mercy
on Brother Juniper. The executioners promised to wait a few mo‹
ments, believing, no doubt, that he was some kinsman of the pri‹

189

soner. So the devout and pious guardian went to the tyrant Nicholas, weeping bitterly, and said: "My lord, I am so filled with grief and amazement that my tongue can scarcely utter it, for it seems to me that in this our land has been committed to-day the greatest sin and the greatest evil which has been wrought from the days of our fathers even until now, and I believe that it has been done through ignorance." Nicholas heard the guardian patiently, and inquired: "What is this great sin and evil which has been committed to-day in this land?" And the guardian answered: "It is this, my lord, that you have condemned — and, as I assuredly believe, unjustly — to a most cruel punishment one of the holiest friars at this time in the Order of St Francis, to whom you profess a singular devotion." Then said Nicholas: "Now tell me, father guardian, who is he; for perhaps, knowing him not, I have committed a great fault?" "He," said the guardian, "whom you have condemned to death is Brother Juniper, the companion of St Francis." Then was the tyrant amazed, for he had heard the fame of Brother Juniper's sanctity; and, pale with fear, he hastened together with the guardian to Brother Juniper, and loosed him from the horse's tail and set him free, and in the presence of all the people he prostrated himself on the ground before Brother Juniper, and with many tears confessed his fault, and the cruelty of which he had been guilty towards that holy friar; adding: "I believe indeed that the days of my wicked life are numbered, since I have thus without reason cruelly tortured so holy a man. For, in punishment of my evil life, God will send me in a few days an evil death, though this thing I did ignorantly." Then Brother Juniper freely forgave the tyrant Nicholas: but a few days afterwards God permitted a most cruel death to overtake him. And so Brother Juniper departed, leaving all the people greatly edified.

CHAPTER IV

HOW BROTHER JUNIPER GAVE ALL THAT HE HAD TO THE
POOR FOR THE LOVE OF GOD

BROTHER Juniper was so full of pity and compassion for the poor, that when he saw anyone poor or naked he immediately took off his tunic, or the hood of his cloak, and gave it to him. The guardian therefore laid an obedience upon him not to give away his tunic or any part of his habit. A few days afterwards, a poor half-naked man asked an alms of Brother Juniper for the love of God, who answered him with great compassion: "I have nothing which I could give thee but my tunic, and my superior has laid me under obedience not to give it, nor any part of my habit, to anyone. But if thou take it off my back I will not resist thee." He did not speak to a deaf man; for the beggar forthwith stripped him of his tunic, and went off with it. When Brother Juniper returned home, and was asked what had become of the tunic, he replied: "A good man took it off my back, and went away with it." And as the virtue of compassion increased in him, he was not contented with giving his tunic, but would give books, or cloaks, or whatever he could lay his hands on, to the poor. For this reason the brethren took care to leave nothing in the common rooms of the convent, because Brother Juniper gave away everything for the love of God and to the glory of his name.

CHAPTER V

ONE Christmas-day Brother Juniper was in deep meditation before the altar at Scesi, the which altar was right fairly and richly adorned; so, at the desire of the sacristan, Brother Juniper remained to keep guard over it while he went to his dinner. And as he was absorbed in devout meditation, a poor woman came asking an alms of him for the love of God. To whom Brother Juniper made answer: "Wait a while, and I will see if I can find anything for thee on this grand altar." Now there was upon the altar an exceedingly rich and costly frontal of cloth of gold, with silver bells of great value. "These bells," said Brother Juniper, "are a superfluity"; so he took a knife and cut them off the frontal, and gave them to the poor woman out of compassion. The sacristan, after he had eaten three or four mouthfuls, bethought him of the ways of Brother Juniper, whom he had left in charge; and began exceedingly to doubt whether, in his charitable zeal, he might not do some damage to the costly altar. As soon as the suspicion entered his head, he rose from table, and went back to the church, to see if any of the ornaments of the altar had been removed or taken away; and when he saw that the frontal had been cut, and the little bells carried off, he was troubled and scandalised beyond measure. Brother Juniper, seeing that he was very angry, said to him: "Be not disturbed about those little bells, for I have given them to a poor woman who had great need of them, and here they were good for nothing but to make a pompous display of worldly vanity." When the sacristan

192

had heard this, he went with all speed to seek the woman in the church, and throughout the city; but he could neither find her nor meet with anyone who had seen her. So he returned, and in great wrath took the frontal, and carried it to the general, who was at Assisi, saying: "Father general, I demand justice on Brother Juniper, who has spoilt this hanging for me, the very best I had in the sacristy. See how he has destroyed it by cutting away all the silver bells, which he says he has given to a poor woman!" And the general answered him: "It is not Brother Juniper who has done this, but thine own folly; for thou oughtest by this time to have known his ways: and I tell thee, I marvel only that he did not give away the whole frontal. Nevertheless, I will give him a sound correction for this fault." And having called the brethren together in chapter, he sent for Brother Juniper, and, in the presence of the whole community, reproved him most severely concerning the said bells; and, waxing wrathful as he spoke, he raised his voice till it became hoarse. Brother Juniper cared little or nothing for these words, for he delighted in reproaches, and rejoiced when he received a good humiliation; but his one thought in return was to find a remedy for the general's hoarseness. So when he had received his reproof, he went straight to the town for flour and butter, to make a good hasty-pudding, with which he returned when the night was far spent; then lighting a candle, he went with his hasty-pudding to the door of the general's cell and knocked. The general came to open it, and seeing him with a lighted candle and a pipkin in his hand, asked: "Who is there?" Brother Juniper answered him: "Father, when you reproved me to-day for my faults, I perceived that your voice grew hoarse, and I thought it was from over-fatigue. I considered therefore what would be the best remedy, and have had this hasty-pudding made for you; therefore I pray you eat of it, for I tell you that it will ease your throat and your chest." "What an hour of the night is this," said the general, "to come and disturb other people!" And Brother Juniper made answer: "See, it has been made for you; I pray you eat of it without more ado, for it will do you good." But the general, being angry at the lateness of the hour, and at Brother Juniper's persistence, answered him roughly, bidding him go his way, for at such an hour he would not eat. Then Brother Juniper, seeing that neither persuasions nor prayers were of any avail, said: "Father, since you will not eat the pudding which was made for you, at least do this for me: hold the candle for me, and I will eat it." Then the general, being a devout and kindly man, seeing the piety and simplicity of Brother Juniper, and how he had done all this out of devotion, answered: "Well, since thou wilt have it so, thou and I will eat together." And so the two of them ate this hasty-pudding together, out of an importunate charity, and were refreshed by their devotion more than by the food.

CHAPTER VI

HOW BROTHER JUNIPER KEPT SILENCE
FOR SIX MONTHS

BROTHER Juniper once determined with himself to keep silence for six months together, in this manner. The first day for love of the Eternal Father. The second for love of Jesus Christ his Son. The third for love of the Holy Ghost. The fourth in reverence to the most holy Virgin Mary; and proceeding thus, each day in honour of some saint, he passed six whole months without speaking.

194

CHAPTER VII

HIS REMEDY FOR TEMPTATIONS OF THE FLESH

ONE day as Brother Giles, Brother Simon of Assisi, Brother Ruffino, and Brother Juniper were discoursing together concerning God and the salvation of the soul, Brother Giles said to the other brethren: "How do you deal with temptations to impurity?" Brother Simon said: "I consider the vileness and turpitude of the sin till I conceive an exceeding horror of it, and so escape from the temptation." And Brother Ruffino said: "I cast myself on the ground, and with fervent prayer implore the mercy of God and of the Mother of Jesus Christ till I am freed from the temptation." And Brother Juniper answered: "When I feel the approach of a diabolical suggestion, I run at once and shut the door of my heart, and, to secure its safety, I occupy myself in holy desires and devout meditations; so that when the suggestion comes and knocks at the door of my heart, I may answer from within: 'Begone; for the room is already taken, and there is no space for another guest'; and so I never suffer the thought to enter my heart; and the devil, seeing himself baffled, retires discomfited, not from me alone, but from the whole neighbourhood." Then Brother Giles made answer and said: "Brother Juniper, I hold with thee; for there is no surer way of overcoming this enemy than flight; inasmuch as he attacks us within by means of the traitor appetite, and without through our bodily senses; and so by flight alone can this masterful foe be overcome. And he who resists it in any other way, after all the toil of the conflict, rarely comes off victorious. Fly, then, from this vice, and thou shalt gain the victory."

CHAPTER VIII

HOW BROTHER JUNIPER MADE HIMSELF CONTEMPTIBLE
FOR THE LOVE OF GOD

BROTHER Juniper, desiring to make himself despicable in the sight of men, stripped himself one day of all but his inner garment; and, making a bundle of his habit and other clothes, he entered the city of Viterbo, and went half-naked into the market-place, in order to make himself a laughing-stock. When he got there, the boys and young men of the place, thinking him to be out of his senses, ill-treated him in many ways, throwing stones and mud at him, and pushing him hither and thither, with many words of derision; and thus insulted and evil entreated, he abode there the greater part of the day, and then went his way to the convent.

Now when the friars saw him they were full of indignation, and chiefly because he had gone thus through the city with his bundle on his head; wherefore they reproved and threatened him sharply. One said: "Let us put him in prison." Another: "He deserves to be hanged." And others: "He cannot be too severely punished for the scandal he has given to-day in his own person, to the injury of the whole Order." And Brother

Juniper, being full of joy, answered with all humility, "You say well indeed; for I deserve all these punishments, and far worse than these."

CHAPTER IX

HOW BROTHER JUNIPER, IN ORDER TO BE DESPISED,
PLAYED AT SEE-SAW

AS Brother Juniper was once entering Rome, the fame of his sanctity led many of the devout Romans to go out to meet him, but he, as soon as he saw this number of people coming, took it into his head to turn their devotion into sport and ridicule. So, catching sight of two children who were playing at see-saw upon two pieces of wood, he moved one of them from his place, and mounting on the plank in his stead, he began to see-saw with the other. Meanwhile the people came up and marvelled much at Brother Juniper's see-sawing. Nevertheless they saluted him with great devotion, and waited till he should have finished his play to accompany him honourably to the convent. Brother Juniper took little heed of their salutation, reverence, or patient waiting, but gave his whole attention to his see-saw. And when they had waited thus for a long time, they began to grow tired, and to say, "What folly is this?" Some few, who knew his ways, were moved to still greater devotion; but at last they all departed, leaving Brother Juniper on the see-saw. When they were gone, Brother Juniper remained full of consolation, because he saw in what contempt they held him. Then came he down from his see-saw, and entering Rome with all meekness and humility, came to the convent of the Friars Minor.

CHAPTER X

HOW BROTHER JUNIPER ONCE COOKED FOR THE BRETHREN
ENOUGH TO LAST FOR A FORTNIGHT

IT happened once, when Brother Juniper was in a house of the brethren, that, for some reasonable cause all the friars were obliged to go out, and Brother Juniper alone remained at home. Then the guardian said to him: "Brother Juniper, we are all going out, therefore, by the time we come back, I wish thee to prepare a little food for the refreshment of thy brethren." "Most willingly," replied Brother Juniper; "leave it to me." When all the brethren, as has been said, were gone out, Brother Juniper said to himself: "What superfluous carefulness is this, that a brother should be lost in the kitchen, and deprived of all opportunity for prayer! Of a surety, as I am now left in this charge, I will cook enough to serve the brethren, were they as many more, for a fortnight to come." So he went to the town and borrowed some large pots for cooking; then he got fresh meat and salt, chickens, eggs, and vegetables; he begged wood also, and made a great fire, upon which he set every thing together to boil: the fowls in their feathers, the eggs in their shells, and the rest in like manner. Meanwhile one of the friars, to whom Brother Juniper's simplicity was well known, returned to the house; and seeing these great caldrons on such an enormous fire, he sat down in amazement to watch with what care and diligence Brother Juniper proceeded in his cookery. And having observed him for some time to his great recreation, this friar went out of the kitchen, and told the other brethren that Brother Juniper was certainly preparing a wedding banquet. The brethren took it for a jest; but presently Brother Juniper took his caldrons off

198

the fire, and bade them ring the bell for dinner. Then the brethren took their places at the table, and he came into the refectory, all rubicund with his toil and with the heat of the fire, and said to the brethren: "Eat a good dinner now, and then we will go to prayer: and let no one think of cooking for a long time to come, for I have cooked more than enough to last us all for more than a fortnight." And so saying, he set down his hotch-potch before them; but there was never hog in the Campagna of Rome so hun-

gry that he could have eaten it. Brother Juniper praised his way of cooking because it was so great a saving of time; and seeing that the other friars ate none of it, he said: "These fowls are good for the head; and this food will keep the body in health, so wholesome is it"; so that the brethren were all in admiration at the devotion and simplicity of Brother Juniper. But the guardian, being angry at such folly, and grieved at the waste of so much good food, reproved Brother Juniper severely. Then Brother Juniper fell on his knees before the guardian, and humbly confessed his fault to him and all the brethren, saying: "I am a very wicked man. Such a one committed such a sin, for which he was condemned to lose his eyes. Such another was hanged for his crimes. But I deserve far worse for my evil deeds. And now I have wasted so much of the gifts of God and the substance of the Order." And thus lamenting he departed; nor would he come into the presence of any one of the brethren for the rest of that day. Then said the father guardian: "My dearest brethren, I would that every day this brother might spoil as much of our substance, if we had it, as he has done to-day, were it only for the edification he has given us by the simplicity and charity with which he has done this thing."

CHAPTER XI

HOW BROTHER JUNIPER WENT ONE DAY TO ASSISI FOR HIS OWN CONFUSION

ONCE when Brother Juniper was dwelling in the valley of Spoleto, knowing that there was to be a great solemnity at Assisi, and that many were resorting thither with great devotion, it came into his head to go there also; and you shall hear in what guise he went. He stripped himself of all but his inner garment, and thus, passing through the midst of the city of Spoleto, he came to the convent. The brethren, much displeased and scandalised, rebuked him sharply, calling him a fool, a madman, and a disgrace to the Order of St Francis, and declaring that he ought to be put in chains as a madman. And the general, who was then on the spot, calling all the friars together, gave Brother Juniper a very sharp correction in the presence of them all. And, after many words, he ended with this severe sentence:

"So great and grievous is thy fault, that I know not what sufficient penance to give thee." Then Brother Juniper answered, as
one who delighted in his own confusion: "Father, I will tell you:
for penance, send me back again from this solemnity in the same
garb in which I came to it."

CHAPTER XII

HOW BROTHER JUNIPER FELL INTO AN ECSTASY DURING
THE CELEBRATION OF MASS

AS Brother Juniper was one day hearing Mass with great devotion, he fell into an ecstasy, and so continued for a long
space of time. And when he came to himself, he said with great
fervour of spirit to the other friars: "Oh, my brethren, who is
there in this world so noble that he would disdain to carry a
basket of mud all the world over, in the hope of obtaining a
house full of gold?" Then he added: "Alas, why will we not endure a little shame to obtain life eternal?"

CHAPTER XIII

OF THE SORROW WHICH BROTHER JUNIPER FELT AT THE
LOSS OF HIS COMPANION BROTHER AMAZIALBENE

BROTHER Juniper had a companion named Amazialbene,
whom he loved most tenderly, and who possessed the virtues of patience and obedience in the utmost perfection; for,
when he was beaten and ill-treated on all sides, he never complained or uttered a word of remonstrance. He was often sent

to places where he met with persons who treated him most cruelly, and he bore it all patiently and without the least resent, ment. At the command of Brother Juniper, he would laugh or weep. At last, as it pleased God to ordain, this Brother Amazial, bene died, in high reputation for sanctity; and when Brother Juniper heard of his death, he felt greater sorrow thereat than he had ever experienced in this life for any earthly thing. And thus did he express in words the great bitterness of his heart, saying: "Alas, woe is me; for there is no good left me now, and all the world is darkened to me by the death of my sweet and most loving brother Amazialbene!" and he added: "Were it not that I should have no peace from the brethren, I would go to his grave and take out his head; and out of his skull I would make me two vessels; from the one I would always eat, in me, mory of him, for my own devotion, and from the other I would drink when I was thirsty."

CHAPTER XIV

OF THE HAND WHICH BROTHER JUNIPER
SAW IN THE AIR

BROTHER Juniper being one day in prayer, and, it may be, proposing to himself to do great things for God, he saw a hand in the air, and heard with his bodily ears a voice, which said thus to him: "O Brother Juniper, with this hand thou canst do nothing." Then he arose immediately, and with his eyes raised to heaven, he went round the convent, repeating aloud: "True indeed, most true indeed!" and this he repeated many times.

CHAPTER XV

HOW ST FRANCIS COMMANDED BROTHER LEO TO WASH
THE STONE

WHEN St Francis was speaking with Brother Leo on Mount Alvernia, he said to him: "Brother little Lamb, wash this stone with water." Then Brother Leo went forth and washed it with water. Then said St Francis, with great joy and gladness: "Wash it with wine"; and it was done. "Wash it," said St Francis again, "with oil"; and Brother Leo did so. Then said St Francis: "Brother little Lamb, wash this stone with balm." And Brother Leo answered: "O sweet father, how am I to get balm in this wilderness?" Then St Francis replied: "Know, Brother little Lamb, that this is the stone on which Christ once was seated when he appeared to me in this place, and therefore did I bid thee wash it four times, and no more, because Jesus Christ then promised me four singular graces for my Order. The first, that all those who shall cordially love my Order, and all the friars who shall persevere therein, shall die a good death. The second, that those who persecute this holy Religion shall be notably punished. The third, that no evil-doer, continuing in his perversity, shall be able to persevere long in this Order. The fourth, that this Religion shall endure until the day of judgement."

PART THREE

THE LIFE OF THE BLESSED
BROTHER GILES, COMPANION OF
ST FRANCIS

CHAPTER I

INASMUCH as the example of holy men serves to detach the minds of devout hearers from transitory pleasures, and to excite them to the desire of eternal salvation, to the honour of God and of his most holy Mother, our Lady St Mary, we will say a word concerning the graces wrought by the Holy Ghost in the soul of our holy brother Giles, who, even while he wore the secular habit, being touched by the Spirit of God, began to strive in all his actions to please God alone.

At that time St Francis appeared as a new herald of Christ to give an example of holy living, of humility, and penance. Then, two years after his conversion, a man named Bernard, endowed with marvellous prudence and very rich in temporal goods, with Peter Cattani, was drawn by his example to the observance of evangelical poverty. By the counsel of St Francis they distributed all their temporal possessions, for the love of God, among the poor, arraying themselves, in the glory of patience and evangelical perfection, with the habit of the Friars Minor; and all their life long did they keep their promise then made with the greatest fervour and perfection. Eight days after their said conversion and distribution, Brother Giles, being still in the secular habit, and seeing the contempt of earthly things manifested by these noble knights of Assisi, to the great admiration of the whole world, on the Feast of St George in the year 1209, very early in the morning, as one in earnest about his salvation, went in great fervour of spirit to the church of St Gregory, where was

the monastery of St Clare. Being greatly desirous to see St Fran‑
cis, he went, as soon as he had finished his prayers, towards the
hospital for lepers, where St Francis dwelt apart in profound
humility, with Brother Bernard and Brother Peter Cattani.

Being come to a crossway, and not knowing which road to take,
he prayed to Christ our precious guide, who led him straight to
the hut. And as he pondered upon the cause of his coming, he
met St Francis returning from the forest, where he had been
praying.

Then Brother Giles threw himself at his feet, and besought him
to receive him into his company for the love of God. And St
Francis, beholding the devout countenance of Brother Giles, an‑
swered and said: "Dearest Brother, God hath conferred a great
grace upon thee. If the emperor were to come to Assisi, and pro‑
pose to make one of its citizens his knight or private chamber‑
lain, would not such an offer be joyfully accepted as a great mark
of honour and distinction? How much more shouldst thou re‑
joice that God has called thee to be his knight and chosen ser‑
vant, to observe the perfection of his holy gospel! Therefore, do
thou stand firm in the vocation to which God hath called thee."
And taking him by the hand he raised him up, and bringing
him into the hut, he called Brother Bernard, and said to him:
"Almighty God has sent us a good brother; let us, therefore, re‑
joice in the Lord, and eat together in charity." When they had
eaten, Brother Francis and this Giles went to Assisi to obtain
some cloth to make him a habit; and by the way they met a poor
woman, who asked an alms for the love of God. St Francis, not
knowing where to find anything for the poor woman, turned to
Brother Giles with an angelic countenance, and said: "For the
love of God, dearest brother, let us give her your mantle." And
Brother Giles obeyed with so willing a heart, that the holy father
thought he saw him and his alms received forthwith into heaven,

whereat he experienced an exceeding interior joy. St Francis having procured the cloth, and caused the habit to be made, received Brother Giles into the Order, and he became one of the most glorious religious whom the world has ever seen in the contemplative life. Immediately after his reception, St Francis went with him into the March of Ancona, singing with him and greatly praising the Lord of heaven and earth. And he said to Brother Giles: "My son, this Religion of ours shall be like unto the fisherman, who casteth his nets into the water, and taketh a great multitude of fishes, whereof he keepeth the larger, casting the smaller back into the sea." Brother Giles marvelled at this prophecy, for the Order at that time numbered only three friars besides St Francis himself. Moreover, St Francis had not yet begun to preach publicly to the people, but only admonished men and women as he met with them by the way, saying, with loving simplicity: "Love God, and fear him, and do worthy penance for your sins." And Brother Giles would say, in his turn: "Do this which my spiritual father says to you, for he speaketh excellently well."

CHAPTER II

HOW BROTHER GILES WENT TO ST JAMES
THE GREAT

BY the permission of St Francis, Brother Giles went once, in the process of time, to St James the Great, in Galicia, and in that whole journey he broke his fast once only because of the great poverty of the country. And as he went asking alms, and finding none who would give to him, he came one evening by chance to a barn, where a few beans lay scattered on the ground. These he gathered up, and supped on them; and in this barn he passed the night, for he loved to abide in solitary places remote from the haunts of men, the better to give himself to watching and prayer. And God so strengthened him by this supper, that if he had eaten of ever so rich a banquet he could not have been so well refreshed. Proceeding then upon his way, he met with a poor man, who asked an alms of him for the love of God. And Brother Giles, charitable as he was, had nothing to give but the habit he wore. So he cut the hood from his cloak, and gave it to that poor man for the love of God, and so journeyed on without a hood for twenty days together. And as he was returning through Lombardy, a man called to him, to whom he went willingly, expecting to receive an alms; but when he stretched out his hand, the man put a pair of dice into it, inviting him to play. Brother Giles replied very humbly, "God forgive thee, my son." And as he passed through the world he met with much mockery and insult, and endured it all in peace.

CHAPTER III

OF BROTHER GILES'S MANNER OF LIFE WHEN HE WENT
TO THE HOLY SEPULCHRE

BROTHER Giles, by the permission of St Francis, went to visit the Holy Sepulchre of Christ; and being come to the port of Brindisi, he was obliged to tarry there many days, because there was no ship ready to sail. So Brother Giles, desiring to live by his labour, got a vessel, and, filling it with water, he went round the city, crying: "Who wants water?" And for his labour he received bread, and all things necessary for the bodily support of himself and his companion. Then he passed over the sea, and with great devotion visited the Sepulchre of Christ and the other Holy Places. And as he returned, he abode for some days in the city of Ancona; and because he was accustomed to live by his labour, he made baskets of rushes, and sold them, not for money, but for bread for himself and his companion; and he carried the dead to their burial for the same wages. And when even this failed him, he begged at the table of Jesus Christ, asking alms from door to door. And with so much labour and in poverty, he returned to St Mary of the Angels.

CHAPTER IV

HOW BROTHER GILES PRAISED OBEDIENCE
MORE THAN PRAYER

AS a brother was one day praying in his cell, his superior sent him an obedience to leave his prayer and go out to beg. The friar went forthwith to Brother Giles, and said to him: "Father, I was at prayer, and the guardian has bade me go forth to beg; now it seems to me far better that I should continue praying." Brother Giles answered: "My son, do you not yet know or understand what prayer is? True prayer is to do the will of our superior; and it is great pride in him who has submitted his neck to the yoke of holy obedience to desire to follow his own will in anything, in order, as he thinks, to perform a work of greater perfection. The perfectly obedient religious is like a horseman mounted on a mettlesome steed, which carries him swiftly and fearlessly on his way; but the disobedient religious, on the contrary, is like a man seated on a meagre, weak, or vicious horse, who is in danger of perishing by the way, or of falling into the hands of his enemies. I tell thee that, though a man were raised to so high a degree of contemplation as to hold converse with angels, yet were he interrupted in that colloquy by the voice of obedience, he ought immediately to leave communing with the angels, and obey the command of his superior."

CHAPTER V

HOW BROTHER GILES LIVED BY THE LABOUR OF
HIS HANDS

WHEN Brother Giles was once living in a convent of the
Friars Minor at Rome, he desired, as he had done ever
since his entrance into the Order, to employ himself in
manual labour, and thus did he spend his day. Early in the morning he heard Mass with great devotion: then he went into a forest about eight miles out of Rome, and bringing home a great
bundle of wood on his back, he sold it for bread and other pro-
visions. One day as he was bringing home his load of wood, a
lady met him and offered to buy it; so, having agreed with her
as to the price, he carried it to her house. The lady, notwithstanding the agreement, seeing that he was a religious, gave him much
more than she had promised. Then said Brother Giles: "Good
lady, I would not have the vice of avarice to gain the mastery of
me, therefore I will not take from thee more than we agreed
upon." And, instead of taking more than the stipulated sum, he
took but half of it, and went his way, leaving the lady in great
admiration. Brother Giles always showed the like scrupulous in-
tegrity in all his dealings. He helped the labourers to gather the
olives and pluck the grapes. Being one day in the market-place,
he heard a man asking another to help him to beat walnuts, of-
fering him a reward for so doing; but the other excused himself
because the place was far off and difficult of access. Then Brother Giles said to him: "My friend, if thou wilt give me a part
of the walnuts, I will come with thee to beat them." So the agreement being made, he went with the man; and first making the

sign of the cross, he climbed the high walnut tree, and in great fear began to beat. When he had finished beating, he gathered up more for his share than he knew how to carry; so taking off his habit, and tying the sleeves and the hood, he made a sack of it, and filling it with walnuts, he took it upon his back and carried it to Rome, and with great joy gave the walnuts to the poor for the love of God. When the corn was reaped, Brother Giles went with other poor persons to gather the ears of corn; and if any one offered him a handful of grain, he would say: "Brother, I have no granary wherein to store it, and for the most part, what I gather I give to the poor for the love of God." Brother Giles had little leisure to help others at such times, for he had to fulfil his appointed task, and also to say the canonical hours, and make his mental prayer. When once he went to the fountain of San Sisto to fetch water for the monks of that place, a man asked him to give him some water to drink. Brother Giles answered: "How can I take the vessel half filled to the monks?" On this the man, being angry, spoke many hard and reproachful words to Brother Giles, who returned very sorrowful to the monks. Then borrowing a large vessel, he came back forthwith to the fountain, and finding the man there, he said: "Take, my friend, and drink as much as thy soul desireth, and be not angry that it seemed to me unjust to take a scant measure of water to those holy monks." Then he, being constrained and conscience-stricken by the charity and humility of Brother Giles, acknowledged his fault, and from that day forth held him in great reverence.

CHAPTER VI

BROTHER Giles was once staying in Rome, at the house
of a Cardinal, when Lent was drawing near; and being unable there to enjoy the quiet of mind which he desired, he
said to the Cardinal: "My Father, I pray you give me permission to go with my companion to spend this Lent in some solitary place"; and the Cardinal answered him: "Alas! dearest brother, whither wouldst thou go? This is a time of great scarcity,
and thou art not well accustomed to these desert places; wherefore I beseech thee remain with me, for I account it a singular
grace to be permitted to provide for thy wants for the love of
God." But Brother Giles being determined to go, went out of
Rome to a high mountain, where there had once been a castle,
and where there was now a forsaken church dedicated to St Lawrence; this he entered with his companion, remaining there
in prayer and meditation. They were not known in the place,
wherefore little reverence or consideration was shown to them,
so that they were in great poverty, and moreover a heavy fall of
snow came on, which lasted many days. They could not leave
the church; they had no food with them, neither was any thing
brought them from without; and thus they remained shut up for
three days and three nights.

Brother Giles, seeing that he could earn nothing for his liveli-
hood, nor go out to beg alms, said to his companion: "My dearest
brother, let us cry aloud to the Lord, that of his loving pity he

would provide for this our extreme necessity; for we have heard how many holy monks, being in great straits, have called upon God to provide for them in their need."

So, after their example, these two holy men betook themselves to prayer, beseeching God with all their hearts to provide a remedy for their distress; and God, who is all-compassionate, had regard to their faith, devotion, and simplicity in manner following: A certain man, casting his eyes upon the church where Brother Giles and his companion were shut up, said to himself by an inspiration from God: "It may be that some devout person is doing penance in that church, and by reason of the snow he can obtain no supply for his wants, and may perhaps die of hunger." Wherefore, by the inspiration of the Holy Ghost he said: "Of a surety I will go and see if what I imagine be true or no." So taking bread and a flask of wine, he went his way, and with great difficulty arrived at the church, where he found Brother Giles and his companion most devoutly absorbed in prayer; but so wasted were they with hunger that they looked rather like dead men than living; and he had great compassion for them, and having warmed and comforted them he returned and told his neighbours of the extremity and necessity of these friars, praying and exhorting them, for the love of God, to provide for their needs.

Many, therefore, after his example, brought them bread and wine for the love of God, besides other things necessary for food, arranging also among themselves that, during that whole Lent, all things needful were provided for them. And Brother Giles, reflecting on the great mercy of God and the charity of these people, said to his companion: "Dearest brother, hitherto we have prayed to God to provide for our necessities, and he has heard us; now it behoveth us to give him thanks, and to pray for those who have fed us by their alms, and for all Christian people."

216

And such grace did God grant to the fervour and devotion of Brother Giles, that many, after his example, forsook this blind world, and many who had no vocation to religion did most austere penance in their own homes.

CHAPTER VII

OF THE DAY OF THE HOLY BROTHER GILES'S DEATH

ON the vigil of St George, at the hour of Matins, fifty-two years being now elapsed since he received the habit of St Francis, the soul of Brother Giles was received by God into the glory of Paradise: to wit, on the Feast of St George.

CHAPTER VIII

HOW A HOLY MAN, BEING IN PRAYER, SAW THE SOUL OF BROTHER GILES PASS TO ETERNAL LIFE

A HOLY man, who was praying when Brother Giles passed from this life, saw his soul, with a multitude of others newly freed from Purgatory, ascend into heaven; and he beheld Jesus Christ, with a multitude of angels, going to meet the soul of Brother Giles, and so ascending again with all those angels and blessed souls, and with the sound of a most ravishing melody, to heaven.

CHAPTER IX

WHILE Brother Giles was lying sick, a few days before his death, a certain friar of St Dominic became sick unto death. Another friar, who was a friend of his, said to the sick brother: "My brother, I desire, if God permit, that after thy death thou return to me and tell me in what state thou art"; and the sick man promised to return if it should be possible. He died on the same day with Brother Giles, and after his death, he appeared to the living Friar Preacher, and said: "It is the will of God that I should fulfil my promise." Then said the living man to the dead: "How is it with thee?" and the dead answered: "All is well; for I died on the very day that a holy Friar Minor, named Giles, passed from this life; to whom for his great sanctity Christ granted that he should carry with him to holy Paradise all the souls that were in Purgatory, among whom was I suffering great torment; and now, by the merits of the holy Brother Giles, I am delivered from them"; and having said this, he forthwith disappeared; and that friar revealed the vision to no man. But after a time this same friar fell sick, and immediately suspecting that God had struck him because he had not revealed the virtue and the glory of Brother Giles, he sent for the Friars Minor; and there came to him ten, two by two; and they being gathered together with the Friars Preachers, he declared to them with great devotion the aforesaid vision; and, diligent inquiry having been made, it was found that the two had indeed passed from this life on one and the same day.

CHAPTER X

HOW GOD GAVE SPECIAL GRACES TO BROTHER GILES,
AND OF THE YEAR OF HIS DEATH

BROTHER Bonaventura of Bagnoreggio said of Brother Giles, that God had given him special graces, not only for himself, but for all those also who should recommend themselves to him with a devout intention in any spiritual need. He wrought many miracles, both in his lifetime and after his death, as appeareth by his legend, and he passed from this life on the Feast of St George, in the year 1252. He is buried at Pe⸗ rugia in the convent of the Friars Minor.

PART FOUR

HERE BEGIN THE CHAPTERS OF CERTAIN
INSTRUCTIONS AND NOTABLE SAYINGS
OF BROTHER GILES

CHAPTER I

OF VICES AND VIRTUES

THE grace of God and the virtues which flow therefrom are a way and a ladder that leadeth to heaven; but vices and sins are a ladder and a way that leadeth to the depths of hell. Vices and sins are a venomous and a mortal poison, but virtues and good works are a salutary medicine. One grace leadeth on to another; and one vice leadeth on to another. Grace asketh not to be praised, and vice cannot endure to be despised. The mind reposeth tranquilly in humility, of whom patience is daughter. Holy purity of heart seeth God, and true devotion enjoyeth him.

If thou lovest, thou shalt be loved.

If thou servest, thou shalt be served.

If thou fearest, thou shalt be feared.

If thou doest good to others, fitting it is that others should do good unto thee.

But blessed is he who truly loves, and desireth not to be loved again.

Blessed is he who serves, and desireth not to be served.

Blessed is he who fears, and desireth not to be feared.

Blessed is he who doeth good to others, and desireth not that others should do good to him.

But because these things are most sublime and high perfection, therefore they that are foolish cannot understand them nor attain thereto. Three things there are that are very sublime and very profitable, which he who has once acquired shall never fail.

The first is, that thou bear willingly and gladly, for the love of Jesus Christ, every affliction that shall befall thee.

The second is, that thou humble thyself daily in every thing thou doest, and in every thing thou seest.

The third is, that thou love faithfully with all thy heart that invisible and supreme Good which thou canst not behold with thy bodily eyes.

Those things which are most despised and decried by worldly men are most truly pleasing and acceptable to God and to his saints; and those things which are most loved and esteemed, and are most pleasing in the eyes of worldly men, are most despised, contemned, and hated by God and by his saints.

This foul disorder proceedeth from human ignorance and malice; for wretched man loveth most those things which he ought to hate, and hateth those which he ought to love.

Said Brother Giles one day to another friar, "Tell me, dearest brother, is thine a good soul?" and the brother answered: "I know not." Then said Brother Giles: "My brother, I would have thee to know that the things which make a soul good and blessed are holy contrition, holy humility, holy charity, holy devotion, and holy joy."

CHAPTER II

OF FAITH

ALL those things which can be thought with the heart, or spoken with the tongue, or seen with the eyes, or felt with the hands, are as nothing in comparison with those which we can neither think, nor see, nor touch. All the saints and wise men who have passed away, and all those who are now in this present life, and all those who shall come after us, — all those who have spoken or written, or shall speak or write of God, — shall never be able to show forth so much of him as a grain of millet in comparison with the whole extent of heaven and earth; nay, a thousand thousand times less. For all that is written of God is but as the lisping prattle of a mother to her babe, who could not understand her words did she speak after any other manner. Brother Giles said once to a secular judge: "Dost thou believe that the gifts of God are great?" And the judge said: "I believe it." To which Brother Giles replied: "I will show thee that thou dost not truly believe it." And then he said to him: "What is the value of thy worldly possessions?" The judge answered: "Perhaps about a thousand pounds." Then Brother Giles said: "Wouldst thou give this property of thine for ten thousand pounds?" The judge answered, without hesitation: "Assuredly, I would do so willingly." Then Brother Giles said: "It is a thing most certain that all the possessions of this world are nothing worth in comparison with heavenly things; wherefore, then, givest thou not these possessions of thine to Christ, that thou mayst purchase riches celestial and eternal?" Then the judge, being wise with the foolish wisdom of the world, made answer to the pure and simple Brother Giles: "Dost thou believe, Brother

Giles, that there is any man whose outward acts accord perfectly with the measure of his internal belief?" Brother Giles replied: "Listen, my beloved: it is most certain that all the saints have truly striven to carry into effect, to the utmost extent of their power, all that they knew and understood to be the will of God; and those things which they were unable to effect in external act, they fulfilled by the holy desire of their will, which supplied their defect of power to perform the action." Said Brother Giles again: "If any man had perfect faith, he would soon arrive at perfection, and attain to a full assurance of his salvation. What harm or what injury could any temporal adversity in this present life do to the man who, with firm faith, looketh forward to that eternal and supreme and most perfect blessedness? And what can any prosperity, or temporal good in this world avail the wretched man who looketh forward to eternal woe! Nevertheless, let no man, how sinful soever he be, despair, so long as he liveth, of the infinite mercy of God; inasmuch as there is not a tree in the world so twisted and knotted and gnarled but may be fashioned and polished and beautified by the hand of man; so likewise there is no man in this world so wicked and so sinful but God can convert him, and adorn him with singular graces and many gifts of virtue."

CHAPTER III

OF HOLY HUMILITY

NO man can attain to any knowledge or understanding of God but by the virtue of holy humility; for the direct way to ascend is first to descend. All the perils and grievous falls which have happened in this world have arisen from nothing else but the uplifting of the head — that is, of the mind — by pride. This is proved by the fall of the devil, who was driven out of heaven; and by that of Adam, our first parent, who was banished from paradise by the uplifting of his head — that is, by disobedience. We see it also in the example of the Pharisee, of whom Christ speaketh in the Gospel, and in many others also.

And so also the contrary truth — namely, that all the great blessings which have ever been bestowed upon the world have proceeded from abasement of the head, that is, from the humiliation of the mind — is proved by example of the blessed and most humble Virgin Mary, the publican, the good thief on the cross and many others in Holy Scripture. And, therefore, good it were if we could find some great and heavy weight, which, being tied round our neck, would draw us down to the earth, and force us to humble ourselves.

A friar once said to Brother Giles: "Father, tell me, how can we avoid this pride?" To whom Brother Giles made this reply: "Rest assured, my brother, that thou canst never hope to be free from pride until thou hast first placed thy mouth where thou dost set thy feet; but if thou wilt well consider the gifts of God, thou wilt clearly see that thou hast reason to bow down thy head. And again, if thou wilt meditate on thy defects and thy mani-

227

fold offences against God, in all this thou wilt find reasons for humbling thyself. But woe to those who desire to be honoured in their unworthiness! He hath one degree of humility, who knoweth himself to be opposed to his own true good. He hath a second, who restoreth the goods of another to their proper owner, and doth not appropriate them to himself. For every virtue and every good thing which a man findeth in himself, instead of appropriating it to himself, he is bound to refer to God, from whom all graces and all good things do proceed. But every sinful passion of the soul, and every vice which a man findeth within himself, he should attribute to himself, considering that they all proceed from himself and his own malice, and from no other source.

"Blessed is the man who knows and accounts himself to be vile in the eyes of God, and also in the sight of men.

"Blessed is he who judges himself always and condemns himself, and none but himself; for he shall not be condemned in that last and terrible eternal judgement.

"Blessed is he who shall submit himself wholly to the yoke of obedience and the judgement of others, as the holy Apostles before and after they received the Holy Spirit."

Brother Giles said also: "Let him who would acquire and possess perfect peace and quiet of mind account every man his superior, and hold himself the inferior and subject to all.

"Blessed is the man who, in his works and in his words, desires neither to be seen nor known for anything else but for that wherewith God hath adorned him.

"Blessed is the man who knows how to keep and hide within his heart divine revelations and consolations; for there is nothing so secret but God can reveal it when it pleaseth him. If the most holy and perfect man in the world were to esteem and account himself to be the vilest and most miserable sinner in the world, this would be true humility.

228

"Holy humility loves not to talk, nor the holy fear of God to use many words."

Brother Giles said again: "It seems to me that holy humility is like the thunderbolt; for, even as the thunderbolt striketh a terrible blow, crushing, breaking, and burning that whereon it lights, yet can we never find the thunderbolt itself, so does humility strike and disperse, burn up and consume every evil and vice and sin, and yet itself can nowhere be seen.

"He who possesses humility, by that humility finds grace with God, and perfect peace with his neighbour."

CHAPTER IV

OF THE HOLY FEAR OF GOD

HE who fears not, shows that he has nothing to lose. The holy fear of God orders, governs, and rules the soul, and prepares it to receive his grace.

If a man possesses any grace or any divine virtue, it is holy fear which preserves it to him. And he who has not yet acquired grace or virtue, acquires it by holy fear.

The holy fear of God is a channel of divine grace, inasmuch as it quickly leads the soul wherein it dwells to the attainment of holiness and all divine graces. No creature that ever fell into sin would have so fallen had it possessed the holy fear of God. But this holy gift of fear is given only to the perfect, because the more perfect any man is, the more timorous and humble he is.

Blessed is the man who looks upon this world as his prison-house, and bears in mind continually how grievously he has offended his Lord.

Greatly ought a man to fear pride, lest it should give him a sudden thrust, and cause him to fall from the state of grace in which he is; for no man is ever secure from falling, so beset are we by foes; and these foes are the flatteries of this wretched world and of our own flesh, which, together with the devil, is the unrelenting enemy of our soul. A man has greater reason to fear being deluded and overcome by his own malice than by any other enemy. It is impossible for a man to attain to any divine grace or virtue, or to persevere therein, without holy fear.

He who has not the fear of God within him is in great danger of eternal perdition. The fear of God makes a man to obey humbly, and to bow his head beneath the yoke of obedience: and the more a man fears God, the more frequently he adores him.

The gift of prayer is no small gift, to whomsoever it is given.

The virtuous actions of men, how great soever they may seem to us, are not to be reckoned or rewarded after our judgement, but according to the judgement and good pleasure of God; for God looketh not to the number of the works, but to the measure of humility and love. Our surest way, therefore, is always to love and to keep ourselves in humility; and never to trust in ourselves that we do any good, but always to distrust the thoughts which spring up in our own mind under the appearance of good.

CHAPTER V

OF HOLY PATIENCE

HE who with steadfast humility and patience endureth tribulations for the fervent love of God, shall soon attain to great graces and virtues; he shall be lord of this world, and shall have an earnest of that glorious world which is to come.

Everything which a man doth, be it good or evil, he doeth it unto himself. Therefore, be not thou offended with him who injures thee, but rather, in humble patience, sorrow only for his sin, having compassion on him, and praying fervently for him to God. For, in so far as a man is strong to suffer and endure injuries and tribulations patiently for the love of God, so great, and no greater, is he before God; and the weaker a man is to endure sufferings and adversities for the love of God, the less is he in the sight of God.

If any man praise thee, speaking well of thee, render thou that praise unto God alone; and if any man reproach thee, speaking evil of thee, do thou help him by speaking of thyself still worse.

If thou wouldst maintain thine own cause, strive to make it appear evil, and maintain that of thy companion good, ever accusing thyself and sincerely excusing thy neighbour. When anyone strives and contends with thee, if thou wouldst conquer, lose thy case, and losing it thou shalt conquer; for if thou wilt go to law to obtain the victory, when thou believest thou hast obtained it, thou shalt find thyself shamefully defeated. Wherefore, my brother, believe me assuredly that the certain way to gain is to lose. But if we endure not tribulation well, we shall never attain to consolation eternal. It is a meritorious thing and far more blessed to endure injuries and reproaches patiently, without murmuring, for the love of God, than to feed a hundred poor men, or to keep a perpetual fast. But what profits it a man, or how does it benefit him, to afflict his body with many fasts, vigils and disciplines, if he cannot endure a little injury from his neighbour? And yet from this might he derive greater reward and higher merit than from all the sufferings he could inflict upon himself of his own will; for to endure reproaches and injuries from our neighbour with humble and uncomplaining patience, will purge away our sins more speedily than they could be by a fountain of many tears.

Blessed is the man who has ever before the eyes of his mind the remembrance of his sins and of the favours of God; for he will endure with patience all tribulations and adversities for which he expects so great consolation. The man who is truly humble looketh for no reward from God, but endeavours only to satisfy him in all things, knowing himself to be his debtor; every good thing which he hath he acknowledges to come from the free bounty of God, while every evil that befalleth him proceedeth from his sins alone.

A friar once said to Brother Giles: "Father, what shall we do if some great adversity or tribulation befall us in these times?" To whom Brother Giles replied: "My brother, I would have thee to know, that if we be such as we ought to be, though the Lord should rain down stones and lightning from heaven, they could not harm or injure us; because, if a man be in truth such as he ought to be, every evil and tribulation will be turned to his good; for we know how the Apostle saith, that all things shall be turned to good for them that love God; and in like manner all things shall turn to the condemnation and punishment of the man of evil will.

"If thou wouldst be saved and attain to eternal glory, desire not revenge, nor the punishment of any creature; for the inheritance of the saints is ever to do good and to receive evil. If thou didst but know, indeed, how much and how grievously thou hast offended thy Creator, thou wouldst know that it is meet and right that all creatures should persecute thee, inflicting pain and sorrow upon thee, that so the offences which thou hast offered to their Creator might be avenged.

"It is great and high virtue for a man to overcome himself; for he who overcometh himself shall overcome all his enemies and persevere in all good. But still greater virtue would it be if a man suffer himself to be overcome by all other men, for thus would he become victor over all his enemies, to wit, sin, the devil, the world and his own flesh. If thou wilt be saved, renounce and despise every consolation which all the things of this world and all mortal creatures can give thee, because greater and more frequent are the falls which arise from prosperity and consolation than those which come from adversity and tribulation."

A certain Religious once complained of his superior in the presence of Brother Giles, because of a severe obedience which he had received from him; to whom Brother Giles made answer: "Dearest brother, the more thou complainest, the heavier dost thou make thy burden, and the harder will it be to carry; but the more humbly and devoutly thou submittest thy neck to the yoke of holy obedience, the sweeter and the lighter will that yoke be to bear. But it seems to me that thou art not willing to bear reproach in this world for the love of Christ, and yet desirest in the next world to be with Christ; thou art not willing in this world to be persecuted and evil spoken of for Christ, yet in the other world thou wouldst fain be blessed and welcomed by Christ; thou willest not to labour in this world, and thou wouldst repose and take thy rest in the other. Brother, brother! I tell thee that thou dost grievously deceive thyself, for it is by the way of shame, humiliation and reproach that a man attaineth to true celestial glory; and by patiently enduring derision and contumely for the love of Christ, doth a man attain to the glory of Christ. For the worldly proverb saith well: 'He who gives not what costs him something, shall not receive that which he desires.'

"The horse is a noble and useful creature; for in his swiftest course he suffers himself to be ruled, guided, and turned hither and thither, backwards and forwards, according to the will of the rider; so likewise should it be with the servant of God, who should suffer himself to be ruled, guided, turned and bent, according to the will of his superior; nay, of all others, for the love of Christ.

"If thou wilt be perfect, strive earnestly to be virtuous and gracious, fighting valiantly against all vices, and bearing patiently all adversities, for the love of thy Lord, who was troubled, afflicted, reproached, beaten, crucified and slain for thy love, and not for his own fault, nor for his own glory, nor for his own profit, but only for thy salvation. And to the end that thou mayest do this which I say, it is needful above all that thou overcome thyself; for little will it profit thee to lead and draw other souls to God, if thou be not first drawn and led to him thyself."

CHAPTER VI

OF SLOTH

THE slothful man loseth both this world and the next, because he brings forth no fruit in himself, and is of no profit to others.

It is impossible for a man to acquire any virtue without diligence and great labour. When thou canst stand in a place of safety, stand not in a place of danger.

He standeth in a safe place who painfully and diligently labours and toils in God, and for the Lord his God, not for fear of punishment or hope of reward, but for the love of God. The man who refuses to labour and suffer for the love of Christ, truly refuses to share the glory of Christ; and thus, inasmuch as diligence is useful and profitable to us, so is negligence hurtful and dangerous.

As sloth is the way to hell, so is holy diligence the way to heaven.

Most solicitous and diligent ought a man to be in acquiring and preserving virtue and the grace of God by constant faithful co-operation with the grace vouchsafed to him; for it often happens that he loses the fruit among the leaves, and the grain amid the straw. On some our good God graciously bestows fruit with but few leaves; to others He gives fruit and leaves together; others, again, there are, who have neither fruit nor leaves. It seems to me a greater thing to know well how to guard and secretly to preserve the fruits and graces vouchsafed to us by God, than to know how to obtain them; for though a man know well how to acquire and gather up wealth, yet, if he know not well how to store it up and to preserve it, he will never be rich; while another, who carefully treasures up what by little and little he has acquired, becomes a man of great wealth.

Oh, how great a quantity of water would the Tiber contain, did none of it flow away in other channels!

Man asks of God an infinite gift, a gift which hath no measure and no bound, yet he will but love God by measure and within bounds. He who desires to be loved by God, and to receive from him an infinite, immense and superabundant reward, ought to love God supremely and immensely, and to serve him without limit or cessation. Blessed is he who loves God with all his heart and with all his mind, who labours and suffers with mind and

235

body for the love of God, and yet seeks no reward under heaven, but accounts himself only to be his debtor.

If one man were exceedingly poor and needy, and another were to say to him: "I will lend thee something very precious for the space of three days; and know, that if thou turn this thing to good account within the space of these three days, thou shalt gain infinite treasure, and become rich for evermore"; certain it is that this poor man would be most diligent in turning that precious thing to the best possible account. And so I say to thee, that the thing which God hath lent to us is our body, which in his goodness he hath lent us for three days; inasmuch as our whole life here below may be compared to three days.

If, then, thou wouldst be rich, and eternally enjoy the sweetness of his divine presence, strive to make the best profit thou canst of this loan from the hand of God for the space of these three days, to wit, of this thy body, which he hath lent thee for the brief space of thy mortal life; for if thou art not diligent to labour and traffic in this present life whilst yet thou hast time, thou shalt never enjoy everlasting riches, nor repose eternally in the peaceful rest of heaven.

But if all the wealth of the world were in the hands of a man who made no use of it, either for himself or others, what would it profit either him or them? Assuredly it would be of no use or benefit whatsoever.

On the other hand, a man who possesses little, by turning that little to good account, may bring forth abundant fruit, both for himself and for others.

There is a proverb of this world which says: "Never set an empty pot to boil on the fire, expecting thy neighbour to come and fill it." And in like manner the good God will not have thee to leave any grace empty and unused; because he never gives a single grace to any man that it should remain unused, but he gives it, on the contrary, that it should be filled and used by the performance of good works; for a good will is not sufficient unless a man fulfil it, carrying it into effect by good works.

Said a beggar man once to Brother Giles, "Father, I pray thee, give me some little consolation"; to whom Brother Giles made answer: "My brother, strive to stand well with God, and then shalt thou have the consolation thou needest; for unless a man prepare within his soul a fair dwelling, in which God may abide and rest, he will never find peace or home or consolation amongst creatures."

When any man wisheth to do evil, he needeth not much counsel how to do it; but to do well he taketh much counsel, and maketh long delay. Brother Giles said once to his companions: "My brethren, it seems to me that there is no one nowadays who wishes to do those things which he sees to be most profitable to him both in soul and body. Believe me, my brethren, for I can swear it in all truth, that the more a man shuns and avoids the yoke of Christ, the more grievous he makes it to himself, and the more heavily it weighs upon him; while the more generously a man takes it up, lending himself willingly to its weight, the lighter and the sweeter will he find it to bear. Now it is the will of God that man should labour in this world for the good of the body, provided he neglect not the good of his soul; for soul and body, without any manner of doubt, shall be united together to suffer or to enjoy for all eternity; to wit, either to suffer eternally in hell inconceivable pains and torments, or to enjoy with the saints and angels in Paradise perpetual joys and unspeakable consolations, as the reward of good works. But if a man do good without humility, it shall be turned into evil; for many there are who have done works good and praiseworthy to the eye, but because they wanted humility the works have become corrupt, thus showing that they sprang from pride; for such as have their root in humility never decay."

237

A friar once said to Brother Giles: "Father, it seems to me that we have not yet learned to know our true good." And Brother Giles replied: "My brother, it is certain that every one practises the art which he has learned, for no man can do good work unless he has first learned. I would have thee to know then, my brother, that the most noble art in the world is that of well-doing; and who can know it except he first learn it?"

Blessed is the man whom no created thing can disedify; but more blessed is he who receiveth edification from everything which he sees and hears.

CHAPTER VII

OF THE CONTEMPT OF TEMPORAL THINGS

MANY sorrows and troubles shall befall the miserable man who sets his heart and desires upon earthly things, for which he forsakes and loses the things of heaven, and at last those of earth also. The eagle flieth very high; but if a weight be laid upon his wings, he can no longer soar aloft; and so by the weight of earthly things man is hindered from soaring on high, to wit, from attaining to perfection; but the wise man, who lays the weight of the remembrance of death and judgement on the wings of his heart, cannot fly and range freely amid the vanities of this world, lest they prove to him occasion of damnation. We see daily how men of the world toil and labour hard, placing themselves in many bodily dangers, to acquire its false riches; and then, after they have thus laboured and acquired, in a moment they die, and leave behind them all that they have gathered together in their lifetime. Therefore there is no dependence to be placed on this deceitful world, which deceiveth every man who trusteth in it, for it is a liar. But he who desires to be truly great and rich indeed, let him love and seek the true and eternal riches, which never satiate or weary or grow less.

Let us take example from the beasts and birds, who, when they receive their food are content, and seek only what they need from hour to hour: and so also ought man to be content with what is barely sufficient temperately to supply his needs, asking no more. Brother Giles said that St Francis loved the ants less than any other animal, because of the great care they take in the summer to gather and lay up a store of grain against the winter; but that he said that he loved the birds far better, because they gathered nothing one day for another.

But the ant giveth us an example that we should not remain idle in the summer-time of this present life, lest we be found empty and without fruit in the winter of the last and final judgement.

CHAPTER VIII

OF HOLY CHASTITY

OUR frail and miserable flesh is like to the swine, that loves to wallow in the mire, and find its delight therein. Our flesh is the devil's knight; for it resists and fights against all those things which are pleasing to God and profitable for our salvation. A certain friar said to Brother Giles: "Father, teach me how to preserve myself from sins of the flesh." And Brother Giles answered him: "My brother, he who wishes to move a large stone, or any other great weight, and carry it to any other place, must try to move it rather by ingenuity than by force. And so, if we desire to overcome the vice of impurity and to acquire the virtue of chastity, we must set to work rather by the way of humility and by a good and discreet method of spiritual discipline, than by a rash penance and presumptuous austerity. Every vice troubles and obscures the fair glory of holy chastity; for it is like a bright mirror which is clouded and darkened, not only by contact with impure and defiling things, but even by the mere breath of man. It is impossible for a man to attain to any spiritual grace, so long as he is inclined to carnal concupiscence; and therefore, whithersoever thou turn thyself, thou shalt never be able to attain to spiritual grace until thou canst master all the vices of the flesh. Wherefore, fight valiantly against thy frail and sensual flesh, thine own worst enemy, which wages war against thee day and night. And know that he who shall overcome this mortal enemy of ours has most certainly defeated and discomfited all his other enemies, and shall attain to spiritual grace, and every degree of virtue and perfection."

Said Brother Giles: "Amongst all other virtues, I would set the virtue of chastity first, because sweet chastity containeth all perfection in itself; but there is no other virtue which can be perfect without chastity."

A friar asked Brother Giles, saying: "Father, is not the virtue of charity greater and more excellent than that of chastity?" And Brother Giles said: "Tell me, brother, what is there in this world more chaste than holy charity?"

Brother Giles often sang this sonnet:

> *O holy chastity, how good art thou!*
> *Truly precious art thou and thy savour is sweet!*
> *They who have not tasted thee know thee not;*
> *Wherefore the foolish understand not thy worth.*

A friar said once to Brother Giles: "Father, thou dost so often commend the virtue of chastity, that I would fain ask of thee what it is?" And Brother Giles answered: "My brother, chastity is, in very truth, the careful and continual custody of our corporal and spiritual senses, in order to preserve them pure and unstained for God alone."

CHAPTER IX

OF TEMPTATIONS

MAN is unable to possess in peace the great graces which he receives from God, because many things that are contrary, disturbing and hostile arise against those graces; for the more acceptable any man is to God, the more vehemently is he assailed and buffeted by the Evil One. In order, therefore, to correspond with the grace which he receives from God, he must maintain an unceasing warfare; for the fiercer the conflict, the more glorious shall be the victor's crown. But we have not many conflicts, nor many impediments, nor many temptations, because as yet we have advanced but a little way in the spiritual life.

True it is, however, that if a man walk warily and well in the way of God, he shall feel neither fatigue nor weariness in his journey; but the man who travels by the broad way of the world shall never be free from labour, weariness, anguish, tribulation and pain, even to the day of his death.

Then said one of the friars to Brother Giles: "Father, it seems to me that thou teachest us two things, the one contrary to the other; for thou sayest first, the more virtuous a man is, and the more acceptable to God, the greater conflicts has he to endure in the spiritual life; and next thou sayest the contrary, to wit, that the man who walks well and warily in the way of God, shall feel neither weariness nor fatigue in his journey." To whom Brother Giles thus explained the contrariety of these two sayings: "It is most certain, my brother, that the devils bring a more fearful array of temptations against those who have a good will than against those who have not. But what harm can the devils and all the evils of this world do to the man who goes forward discreet‹ ly and fervently in the way of God, and therein labours and toils faithfully, knowing and seeing as he does that his reward shall a thousand times over-pay his labour? And further, I tell thee, of a truth, that he who is enkindled with the fire of divine love, the more fiercely he is assailed by temptations to sin, the more deeply will he hold it in abhorrence and detestation. The worst devils ever hasten to tempt a man when he is under some bodily weakness or infirmity, or when he is in some great sor‹ row or anguish, or in a state of tepidity, or when he is hungry or thirsty, or has received some insult or affront, or some injury, spiritual or temporal; for these wicked spirits know well that at such times, and in such circumstances, he is most open to temp‹ tation. But I say to thee, of a truth, that for every temptation and for every vice which thou shalt overcome, thou shalt acquire a virtue; and for each vice, in the conquest whereof thou shalt overcome thyself, thou shalt obtain a larger grace and a brighter crown."

A friar once asked counsel of Brother Giles, saying: "Father, I am assailed often by an evil temptation, and I have many times besought the Lord to deliver me from it, yet he takes it not from me; counsel me, father; what ought I to do?" To whom Brother Giles made the reply following: "My brother, when a king ar‹ rays one of his knights in strong armour of proof, it is a token that he requires him to fight valiantly against his enemies for love of him."

Another friar said to him: "Father, what can I do to attain to greater fervour and love of prayer? for when I go to pray I am hard, cold, dry, and without devotion." Brother Giles answered him thus: "A king has two servants: one of them has armour of proof, and the other has none; both desire to go forth and fight against the enemies of the king. He that is well armed enters into the battle and fights valiantly; but the other, who is unarmed, says thus to his lord: 'My liege, you see that I am unarmed and defenceless; but for your love I will gladly enter into the battle and fight there all unarmed as I am.' Then the good king, seeing the love of his faithful soldier, says to his servants: 'Go with this my true follower, and provide him with all the armour necessary for his defence, that he may enter securely into the conflict; and emblazon his shield with my royal bearings, that he may be known as my loyal knight.' And thus oftentimes it cometh to pass, when a man goes to prayer, that he feels himself to be naked, indevout, cold, and hard of heart; but when he puts a force upon himself, and for love of our Lord enters boldly into the battle-field of prayer, our loving Lord and King, beholding the gallant bearing of his faithful knight, gives him, by the hands of his ministering angels, fervent devotion and good will. When a man has begun some great and laborious work, such as clearing the ground and cultivating the vine that it may bring forth its fruit in due season, he is often tempted by the great toil and manifold hindrances he meets with to weary him of his work, and even to repent him that ever he began it. But if notwithstanding he persevere until the harvest-time, he will forget all that he has endured in his joy at the fruit of his labours. In like manner he who is strong to resist temptation shall attain to great consolations; for, as St Paul tells us, after tribulation shall be given consolation and the crown of eternal life. And not only they who resist temptation shall obtain the rewards of heaven, but they shall be recompensed even in this life; as says the Psalmist: 'Lord, according to the multitude of my temptations and my sorrows, thy consolations shall rejoice my soul.' So that the greater the conflict and the temptation, the more glorious shall be the crown."

A certain friar asking counsel of Brother Giles concerning a temptation, said to him: "O father, I am beset by two evil temp⁄ tations: the one is, that when I do anything good, immediately I am tempted to vainglory; the other, that when I do anything evil, forthwith I fall into such sadness and despondency, that I am almost in despair." To whom Brother Giles replied: "My brother, thou dost well and wisely to mourn for thy sins; but I counsel thee to do so discreetly and temperately, and always to remember that the mercy of God is greater than all thy sins. And if the infinite mercy of God receiveth to penance a man who is a great sinner, and who sins wilfully, when he repents: thinkest thou that the good God will forsake the man who sins not wilfully, if he also be contrite and penitent? I counsel thee likewise not to refrain from doing well, for fear of vainglory; for if the husbandman were to say in the seed-time: 'I will not sow my seed, lest perhaps the birds come and eat it up', assuredly he would reap no fruit that year. But if he sow his seed, although the birds may consume a portion thereof, he will gather in the greater part when the harvest comes. And so with the man who is temp⁄ ted to vainglory but continually resisteth the temptation, I say that he does not by reason of it lose the merit of his good work."

A friar said to Brother Giles: "Father, I have read that St Ber⁄ nard once said the seven Penitential Psalms with so great devo⁄ tion and tranquillity of mind, that he thought of nothing else the whole time but of the words of the psalms he was saying." And Brother Giles answered him thus: "My brother, I think more of the prowess of the knight who holds and valiantly de⁄ fends a castle which is assailed and compassed around by ene⁄ mies, so that he suffers none of them to effect an entrance, than if he were dwelling therein in peace, undisturbed by any hos⁄ tile assault."

CHAPTER X

OF HOLY PENANCE

A MAN ought continually to afflict and mortify his body, and willingly to endure every injury, tribulation, anguish, shame, contempt, reproach, adversity and persecution, for the love of our good Master and Lord, Jesus Christ, who gave us an example of all this in his own person; for, from the moment of his glorious Nativity until that of his most cruel Passion, he continually endured anguish, tribulation, pain, contempt, sorrow and persecution, and that only for our salvation. Wherefore, if we would attain to a state of grace, it is necessary above all things that, so far as possible, we walk in the footsteps of our good Master, Jesus Christ. A secular once said to Brother Giles: "Father, how can we that live in the world attain to a state of grace?" And Brother Giles replied: "My brother, a man must first repent of his sins with great contrition of heart; next, he must confess them to the priest with bitter and heartfelt sorrow, accusing himself of them sincerely, without excuse or concealment; next, he must perfectly perform the penance enjoined him by the confessor; also he must guard himself from every vice, from all sin and from all occasions of sin; he must likewise exercise himself in good works towards God and his neighbour; and by so doing, a man shall attain to a state of grace and virtue."

Blessed is the man who feels a continual sorrow for his sins, weeping over them day and night in bitterness of heart, only because of the offence he has thereby offered to God.

Blessed is the man who shall have always before his eyes the sorrows, pains, and afflictions of Jesus Christ, and who for his love shall neither desire nor receive any temporal consolation in this bitter and tempestuous world, until he cometh to the celestial consolation of life eternal, wherein all his desires shall be fulfilled in fulness of joy.

CHAPTER XI

OF HOLY PRAYER

PRAYER is the beginning, the middle and the end of all good; prayer illuminates the soul, and enables it to discern between good and evil. Every sinner ought to pray daily with fervour of heart, that is, he should pray humbly to God to give him a perfect knowledge of his own miseries and sins, and of the benefits which he has received and still receiveth from the good God. But how can that man know God who knoweth not how to pray? And for all those who shall be saved, it is needful above all things that, sooner or later, they be converted to the use of holy prayer. Brother Giles said thus: "If a man had a son who, for his evil deeds, had been condemned to death or banishment, most certainly he would use every means in his power, labouring day and night, to obtain from the emperor the pardon of his son, and his release from banishment or death; he would make many prayers and supplications, he would give presents or pay fines to the utmost of his power, either in his own person or by the hands of his kindred and friends. Now, if a man do all this for the mortal life of his son, how much more careful and diligent ought he to be in praying to God, and in begging both good men in this world and the saints in heaven to pray for his own soul which is immortal, when it is banished from the heavenly city, or when it lies under sentence of eternal death for its many sins!"

A certain friar said to Brother Giles: "Father, it seems to me that a man ought to feel great sorrow and grief of heart when he experiences not the grace of devotion in his prayer." Brother Giles answered him: "My brother, I counsel thee to proceed calmly and gently; for if thou hadst a little good wine in a bottle, and if in that same bottle there were dregs below the good wine, thou wouldst assuredly take care not to shake or move it, for fear of mixing the good wine with the dregs. Now, until thy prayer be freed from all vicious and fleshly lust, thou shalt receive no divine consolation; because that prayer is not pure in the sight of God which is mingled with the dregs of carnal things. Where-fore a man should strive as much as possible to free himself from all the dregs of worldly concupiscence, that his prayer may be pure before God, and that he may derive therefrom devotion and divine consolation."

A friar put to Brother Giles this question: "Father, why is it that a man is more disturbed by temptations during prayer than at any other time?" To which Brother Giles made answer as follows: "When a man has to bring any question for the deter-mination of the judge, and goes to him for aid or counsel, his adversary no sooner hears of it than he straightway appears to op-pose and resist his appeal, and to throw every obstacle in the way of his cause. So it is when a man goes to prayer, for he goes to seek help from God in the cause of his soul; and immediately there cometh his adversary the devil with his temptations, to make great opposition and resistance, using every effort, artifice and labour to hinder his prayer, lest it should prove acceptable in the sight of God, and to take from it all merit and all consola-tion. And this we may plainly see; for when we are speaking of worldly things we feel perhaps no temptation, nor experience any distraction of mind; but when we go to prayer to delight and console ourselves, we are suddenly pierced with many arrows, to wit, by divers temptations, which the devil putteth in our way in order to distract our mind, that the soul may have no delight or consolation in its converse with God." Brother Giles said, furthermore, that a man in prayer ought to be like a good knight in battle, who, however hard pressed by his enemy, scorneth to leave the field, but resisteth manfully, striving to overcome his foe, that he may rejoice and triumph in the glory of victory. But if he should leave the battle for fear of wounds or death, assuredly he would meet with nothing but shame, confusion and dishonour. And so ought we to do, for we ought not to intermit our prayer for every temptation which may present itself, but resist courageously; for, as the Apostle says: "Blessed is the man that endureth temptation; for, when he hath overcome, he shall receive the crown of eternal life." But if, because of temptations, a man abandon prayer, he will certainly be defeated, dishonoured and overcome by his adversary the devil.

Another friar said to Brother Giles: "Father, I see some men who have received from God the gift of tears, which they shed abundantly and devoutly in their prayer; and I can experience none of these graces when I pray to God." To whom Brother Giles made answer: "My brother, I counsel thee to labour humbly and faithfully in this thy prayer, for the fruits of the heart cannot be gathered in without labour and fatigue being used thereon; and even after this labour and toil the desired fruit follows not immediately, nor until its appointed season; so also God gives not these graces in prayer immediately nor until the fitting time is come, and the mind is wholly purged from all carnal vices and affections. Therefore, my brother, do thou labour humbly in prayer; for God, who is all good and gracious, knoweth all things, and discerneth what is best for thee; and when the fit time and season is come, he will, in his loving mercy, give thee abundant fruit of consolation."

Another friar said to Brother Giles: "What art thou doing, Brother Giles? What art thou doing, Brother Giles?" And he answered: "I am doing evil." And that friar said to him: "What evil doest thou?" Then Brother Giles, turning to another friar, said to him: "Tell me, my brother, which, thinkest thou, is the readier, our Lord God to give us his grace, or we to receive it?" And that friar made answer: "Most assuredly God is readier to give us grace than we to receive it." Then said Brother Giles: "Do we well in this?" And that friar said: "Nay; but we do evil." Then Brother Giles turned to the friar who spake first, and said: "See, brother, this shows us clearly that we do evil, and that I spoke truly when I answered thee, to wit, that I was doing evil." Brother Giles said also: "Many works are praised and commended in Holy Scripture, such as the works of mercy and other holy works; but when the Lord speaketh of prayer, he saith thus: 'Our heavenly Father seeketh men to adore him on earth in spirit and in truth.'" Again Brother Giles said: "The true Religious are like wolves; because they never come into public and frequented places save upon great necessity, and seek immediately to return to their secret haunts rather than to remain long among men. Good works adorn the soul." A friar who was a very familiar companion of Brother Giles said to him: "Father, why goest thou not sometimes to speak of the things of God, to teach and to labour for the salvation of souls?" To whom Brother Giles replied: "My brother, I desire to fulfil my duty to my neighbour with humility, and without injury to my own soul; and that is done by prayer." "At least," said the friar, "go sometimes to visit thy parents." And Brother Giles answered: "Knowest thou not what our Lord saith in the Gospel, 'He who shall leave father, or mother, or brethren, or sisters, for my sake, shall receive an hundredfold'?" And he added, moreover: "A nobleman entered the Order of Friars Minor whose possessions valued, perhaps, sixty thousand pounds; great, then, shall be the reward of those who leave much for the love of God, since it is to be re-turned to them an hundredfold. But we who are blind, when we see any man virtuous and pleasing to God, understand not his perfection because of our own blindness and imperfection. Were we truly spiritual, we should seldom desire to see or speak with any one, except upon great necessity; for the truly spiritual man desireth to dwell apart from creatures, and to be united to God in contemplation."

Then Brother Giles said to a certain friar: "Father, I would fain know what is contemplation?" And the friar answered: "Fa-ther, truly I know not." Then Brother Giles said: "To me it seems that contemplation is a divine fire, a sweet devotion infused by the Holy Ghost, a rapture and suspension of the mind inebriated by the unspeakable savour of divine sweetness, and a sweet and tranquil enjoyment of the soul which is rapt and suspended in loving admiration of the glories of heaven, and an inward and burning consciousness of that celestial and unspeakable glory."

CHAPTER XII

OF HOLY SPIRITUAL PRUDENCE

O THOU servant of the heavenly King, who wouldst learn the mysteries and the profitable & virtuous lessons of holy spiritual doctrine, open wide the ears of thine understand-ing, receive with earnest desire of heart, and carefully lay up in the treasure-house of thy memory the precious store of these spi-ritual doctrines, warnings and admonitions, which now I unfold to thee; by the which thou shalt be illuminated and directed in thy journey on the way of the spiritual life, and shalt be defended

251

from the malignant and subtle assaults of thy material and im-material enemies: and so, with humble boldness, thou shalt steer thy course safely through the stormy sea of this present life, un-til thou shalt attain to the desired haven of salvation. Listen, then, my son, and note well what I say to thee.

If thou wouldst see well, pluck out thine eyes and become blind; if thou wouldst hear well, become deaf; if thou wouldst speak well, become dumb; if thou wouldst walk well, stand still, and travel only with thy mind; if thou wouldst work well, cut off thy hands, and labour with thy heart; if thou wouldst love well, hate thyself; if thou wouldst live well, mortify thyself; if thou wouldst gain much and become rich, lose and become poor; if thou wouldst enjoy thyself and take thine ease, afflict thyself, and con-tinually fear and distrust thyself; if thou wouldst be exalted and had in honour, humble and reproach thyself; if thou wouldst be reverenced, despise thyself, and do reverence to those who de-spise and reproach thee; if thou wouldst always receive good, con-tinually endure evil; if thou wouldst be blessed, desire that all men should curse thee and speak evil of thee; if thou wouldst enjoy true and eternal repose, labour and afflict thyself, and de-sire every kind of temporal suffering. Oh, what great wisdom is it to know and do all these things! but, because it is so high and so sublime, it is granted by God to few. But I say, of a truth, that if any man will study these things and carry them into effect, he will have no need to go to Paris or to Bologna to learn any other theology. For, if a man were to live a thousand years, and have no external action to perform, nor any word to speak with his tongue, I say that he would have enough to do within his own heart, in labouring internally at the purifying, governing, and justifying of his heart and of his mind.

A man should not desire either to see, to hear, or to speak any thing but for the profit of his soul. The man who knows not himself is not known. Woe to us, then, when we receive the gifts and graces of the Lord, and know not how to acknowledge them! Woe still greater to those who neither receive nor acknowledge them, nor care to receive or possess them! Man was made to the image of God, and changes as he wills; but the good God changeth never.

CHAPTER XIII

OF KNOWLEDGE USEFUL AND USELESS

THE man who would know much, must labour much and humble himself much, abasing himself and bowing his head until his mouth be in the dust; and then will the Lord bestow on him great wisdom and knowledge. The highest wisdom is to do always that which is good; acting virtuously, and guarding carefully against every sin and every occasion of sin, and ever keeping in mind the judgements of God. Brother Giles said once to a man who desired to go to a school to learn secular knowledge: "My brother, wherefore wouldst thou go to this school? I would have thee to learn that the sum of all knowledge is to fear and to love, and these two things are sufficient for thee; for so much knowledge as he can use, and no more, is sufficient for a man. Busy not thyself in learning those things which may be useful to others, but study always and seek to use those which are profitable to thyself. For we often greatly desire knowledge by which we may aid others, and think little of that by which we may profit ourselves; and I say to thee, that the word of God dwelleth not with the speaker, nor with the hearer, but with the faithful doer thereof. Some men who cannot swim cast themselves in the water to save others from drowning, and so all of them are lost together. If thou dost not work out thine own salvation, how shalt thou work out that of thy neighbour? And if thou doest not thine own work well how shalt thou do the work of another man? for it is not credible that thou shouldst love the soul of another better than thine own.

"The preachers of God's word ought to be standard-bearers, lights and mirrors to the people. Blessed is the man who so guideth others in the way of salvation, that he ceaseth not to walk therein himself. Blessed is the man who so teacheth others to run therein, that he ceaseth not to run himself. More blessed is he who so helps others to become rich that he fails not also to enrich himself. I believe that a good preacher admonishes and preaches to himself far more than to other men. It seems to me that he who would convert and draw the soul of sinners into the way of God, ought to stand in continual fear lest he should be perverted by them, and drawn by the way of sin and the devil's road to hell."

CHAPTER XIV

OF GOOD AND EVIL SPEAKING

THE man who speaketh good words and such as are profit-able to the soul is truly the mouth of the Holy Ghost; and the man who speaketh evil and useless words is certainly the mouth of the devil.

When good spiritual men meet at times to converse together, they should always discourse concerning the beauty of virtue, that they may increase in the love thereof, and that virtue may increase in them; that so delighting in it more and more, they may exercise themselves the more diligently in all virtues, and by this continual exercise may attain to a greater love of them; and by this love and this continual exercise and delight in virtue, they may ascend to an ever-increasing and more fervent love of God, and to a higher degree in the spiritual life, thus obtaining from the Lord greater gifts and a larger measure of divine grace.

The more strongly a man is tempted, the more needful it is that he speak continually of holiness and virtue; for as by means of unholy talk of evil things a man is easily led to do evil, so oftentimes by speaking of virtue a man is led and disposed to virtuous actions. But what shall we say of the good which pro-ceedeth from virtue? It is such and so great that we cannot wor-thily express its sublime, admirable and infinite excellence.

And again, what shall we say of evil, and of the eternal penalty which follows sin? For it is an abyss so fearful and so deep, that it is beyond the power of our mind to think, or of our mouth to speak. I do not think that there is less virtue in keeping silence well, than in speaking well; and therefore it seems to me that a man ought to have a neck as long as a crane's, that, when he has to speak, his words may have a long way to travel before they reach his mouth; to wit, that when a man would speak, let him think and think again, and examine and re-examine very dili-gently, the how and the why, the time and the manner, the state and condition of his hearers, and his own motive and intention.

CHAPTER XV

OF HOLY PERSEVERANCE

WHAT will it profit a man to fast much, and pray, to give alms, to afflict his body, and to have his soul filled with heavenly thoughts, if, after all, he come short of the desired and blessed haven of salvation, that is, of holy and steadfast perseverance? We may sometimes behold a fair and tall ship upon the waters, strong and newly built, and laden with a rich and regal freight; yet suddenly, by the rising of a tempest, or by lack of skill in the helmsman, that proud vessel sinks and perishes miserably, never reaching the desired haven. What avail then all its riches and strength and beauty, now woefully lost in the depths of the sea?

Again, we may sometimes see a small and battered vessel, carrying but little wealth on board, but steered by a good and wary pilot, pass safely through all the perils of the waves, and anchor safely in the longed-for harbour; and so it is with voyagers on the world's tempestuous sea. "And therefore," said Brother Giles, "a man should always fear; and though he be in great prosperity, or in high dignity, or in a state of great perfection, or of great perfection in his state, yet if he have not a good pilot, to wit, holy discretion, he may perish miserably in the deep abyss of sin: wherefore we see plainly that perseverance is of all things the most needful for us; for, as the Apostle says: 'Not he who beginneth is crowned, but he who persevereth unto the end.' When a tree has been planted, it does not grow immediately; and after it is grown, it does not immediately bear fruit; and when it has borne fruit, not all its fruit is tasted by its master, but some falls

256

to the ground and is spoiled, some is eaten by worms; yet if it abide until the due season, the greater part will be gathered by the owner of the tree. And what would it profit me," continued Brother Giles, "though I had enjoyed the delights of the kingdom of heaven for a hundred years, if thereafter I should not persevere and make a good end?" He said also: "I account these to be the two greatest gifts and graces which God can bestow on us in this life, to wit, lovingly to persevere in his service, and ever to preserve ourselves from falling into sin."

CHAPTER XVI

OF TRUE RELIGIOUS LIFE

BROTHER Giles said of himself: "I would rather have a small measure of the grace of God as a Religious in Religion, than have many graces from God as a secular living in the world; for in the world are many more perils and hindrances, and far fewer remedies, than in Religion." He said also: "It seems to me that a sinful man fears his good far more than he fears his loss or injury; for he fears to enter Religion and to do penance, yet he does not fear to offend God and lose his own soul by remaining hard and obstinate in the world, awaiting his eternal damnation in the mire and misery of his sins."

A man of the world asked Brother Giles: "Father, what wouldst thou advise me to do — to enter Religion, or to remain and do good works in the world?" To whom Brother Giles thus replied: "My brother, it is certain that if a man knew of a great treasure lying hidden in a common field, he would not ask counsel of any one to ascertain whether or no he should take possession of it and carry it to his own house: how much more ought a man to strive and hasten with all care and diligence to possess himself of that heavenly treasure which is to be found in holy religious orders and spiritual congregations, without stopping to ask counsel of so many!" The secular, on receiving this answer, immediately distributed all that he possessed to the poor; and having thus stripped himself of all things, entered forthwith into Religion.

Brother Giles said: "Many men enter Religion, and do not put into effect and operation those things which belong to the perfection of that holy state; but these are like the ploughman who arrayed himself in the armour of Orlando, and knew not how to manage it, or how to fight under its weight. It is not every man who can ride a restive and vicious horse; and if he attempt to mount it, he will perhaps be thrown when the animal rears or runs away."

Brother Giles added, moreover: "I account it no great matter for a man to enter into the king's court; nor do I think it any great thing for a man to obtain certain graces or favours from the king; but it is a very great thing for him to be able to dwell and converse discreetly in the king's court, persevering wisely and prudently in his service.

"Now the court of the great King of Heaven is holy Religion, and there is no great labour in entering it, and receiving therein certain graces and favours from God; but the great thing is, that a man should know how to live well therein, and to persevere therein discreetly until the day of his death."

Brother Giles said also: "I would choose rather to be in the secular state, continually and devoutly desiring to enter into holy Religion, than to be clothed in the religious habit without the exercise of good works, but persevering in sloth and negligence. And therefore ought the Religious ever to strive to live well and virtuously, knowing that he can be saved in no other state but that of his profession."

On another occasion Brother Giles said: "It seems to me that the Order of the Friars Minor was instituted by God for the utility and great edification of the people; but woe to us friars if we be not such men as we ought to be! Certain it is that there can be found in this life no men more blessed than we; for he is holy who followeth the holy, and he is truly good who walketh in the way of the good, and he is rich who goeth in the path of the rich; and the Order of Friars Minor is that which follows more closely than any other the footsteps and the ways of the Best, the Richest, and the Most Holy who ever has been or ever will be, even our Lord Jesus Christ."

CHAPTER XVII

OF HOLY OBEDIENCE

THE more strictly a Religious holds himself bound by the yoke of holy obedience for the love of God, the more abundantly will he bear fruit unto God; the more entirely subject he is to his Superior for the glory of God, the freer and the purer shall he be from sin. The truly obedient Religious is like a knight well mounted and well armed, who fearlessly and securely makes his way through the ranks of the enemy, because none of them can harm him. But he who obeys with murmuring and unwillingness is like a soldier who, entering the battle unarmed and ill-mounted, is soon thrown to the ground and wounded by his enemies, and, it may be, made captive or slain.

The Religious who wishes to live according to his own will, shows that he desires to build his eternal abode in the lowest depths of hell. When the ox bows his head beneath the yoke, he ploughs the ground well, so that it will bring forth good fruit in due season; but when the ox strays about at his own pleasure, the land remains wild and uncultivated, and brings forth no fruit at the harvest. And so the Religious who bows his head beneath the yoke of holy obedience, bears much fruit in due season to the Lord his God; but he who obeys not his Superior from his heart, remains barren and wild and fruitless in his profession. Wise and magnanimous men bow their heads promptly, fearlessly and without hesitation beneath the yoke of holy obedience; but foolish and cowardly men struggle to withdraw their neck from the yoke, and refuse to obey any creature. I hold it to be greater perfection in a servant of God simply to obey his Superior for the reverence and love of God, than it would be to obey God himself were he to command him in his own Person; for he who is obedient to a Vicar of the Lord would assuredly be still more obedient to the Lord himself, were he to lay his commands upon him.

And so it seems to me that in the case of a man who has promised obedience to another, were he vouchsafed the grace of conversing with angels, and were he, whilst thus conversing, to be called by him to whom he has promised obedience, it would be his duty immediately to leave his communing with angels, and go to perform the obedience given him for the glory of God.

He who having placed his neck under the yoke of holy obedience desires to withdraw from that obedience, in order to follow a life of greater perfection, in that man, I say, if he be not already well established in the virtue of obedience, such a desire is but a sign of great pride and presumption lurking secretly within his soul. Obedience is the way to attain to every good and every virtue; and disobedience is the way to every evil and to every vice.

CHAPTER XVIII

OF THE REMEMBRANCE OF DEATH

IF a man had ever before the eyes of his mind the remembrance of death and of the final eternal judgement, and of the pains and torments of the lost souls, certain it is that he would never have a will to sin or to offend God. And if it were possible for a man to have lived from the beginning of the world until now, and in all that time to have endured every kind of adversity, tribulation, grief, sorrow and affliction, and so to die, and then his soul go to receive the eternal bliss of heaven, what harm would he have received from all the evil which he had endured during all that time past?

Again, if for the same space of time a man had enjoyed every kind of earthly pleasure and consolation, and then, when he came to die, his soul were to fall into the eternal torments of hell, what would all the good things profit him which he had enjoyed in the time past?

A beggar man said once to Brother Giles: "I tell thee, I would right gladly live a long time in this world, and have great riches and abundance of all things, and be held in great honour." To whom Brother Giles made answer: "My brother, wert thou to be lord of the whole world, and wert thou to live therein a thou‑sand years in every kind of temporal enjoyment, pleasure, delight and consolation, tell me, what guerdon or what reward couldst thou look for from this miserable flesh of thine, which thou wouldst so diligently serve and cherish? But I say to thee, that he who lives according to the will of God, and carefully keeps himself from offending God, shall receive from God, the Supreme

Good, an infinite eternal reward, great and abundant riches and great honour, and long eternal life in that perpetual celestial glory; unto which may our good God, Lord, and King, Jesus Christ, bring us all, to the honour of the same Lord Jesus Christ, and of his poor little one Francis."